T0155054

The Vicodin Thieves

CONTENTS

Part One

THE INTIMATE EXECUTION OF AMERICA'S YOUNGEST MAYOR

After more than fourteen years, recently discovered evidence sheds new light on the unsolved murder of Alhambra's former mayor
—*Pasadena Weekly*, February 23rd, 2006

THEY FOUND HIM ON the sidewalk, a block from his boyhood home, with a shotgun blast to his handsome face and a ghastly bullet wound through his chest.

Townsfolk skipped a breath hearing that he had been killed, let alone in an execution-style butchery that terrified the neighborhood. Stephen Ballreich was hardly your ordinary murder victim, his history had been so extraordinary in the concrete suburbia normally ruled by stiff, paunchy men from older generations. When he assumed Alhambra's mayoral seat in 1977 at the age of twenty-six in post-Watergate America, it slingshot him to instant celebrity as America's youngest mayor and Golden Boy of the San Gabriel Valley.

Charismatic and hard charging, a natural before any crowd, the blond-haired, blue-eyed Ballreich had a seemingly limitless future. Congress, a run at governor: Republican pundits believed it was all his for the asking. Carelessness, however, would cost him his chance to shine on a bigger stage.

Shortly after his landside re-election in 1978, the electricity that had once distinguished him curdled into scathing headlines against him, as activists accused him of misspending about $2,700 of city travel funds on a trip to Washington, D.C. the previous year. The District Attorney's office declined to press charges, but the scandal punctured Ballreich's confidence, if not his mystique as a prodigy that others should have seen coming. He abruptly resigned his post, relocating for ten years to Arkansas, where he would later brag about hobnobbing with Bill and Hillary Clinton.

Ballreich returned to Southern California in 1988 as a political consultant and a single dad, still dynamic as ever, though no prodigal son. Savagely killed at forty-one, he was never able to do what he confided to his girlfriend: seek office again to fulfill the promise so many saw in him.

A COLD RED SCENT

IF ALL THIS SEEMS like a distant memory about a once-famous person, it is. Stephen (Steve) Lynn Ballreich was mowed down across the street from the leafy grounds of the Ramona Convent where he once played as an outgoing kid around 8:00 P.M. on November 14th, 1991, months after the American military ousted Saddam Hussein's forces from Kuwait.

Some fourteen years later, the Los Angeles County Sheriff's Department remains stumped about who murdered him in such a public fashion. It is officially a cold case with no active suspects and no motive ever established. Several veteran homicide detectives assigned to investigate it have come and gone. One drifted into a retirement on the East Coast feeling "haunted" by its unresolved status, a source said. "All the leads have been exhausted," acknowledged Sheriff's homicide detective Susan Coleman. "We've been hindered by a lack of witnesses and evidence."

So much time has elapsed that a jaded sense exists today that the case is practically unsolvable. Even Ballreich's own mother has stopped calling officials for updates. Adding to the cynicism is the virtual information blackout imposed by authorities. Neither the Alhambra Police Department, which first responded to the shooting, nor the Sheriff's Department that took over the investigation will release the crime report. They say publicizing it could jeopardize what leads they have, including clues lifted from the murder site, a modest, tree-lined block between Valley Boulevard and the San Bernardino Freeway.

At the top of the missing evidence is the murder weapon itself: a twelve gauge shotgun that cannoned two or three close-range pellet-salvos into Ballreich as he walked or jogged in the 1700 block of Marguerita Avenue during the primetime television hour. Another crucial item that authorities failed to locate, at least initially, was an address book kept at his apartment.

"I ask some of the police chiefs once in a while when I am trying to be funny how the Ballreich case is coming," said former Councilman Parker Williams, who served with him at City Hall in the 1970s and was later prosecuted in a bribery scandal. "You know without asking that nobody has any information...I think it's just tragic."

While several of Ballreich's longtime friends question whether the Sheriff's Department pursued the case as tenaciously or competently as it could have—especially in light of a newly disclosed 1989 death threat he allegedly received and his entanglement with possessive women—it has never been a slam-dunk whodunit. Ballreich's habit of infuriating people he once impressed, gambling fever and oft-murky doings made him a jigsaw-like personality excruciating for police to piece together.

The more you dig into his existence, the more you appreciate the detectives' quandary. It wasn't so much who wanted Stephen Ballreich dead but, at times, who didn't?

Williams, like others, said authorities told him that Ballreich's killer probably first shot him in the back from a slowing car, and then stood over him as he lay supine on the sidewalk to bury a second round into his face. The point-blank force from it penetrated his skull, blowing off the back, according to the autopsy report, a copy of which the *Pasadena Weekly* obtained.

In the days following the bloodshed, wild theories circulated around town that a hit man commissioned by an obsessed woman, jealous husband, or incensed father had masterminded it, or that it had tumbled from a snowballing debt. Fringe scenarios envisioned the ex-mayor, with a slightly receding hairline and a trademark blond moustache, was targeted because of politics. Had someone put out a contract on Ballreich because he had learned something sinister or switched allegiances? "Obviously, because of his political activity, we're having to check that out," Curt Royer, a Sheriff's sergeant who had become one of the lead investigators, told the *Los Angeles Times*.

For many, the fact that he perished where he did was more than a gut-wrenching coincidence. People close to him knew that he was so fond of his childhood block that he often drove from his sparsely furnished South Pasadena apartment, where he had been living upon his return from Arkansas, to jog there after work. Someone out to knock him off, who appreciated Ballreich's sentimental attachment, could have easily exploited it. Authorities tried tempering the rabid speculation about that and similar theories by suggesting it might have been a more mundane robbery or a gang assault responsible.

Again, those acquainted with Ballreich's background doubt it was a crime of opportunity. Besides, he was an athletic 6'1", 239-pound Caucasian outfitted in a red jacket, sweatpants, and sneakers when he took his last stride. He did not fit the profile of someone a gang would hurt, even for a suburb a short hop from East L.A.'s deadliest barrios.

Ballreich's behavior in the months leading up to his demise, on the other hand, paint a picture of a man frantic for cash and eager to commit to paper where his assets would go should he perish. Shortly before he did, Ballreich evidently spread $5,000 cash on the floor of his apartment. On the Wednesday he was murdered, one source said, an occupant from his apartment complex saw him peel out in his car in a rush to get to a meeting spot.

Overall, if you polled those in Ballreich's inner-circle, the way he died seemed to them to holler the motive in capital letters—VENGEANCE!

The local Baptist church that hosted his funeral drew 150 mourners, many of them numb. Eulogies by dignitaries and officials from this gray, cliquish city where mercurial rock producer Phil Spector murdered a date in 2003 and Hillary Rodham Clinton's mother grew up, lamented what was lost and what could have been. His landlady, who seemed to have an abiding fondness for him, praised his uniqueness. Talmadge Burke, a pillar of Alhambra's political establishment and one of California's longest serving politicians, was devastated, though he was as different as could be from the victim. "He loved beauty and the aesthetics of Alhambra," Burke quipped to a local newspaper. "He [was] always helpful. He liked people of all ages. It's difficult to say goodbye."

Less mentioned amid the black suits and sodden tissues was the deceased's compulsion for illicit romances and fast living, a "thrill junkie" who cleaned up beautifully in a suit and tie. Those proclivities slid with him into the grave or, perhaps, dispatched him there.

A HORRIBLE VOID

Jo Hartman, a special education teacher in Santa Maria, remembered the heartbreak of 1991, when she breezed into her apartment to notice her answering machine blinking crazily. Played back, the messages had an awful theme—the local news was all over the story of her boyfriend's death.

Ballreich and Hartman got to know each other in tenth-grade algebra. Mischievous humor and chemistry kept them close but Hartman would not let it go further, aware of the girls who swooned for Ballreich without him even trying. One buddy compared him to actor Tom Selleck with a Marlboro Man swagger. You needed a calculator to keep up with his conquests. It was in March 1991, after a fundraiser for a Pasadena candidate that Ballreich was guiding, when romance sparked between them. There was an inevitability to it. Once involved, they laughed they were the real life version of the movie *When Harry Met Sally*.

Ballreich, twice divorced by now, talked marriage, Hartman said. She wavered. They had quarreled over money she owed him and his devil-may-care style. Hartman also recognized that Ballreich sometimes drank excessively, and had other weaknesses going way back. She was not the first to come to that conclusion. Binges and reckless abandon fueled the paradox about him, as if periodic self-destruction was programmed into his genes. Ballreich could be tender and fun loving, the star of the room, just as he could be deceitful, slippery, or a flake that stood up friends within the course of the same week.

Steven Born learned this about him in the early-1970s. They had met as volunteers for the Young Republicans doing grunt work on a San Fernando Valley congressional campaign. Born watched his friend alienate peers with sordid behavior that undercut what he said was Ballreich's uncanny "power of persuasion." Born and others from that era perceived a guy with an outsized personality with difficulty tapping the brakes of self-control when it came to laying wagers, hitting on attractive females, or barroom brawling.

"That was part of the problem: [Steve] could manipulate people so well," said Born, a science teacher. "He remembered everybody's name. He could get people to do things and work hard on campaigns, even for inferior candidates. He was a wonderful salesman. There was that part of him that did really care about people. Then he'd switch on the selfish part and regret it later. It was like he was telling himself he had to do that to be a good person."

In July 1991, the last time Hartman saw him alive, Ballreich unexpectedly—and for reasons still unexplained—asked her to witness a legal will that he had drafted. It was strange, foreboding, and uncharacteristic. "Here was someone who didn't plan things out," she said. "Common sense would make you question why he was concerned about not being around."

By fall of '91, the pair had started to warm up again romantically. He was sanguine about his future, telling Hartman that he wanted to "toss his hat in the political ring" a final time without specifying which race. Simultaneously, he prodded her to repay the $1,000 that he had lent her that summer, phrasing the money "imperative" for him to recoup. His last communication with her was contained in an amusing Halloween card that he mailed. Her final words to him were a phone message that went unreturned. She left it on November 14th at 6:51 P.M., roughly ninety minutes before his murderer aimed that shotgun at him. "I was in despair, beyond despair with the news," Hartman said. "At first I didn't believe it. At the reception after the funeral is when it hit me. He was really gone! It was that horrible void."

Hartman said she spoke to the police several times trying to help them apprehend the killer. Another longtime friend, who asked that their name be withheld out of safety concerns, joined the effort to winnow down suspects. This friend sent detectives a detailed, nine-page memo listing Ballreich's friends, associates, and lovers, theorizing who might have wanted get payback on him and why. The memo, a copy of which the *Pasadena Weekly* has obtained, points most strongly at two women with whom he had been involved. (The *Weekly* does not divulge the names of people if they have not been arrested or sentenced for a crime.)

Ballreich had met one of the women when he was a twenty-something mayor and she was a petite, attractive teenager from a local high school. They dated periodically and often brazenly. The illicit relationship ignited doubts about Ballreich's character among his older Council peers. "He screwed himself up at an early age with drinking, gambling, liking young girls," said Barbara Messina, a former councilwoman and current Alhambra School Board member. "He had too much too soon and couldn't handle it. [But] he'd brought the community together and started Project Pride. He could've charmed a snake out of a tree."

RED FLAGS

OR, ALTERNATIVELY, INVITED VIPERS into his nest after he had returned home from Arkansas. According to his friend's memo, this younger woman later studied the cello at USC, but never finished because of drug problems. She eventually married and moved to the New York area. Despite that separation, she and Ballreich continued their love affair when she visited the West Coast. Their favored hook-up spot was at a Best Western motel in Arcadia near the Santa Anita racetrack, the memo said.

In January 1989, this woman's husband allegedly threatened to kill Ballreich if he persisted with the tryst. Ballreich, worried enough to interview bodyguards, told the friend who penned that memo that the woman was in town at the beginning of November 1991 and that he had seen her. "Obsessed with Steve, extremely possessive, constantly looking for Steve's suspected infidelities despite [the] fact that she, herself, continued to be married," the memo read. "Violently jealous...[Steve] described his continuing concern for her welfare as his 'weakness'..."

Ballreich, Hartman said, never confided in her about any threat, but she knew about the "obsessed" cellist. A few years earlier, when she and Ballreich were still on platonic terms, she had called him about playing tennis. He abruptly told her he couldn't and hung up. Hartman's phone soon rang and Ballreich put the woman on the line. "She said, 'This is so and so and I'd like you never to call Steve again,'" Hartman recalled. "She said, 'He's my fiancé and I want you out of my life.' It was almost like Steve was intimidated. I said Steve's happiness is important to me and if I'm upsetting that, I won't call again. She slammed the phone in my ear. Steve called the next night to say he was 'horribly sorry.' I told him, 'Steve, what are you doing? This was a red flag. '"

When detectives questioned this woman about her whereabouts and activities the day Ballreich died, she warned them that the next time they contacted her she would have a lawyer represent her, Hartman was told. "As soon as she said that, they stopped. To me that would've been pay dirt," Hartman said. "They should have been running this down. I'm not blaming the police. I thought it was one of those hard-to-solve cases. But there was a real suspect and the Sheriff's Department didn't follow through."

She and the friend who authored the memo said they queried the Sheriff's Department if a crime show like *America's Most Wanted* might consider airing a segment about the case to generate leads and publicity. The idea went nowhere, they said, because detectives told them that producers of those shows would not feel Ballreich's rogue personality made him a sympathetic enough victim.

The comings and goings into his apartment during the immediate search for his slayer was another area where Ballreich's friends butted heads with investigators. Hartman, for instance, had used her own key to enter his place on November 16th to retrieve his will, finding that it had gone missing. When she came back the next day, it had magically appeared. Hartman said she informed detectives about it with little effect. Ballreich's other friend experienced the same thing. She reported ten items that had been lifted from his place. Among them were a gold watch, two rings, a bible with his daughter's name in it, a pair of négligées, and, curiously, his address book. "His apartment wasn't taped off," Hartman said. "There was no yellow [police] tape."

The Sheriff's Deputy Coleman disagreed, contending that Ballreich's apartment was secured by all the "appropriate" measures. She declined to elaborate on the items allegedly taken. Other sensitive areas–what tips authorities explored and whether a volatile, older woman from the political world that Ballreich had slept with passed their polygraph test under interrogation–have drawn official silence, too.

"There were several friends, several associates, and several acquaintances who were interviewed by us, but no one has been identified as the suspect," Coleman said. "There are many things that could have happened, and maybe even the thing you expected least. You just can't have guesses. You have to have facts." As with all unsolved murders, she said, detectives have reviewed Ballreich's case within the last five years. Coleman said they failed to uncover any disregarded clues.

Over at Alhambra City Hall, the enduring mystery that has flummoxed police and demoralized his loved ones has elicited paltry attention. Nobody there can cite regular contact with the Sheriff's Department asking to be briefed about the investigation or expressing alarm about its dwindling scent. It is almost as if the city's leadership would prefer the issue fade away because Ballreich's personal failings were a municipal embarrassment best forgotten. If not for his toothy photograph on the wall or yellowing newspaper stories about him, an outsider never would have known that Alhambra's onetime favorite son had ever banged the council gavel.

"I don't mean that to sound cavalier, but there are probably thousands of unsolved murders in L.A. County over fifteen years," said Alhambra mayor Paul Talbot. "Stephen Ballreich's murder, though more sensational, is just as tragic as thousand of others. I'm more interested in the more current types of crimes." The Sheriff's Department has about 1,200 cold cases it is working, including Ballreich's, officials estimated.

Councilman Daniel Arguello, who split with Talbot in a juicy power struggle in the last few years, disagrees that his colleague should be so passive about the taking down of one their own. "This isn't Los Angeles, where you have four million people living there—it's Alhambra!" said Arguello. "It was a very serious crime and nobody knows who did it, even the Alhambra spin doctors who say Ballreich was an evil guy."

PROJECT PRIDE AND THE KID

Ballreich's mother, Jean, said she has lost track of the probe. For the three years after it happened, she stayed in touch with authorities from her home in Prescott, Arizona. A highly devout Christian, now twice widowed, she moved to the Southwest in 1980 to ease her asthma. "At first, I really, really wanted to know," she said. "I would keep calling the Sheriff's Department, and the detective said, 'As long as I'm here,' they would pursue it. There are many things about it that are hard to understand. "But it won't bring [Steve] back. God knows all things, and he knows what happened. If I could talk to whoever did this, I would just say. 'I forgive you,' not because I didn't love my son, but because God will."

She and Stephen's father, Barney, had once foreseen exquisite things for him. From an early age, he schmoozed neighbors on his paper route, had terrific writing and speaking abilities, and possessed an allure everybody recognized. Shackling those talents, his mother said, was a manic-depressive streak and pigheadedness from an early age that he was destined for life in politics and only politics.

The family's Beverly Hills-based jewelry business disinterested him as an occupation. Ballreich's father then died suddenly when he was in his early-twenties. "From the time he was born, a lot of [Stephen's] problem was being too high or too low," in a possible sign of bipolar syndrome. "I couldn't convince a lot of people about that," Jean Ballreich said. "Emotionally, he was unstable. If he hadn't been that way, he might've been the governor of California. I would've loved it if he'd gone into TV."

One matronly Republican Party volunteer recalled meeting Ballreich when he was a gung-ho teenager with a cast on his leg stuffing mailers for a conservative candidate. Ronald Reagan and former Senator Barry Goldwater were his icons. He quoted Thomas Jefferson the way some teenagers quote rock lyrics, though Stephen was a Beatles fan entranced with *The White Album*. He collected vintage political pins, assembling an impressive collection.

Despite obvious brains, his grades were average, his mother said. After graduating from Alhambra High School, he attended various colleges without earning a degree. To earn money—and he always seemed to scrambling for it—he acquired a Burbank restaurant named The Pizza Pantry. He did seasonal campaign work for local Republicans, as well, and may have taken odd jobs under the alias Richard Aldridge, sources said.

He married young, but the union was tumultuous and he and his first wife, Cindy, subsequently divorced. She did not respond to requests for comment. "He wasn't a follow-througher unless it was something he wanted to do," Jean Ballreich said. "Politics ruined his marriage. He gave Cindy a bad time. He did so many contradictory things."

But he achieved some landmark ones, too. In 1974, in the midst of Watergate and Vietnam, Ballreich blindsided the Alhambra status quo by unseating incumbent Councilman T. D'Arcy Quinn. Though it made for a magical storyline, he had used hustle and chutzpah to win, staying up until 4:00 A.M. election-day dropping campaign fliers on doorsteps while his opponent slept. When he rotated in as mayor three years later, after winning re-election in 1978 with a record seventy-five percent of the vote, laurels were thrown at his feet.

Parker Williams said that he introduced Ballreich about this time to renowned political consultant Stuart Spencer, who would later counsel Reagan as President. Spencer, Williams said, believed that Ballreich had a sparkling career ahead if he pushed aside the distractions and focused. Certainly, someone with his zippy charisma was bound for bigger things than a city whose most provocative issue was getting the Long Beach Freeway extension completed so local streets were less bottlenecked. The local Jaycee's named Ballreich, who seemed to have a little John McCain in him, one of California's "five most successful young men."

His signature initiative was Project Pride, a community cleanup regimen. Local television stations did segments showing the Baby Boomer mayor painting over graffiti with ex-gang members. He also pushed for the opening of a boxing club.

Yet only three months after his re-election victory party, a citizen's group called All We Can Afford accused him of misusing and failing to report $2,650 in travel expenses following a March 1978 trip to Washington, D.C. for the National League of Cities. Questions swirled around whether he had receipts for his time at the Mayflower Hotel or whether he had even stayed there.

A District Attorney probe netted no formal charges. Prosecutors never turned up any proof that Ballreich had intentionally broken Alhambra's then-vague travel rules. Ballreich reacted defensively, all the same, bitterly resigning from the council where he had been its telegenic star—a decision he said he later regretted. "I will not subject the city or any member of this City Council to the continual meaningless harassment, such as it has had to endure during the last fifty-five days," he said publicly at the time. His adversaries, he added, had contorted an innocent incident into something criminal.

From there, the city's chastened prince did the unexpected. He boxed up his things and hotfooted it 1,700 miles to Arkansas.

DREAMING GRANDLY

HE WAS THERE DURING most of the 1980s, doing what, nobody is quite certain. Everybody he spoke to from Arkansas heard different stories, the truth grafted, nuanced, or fabricated whole cloth. Maybe he was just airbrushing over his shame about tripping himself up just as new doors were about to open for him. What is known is that he stayed in a house that his mother purchased in a lakeside resort town called Heber Springs in Arkansas' north-central Ozark Mountains. He also spent time in Little Rock, apparently doing campaign work for state Democrats. Interspersing his political work was a stint as a radio talk show host for a station whose call letters or format nobody can pinpoint all these years later.

Longtime friend Born visited him in Heber Springs in 1988. As usual, Ballreich did not show up to their agreed meeting place. Perplexed, Born asked a local where he could find the town's big radio personality. "The guy laughed," Born recalled. "He said, 'Steve fries fish for a living.' I thought typical Steve."

Wherever his paycheck was signed, Ballreich spoke constantly about associating with then-Governor Clinton and his wife, Hillary. Depending on who you ask, he worked for Clinton, advised him, socialized with him, or some combination thereof. There were conspicuous similarities between the two. Both were political junkies and bubbly ambitious during the workweek, good time Charlies hooked to pathological libidos after hours, and magnetic one-on-ones around the clock.

"If you were in a crowded room with Bill Clinton, he'd talk to you like you were the only one there, and Steve was the same way," quipped Glenn Thornhill, who knew Ballreich from his Young Republicans days. "Steve said he knew Bill and Hillary, and hung around in the same circles. Who knows? It could've been bull. But I can see why Steve liked him: Clinton was a successful Steve Ballreich."

While in Arkansas, Ballreich fathered a daughter, Noelle. One source said he wed the mother in a shotgun marriage that did not last long. Before he died, he admitted he had been an absentee father and that at least Noelle would not be influenced by his poor decision-making.

Unfortunately, there was not always so much clarity. Ballreich, for instance, tried convincing folks he was part Irish in spite of the imposing, blonde appearance that confirmed his German heritage. Whether that blarney was a symptom of a delusional personality or a fanciful one, it helped him compartmentalize his life with slick divisions. Even longtime family friends had little inkling of his wild side, or the fact that he had done semi-pro boxing or battled health problems.

One characteristic he was unable to deflect from public consumption was the sexual appetite that incessantly put him in hot water. He acknowledged to a family friend that he had little restraint over his urges around a pretty face, and that when his "hormones percolated" he was a slave to them. "Light and dark," this friend used to describe him. "Light and dark."

Arkansas' weather and backward climate helped propel him West back to Southern California. He returned almost broke, but with his love of politics and patriotism intact. At first, he stayed with friends until he had saved enough money to rent in South Pasadena, the quaint city of Craftsman homes that had been Alhambra's arch-enemy for decades over the Long Beach Freeway controversy.

If he lived cheaply, he dreamed expansively. Ballreich, in early 1989, hooked arms with failed Alhambra Council candidate Allen Co in a novel bid to boost voting rates and political participation within the city's Asian American community. It was a prescient move by a wily tactician; Asian Americans today comprise sixty percent of the town's population. Ballreich told the media at the time that he was shocked at the level of prejudice towards them among whites and the surge of Asian businesses since he had left in 1979. Someone, he said, had to prepare the city of about 90,000 for a multi-ethnic future once its white-bred past slipped away. Co, who later served on the South El Monte Council, did not return phone calls.

Ballreich's interests crackled beyond the coming minority-majority. In 1988, he and Merrill Francis, a longtime Alhambra lawyer and civic leader, launched a political consulting business called Pegasus after the mythical flying horse. Their gimmick: Francis, the Democrat and Ballreich, the centrist Republican, would bring a spectrum of campaign experience to their clients. Together only a few years, they mostly ran local council and school board races, generally with little success, branching out to manage then-Councilman Michael Blanco's losing bid for California Insurance Commissioner.

Though creeping towards middle age, Ballreich was devoted to outdoor exercise, either running or playing tennis practically daily, Francis said. But there were issues. Though few knew it, Ballreich had gone back to Arkansas to have laser heart surgery performed. His autopsy report did reveal coronary blockages.

Francis said he has difficulty recollecting Ballreich's murder because it coincided with the death of his first wife and his mother. Some memories remained un-dimmed. "Steve was very approachable and there was an excitement about him—a sex appeal. He made a strong impression." At the time of his murder, Francis said, his partner was still a "ladies man with a pretty active social life." Among other women he was dating was a youngish one who worked in the court system, Francis added. He did not know if detectives interviewed her. Authorities did disclose to Francis that Ballreich's answering machine tape had given them promising leads. They said the murder had the earmarks of a professional job, what with shots to his face and heart area.

During their years together, Francis said Ballreich spent part of it traveling around the country promoting a patriotic cause for a man who later refused to pay him. Though angry about being stiffed on that job, Ballreich routinely took chances that almost no one else would, be it with spec assignments, pranks, or women half his age. It was as if he required the adrenaline kick to keep him interested. "Steve was a natural risk-taker," Francis said. "He'd bet beyond his paying capability. One time he put up the pink slip on his car on a prize fight... What I'm seeing [today] is that he was a like a piece of quartz shining through many facets."

Francis, now seventy-two, spoke at the funeral and tried assisting police. He does not subscribe to conspiracy theories that others whisper suggesting that Ballreich's murder was politically motivated. "That scuttlebutt didn't mean anything," he said. "But there is disappointment that there hasn't been retribution for whoever killed him."

Ballreich's allegiance to Clinton was as strong as ever after he re-migrated from the South. He told many in 1991, including Francis, that he would not only support the Arkansan for President but would raise money for him. If Ballreich was on the Clinton team, it is news to some of the ex-Presidents key advisers. Los Angeles lawyer John Emerson, who was involved with Clinton's 1992 campaign to win the California primary, said he didn't know who Ballreich was. Linda Dixon, assistant manager for volunteer and visitor services for the Clinton Foundation, parroted the same line. "I've been with President Clinton twenty-three years and I've never heard his name before," Dixon said. "I'm only speaking for myself."

Ballreich's Young Republicans chums kept in contact with him to the end. Over drinks, they razzed him about how a died-in-the-wool conservative could champion a liberal-tilting Southern Democrat. When the needling stopped, these same longtime acquaintances noticed that while Ballreich was still the impulsive, flirtatious guy he'd always been, he had a more serious bent to him, a sort of world-weariness.

DIFFERENT MASKS

HIS DEATH WAS QUICK, brutish, and well orchestrated. Residents who heard the shots summoned Alhambra police. Witnesses relayed they had seen a dark, 1970s-era Camaro flee the scene. Fear clenched Marguerita Avenue in the following days. The nearby elementary school—the same one Ballreich attended in the 1960s—went into lockdown after someone reported a prowler lurking. It was not the last suspicious sighting, not with a cunning murderer running free.

Police discovered Ballreich lying face up with what the coroner's office described as "massive open head trauma." The second wound came from a gunshot that struck him in the upper, left side of his back and exited through his chest, leaving behind a grisly, seven-inch gash. Either blast was lethal. Police extracted gunshot residue from the scene.

The coroner's office reported three salvos were fired, but only described two of them. Ballreich, it said, appeared to have been "walking on the sidewalk" when the gunman pulled up. This may be critical. While he was an avid runner, he was wearing underpants, not an athletic supporter, at the time he died. Some have speculated whether that meant he was meeting somebody under the pretext of exercise. No drugs were detected in his system. Overall, the autopsy determined that Ballreich had been healthy except for coronary occlusions. Still in his wallet was his old Arkansas driver's license.

Detectives mulled the possibility street gangs were involved. Four days before the murder, a twenty year old gang member had been killed about a mile away. They also interviewed members of the Lincoln Club, a Republican political action committee that Ballreich volunteered at and advised. Before he died, he had counseled the PAC about its donations and involvement with various campaigns.

The Sheriff's Department interviewed Lincoln Club employees at the PAC's El Monte offices, a former worker there confirmed. Nerves were already on edge at the small organization after employees complained about a bizarre series of petty crimes directed at them. Staffers had reported a slashed tire, a tampered car gas tank, a stolen purse and signs of an intruder at one of their houses, among other unexplained events. Suspicion fell on a recently fired employee—a woman who had known Ballreich well.

Bill Ukropina, a volunteer with the Lincoln Club and former chairman of its Pasadena branch, said he was unaware that the homicide investigation touched the group. Nor, he said, was he aware of Ballreich's personal issues. "I never saw any side of Steve other than a cordial, professional one," Ukropina said. "He was such a talented guy. He made excellent presentations. He brought a lot to the world, a lot to the community. I miss him."

Ultimately, the Sheriff's Department decided both the Lincoln Club and roving gang violence probably had nothing to do with what happened to him. It was not clear why detectives ruled them out. Perhaps other avenues were more fruitful. Ballreich's landlady, a longtime friend, had watched him rush out of his South Pasadena apartment on the November 1991 afternoon that he was shot. "The day Stephen died, he'd come home, and all of a sudden left in great haste," said this source. "He peeled rubber out, like it was some big emergency. If he was upset and in a hurry, somebody must've called him."

Born, the friend from their days together in the Young Republicans, said police were curious in learning about Ballreich's gambling habits. For years, Ballreich had wagered on football games and prizefights. Williams, the former councilman, acknowledged remembering one of Ballreich's bookies from the 1970s. So, could a new debt from a lingering vice have precipitated what transpired on Marguerita Avenue? There are tantalizing aspects to the idea. The Sheriff's Department, Born said, located somebody who remembered seeing $5,000 in cash in Ballreich's apartment not long before he left it a final time. "The Sheriff's Department thought he was meeting someone the night" said Born. "Why [else] would he have $5,000 on the floor of his apartment? Why not keep it in the bank?"

Which leads us back to the beginning—November 1991. If it was not an indiscriminate drive-by, and it was not something else random, then why was a once high-profile person drawn to his old neighborhood and effectively assassinated? Was it a violent exclamation point about an unforgivable sin or a warning to others? "[Sheriff detectives] had a particular interest in who might know he was running in that area on that street on that day at that time," said Francis, his ex-business partner. "Who knew him well enough to know that? It narrows the circle of people who would be of primary interest."

The question may be unanswerable. When you sweep everything else aside, you realize that Stephen Ballreich died the same way he lived—spectacularly, disturbingly. It is symmetry not lost on longtime buddy Glenn Thornhill. "One of my friends ran into an Alhambra policeman, and the cop said, 'We don't know who did it. Steve Ballreich told so many different stories to so many different people we could be talking to the responsible person and we wouldn't even have a clue.'"

OPERATION BALD-HEADED EAGLE

Was a convicted smog-credit swindler also part of shady international money repatriation schemes with links to the CIA?

—*Pasadena Weekly*, August 20th, 2009

THE REMNANTS OF ANNE Sholtz's old life are evident in the smaller things. They are visible in the GPS tracking bracelet–standard issue for felons in home detention–that looped around her ankle for a year, and in her idled passport. They are traceable in her pillow, which rests today in a leased home miles from the $5 million hillside estate that once broadcast her transformation from Caltech economist to business phenom.

Yes, the wreckage from that existence–the economizing, the isolation from connected friends who now shun her–is graspable. Where the picture turns as murky as Southern California's whiskey-brown smog is how Sholtz, as a then-thirtysomething go-getter, was able to deceive the very air pollution market that she helped to conceive, and the lessons it holds for keeping financial crooks out of the trillion-dollar greenhouse gas trading system that President Obama has trumpeted as a key to curbing global warming.

Unless you are in the arcane field of emissions trading, chances are you have probably never heard of Sholtz before. Last April, the former Pasadena pollution broker was convicted in federal court for masterminding a fraudulent, multi-million dollar deal for credits in Southern California's novel smog exchange. Despite pleas that she sock Sholtz with years behind bars, U.S. Central District Court Judge Audrey Collins gave her just a year in home confinement.

Fortunate with a light sentence in that downtown L.A. courtroom, Sholtz, nonetheless, sustained heavy losses outside of it, squandering, among other potential, her chance to build a unique and lucrative pollution trading business, with access to President Obama or Governor Arnold Schwarzenegger as an industry confidante. Those opportunities gone, she now drives her mother's car, not the Mercedes or SUV she previously did. Rather than expanding her patented ideas into climate change, she checks in with her probation officer.

Blown prosperity for Sholtz; it has been no bonanza for others, either. Between criticism over its secretive, mixed-bag prosecution of her and evidence of Sholtz's role in a scheme to extract millions in overseas U.S. aid with men purporting to be American intelligence and military operatives, the Department of Justice's L.A. office probably wishes she would just fade away. Local smog regulators at the South Coast Air Quality Management District (AQMD), whose market-based regulation proved vulnerable to her deceptions, can relate. The trouble is, some events are just too big to disappear. And the Sholtz case, no matter its relative obscurity or connection to complex regulations, fits that mold because it underscores the need for vigorous oversight of emissions markets against seemingly inevitable Wall Street-style chicanery.

Saying that she hopes to reconcile the events that dragged her from eco-visionary to convicted felon and industry pariah, Sholtz, forty-four, gave the *Pasadena Weekly* her first public comments in seven years. These days she is a freelance auditor examining white-collar fraud (ironically, for the federal court system that processed her case) and proclaims herself "happy" and "debt-free." Just don't mistake that resilience for satisfaction, or expect to hear weepy remorse from her about the ruins smoldering in her wake. Channeling other emotions, Sholtz said that she was "disappointed" in how prosecutors and bankruptcy officials treated her, and was perplexed over why the whistleblower tips she furnished them about bank money laundering and environmental corruption seemed to have fallen on tin ears.

"Years ago, I was depressed I'd made bad decisions, which led to one disastrous deal and my companies unraveling," Sholtz said over lunch at a location that she asked go undisclosed, fearing former associates she claimed have threatened her. "I've never said anything about this whole experience until now. The only reason I'm speaking is because I'm tired of the misperceptions."

BOUND TO HAPPEN

IF TWO REPUBLICAN CONGRESSMEN skeptical about President Obama's carbon-cutting blueprint have their way, Sholtz's story may yet capture national attention. This spring, Congressman Joe Barton (R-Texas) the ranking member of the House's powerful Energy and Commerce Committee, and Congressman Greg Walden (R-Oregon), ranking member of the House's Oversight and Investigations Subcommittee, demanded the U.S. Environmental Protection Agency provide a welter of information about Sholtz to them, based partly on the *Pasadena Weekly*'s coverage. "We believe this case has great relevance in the context of the pending legislation on climate change," Barton and Walden wrote in a May statement. In it, they cited doubts that federal authorities have the money and legal punch to adequately police a national greenhouse gas market.

All the same, those doubts may be road tested. An Obama-backed bill requiring industry and public utilities nationwide to buy and sell federally auctioned permits to discharge carbon dioxide and other greenhouse gases under a so-called "cap-and-trade" regimen narrowly passed the House in June. Formally titled The American Clean Energy and Security Act of 2009, the legislation, which includes numerous new energy efficiency standards and initiatives, represents the most seminal change in U.S. environmental policy since passage of 1970s Clean Air Act. The thirteen hundred-page bill, co-written by House Democrats Henry Waxman (California) and Edward Markey (Massachusetts), next goes to the Senate. The overriding objective is to reduce U.S. greenhouse gases from 2005 baseline levels so that by 2020 aggregate levels are down seventeen percent and by 2050 they have shrunk a colossal eighty-three percent. (Global warming is caused by the atmospheric buildup of carbon dioxide and other gases that reflect some of the Earth's heat back towards the planet instead of dispersing it into space. Many scientists contend the phenomenon is imperiling the Arctic, biodiversity, food production, and weather patterns.)

Hopeful as the White House is about cap-and-trade as a lever to reign in heat-trapping emissions, even enthusiasts acknowledge that the intricacies are jaw-dropping, if not for the sheer mechanics of it, then for the geographic lines, industrial sectors and differing populations it will transect. Roughly six billion tons of emissions could be traded yearly at first, estimated David Kreutzer, an economist at the conservative Heritage Foundation in Washington, D.C. Entities discharging more than twenty-five thousand tons of greenhouse gases annually—non-nuclear power makers, oil refiners, natural gas producers, coal-fired steel plants, among others—will participate.

Detractors believe with the money at stake, white collar cheating is practically inevitable. Between now and 2035, greenhouse gas permits may reach $5.7 trillion in value, Kreutzer said. Some investment houses are already gearing up to act as trade middlemen. Oddly, the watchdog angle was barely touched on during congressional deliberations. Attention mainly focused on provisions allowing companies to soften emission damage offsite, even overseas, if it is cheaper, and the initial giveaway of eighty-five percent of credits to carbon-dependent businesses and regions facing sharply higher energy prices. As the bill stands, market oversight will be spread out among the Federal Energy Regulatory Commission, the EPA, and several unspecified agencies. "Most of the people I talk to think [the market] will be set up for fraud," said policy analyst Joel Kotkin. "There's scamming and then there's scamming."

Simultaneously, seven Western states and parts of western Canada are considering launching their own regional cap-and-trade under a Schwarzenegger administration plan. It is aimed at rolling back carbon dioxide emissions to 1990 levels by 2020. The Western Climate Initiative may be dissolved or modified if a national market is approved. Until then, West Coast officials are studying how to ward off cheaters in areas such as insider trading, excessive speculation, and market manipulation. Sometimes, however, the threat hides in the open.

ANOTHER DIRECTION

L.A.'s implacable smog problem stood to make Sholtz rich, and maybe more influential. A dark haired woman with wide-set eyes and a slight Midwestern twang, she grew up the brainy daughter of an aeronautical engineer. Schooled in Minnesota and elsewhere, Sholtz said her aptitude in math and science won her countless honors and early interest from NASA. It was a job offer teaching economics at Caltech that pulled her from Washington University in St. Louis, where she was in a doctoral program, to Southern California. Her timing was superb.

The Cold War had just ended and California's recession was buzz-sawing thousands of blue collar jobs. Bigwigs then were not debating carbon footprints. They were grouching about regulatory overkill in the fight against chronic smog. Legislators, lobbyists and boosters, convinced that costly rules were suffocating manufacturers, saw their chance to emasculate the AQMD's power. To neutralize the threat, the air district offered something chancy.

The AQMD has not invented the concept of injecting market principles to detoxify the environment and allow industry leeway in deciding how and when to run its smokestacks, towers, generators, and other machinery cleaner and greener. It originated with academics decades earlier, and then was embraced by the first Bush Administration to address acid rain, a harmful, sulfur dioxide-laced mist emitted from Midwestern power plants that drifted over Northeastern states and into parts of Canada. Most consider the congressionally adopted program a success. Whether the same system will translate for a prodigiously larger, national greenhouse gas market is anyone's guess.

It is for this reason that L.A.'s experience is instructive. Instead of continuing to rely on fine print dictates to regulate individual machinery at power stations, oil refineries, cement companies, defense plants, and other manufacturers, as smog officials had done for decades, the AQMD in 1994 gambled on economics. Some tactic was needed to chop emissions by seventy percent to meet national clean air standards. Environmental groups fretted that cap-and-trade here was a recipe for stalling progress, but regulatory chic was in trader's garb. The spectacle of L.A.'s notorious air pollution being traded like a blue chip stock sounded exotic and the world press flocked to the district's eco-conscious Diamond Bar headquarters to hear the details.

GREEN FAIRYTALE

UNDER THE NOW FIFTEEN year old market, 332 of the area's heaviest polluters are allotted credits based on their aggregate emissions of two harmful chemicals: oxides of nitrogen and sulfur. These credits, calculated from baseline production levels, essentially are permits to pollute by the pound. If an entity reduces more of its discharges than required under its cap set by regulators—usually by installing high tech, gunk-trapping equipment—it can sell the differential between what it is allowed to emit and what it actually released into the skies, or expects to, to others in the form of credits. (A company can choose not to trade, just as long as its emissions fall below its limits.) Every year, firms' emission allotments shrink by a certain percentage so pollution dips regionally. Each credit is assigned a period for its one year use, the date it was issued and one of two geographic zones it can be used in.

To date, there have been 5,170 trades worth $980 million in the "Regional Clean Air Incentives Market" (RECLAIM). District officials argue that it is has achieved its goals, shrinking nitrogen oxides seventy-three percent and sulfur oxides fifty-nine percent. Trades are made company to company, or through broker-type middlemen. Here is where symmetry enters. During the RECLAIM design phase, the district solicited technical expertise from lawyers, academics, and others, bidding out consulting contracts to some of them. The Pacific Stock Exchange and Caltech received work performing market analyses, with Sholtz one piece of their brainpower. It was there she hobnobbed with AQMD staff and there she promoted two concepts of her own: a plan to stabilize prices and planning by establishing two staggered cycles for RECLAIM credits expiring in a given year; and to deter fraud by assigning credits identifying numbers, somewhat akin to a bar code, so officials could track their movements. Only the staggering portion of Sholtz's plan was approved.

Jack Broadbent administered RECLAIM for the district back then and remembered Sholtz. "She came across in a very professional manner, pretty slick, part advertising, part substance," said Broadbent, now executive officer of the Bay Area AQMD. "Anne [also] did a good job of ticking a number of us off. She asked what air pollution regulators know about these...ideas." Arrogant or merely self-assured, few seemed as poised to capitalize on RECLAIM as the ever-hustling Midwesterner. While still working out of her apartment and teaching at Caltech, as well as at USC as an environmental law scholar, she founded a smog credit exchange allowing buyers and sellers to arrange favorable deals. Every RECLAIM transaction in this eBay-like auction made her a three percent to six percent commission.

Her company, Automated Credit Exchange, touted itself as the first-ever electronic trading system for pollution credits. Unlike traditional brokerages such as Cantor Fitzgerald, Sholtz's system relied on analytical, NASA space-exploration software licensed through Caltech to create mathematically optimal trades from a mishmash of data. Industrial heavyweights like Disney, Northrop-Grumman, Chevron, and the L.A. Department of Water and Power signed up as clients; the Pacific Stock Exchange, Bank of America, and U.S. Trust served as trade clearinghouses.

In February 1996, Sholtz celebrated her company auctioning a record 2.4 million RECLAIM credits in a single week. A *Los Angeles Times* story the next year exalted Sholtz's ingenuity, quoting one client who called it "absolutely wonderful." She later set up shop with an office on South Raymond Avenue in trendy Old Pasadena. With money and publicity flowing, and nibbles about selling her analytical software to advertisers and officials auctioning federal airwaves, Sholtz appeared destined for the cover of Forbes. There were trips to the United Nations, meetings with Al Gore, her 7,000 square foot estate festooned with Koi ponds in gated Bradbury a few miles east of Pasadena, not to mention exhilaration for what lay ahead.

It was an Horatio-Alger-meets-green-entrepreneur fairytale. Unfortunately, some fairytales end miserably. In 2002, nine of Sholtz's clients complained to the AQMD that the fast-riser known for her wonky lingo and oft-clingy outfits had bamboozled them in what would become a convoluted bankruptcy of her firms, with claims in the $80 million range. The EPA was summoned. Before long, investigators had zeroed in on a particular transaction.

Beginning in fall 1999, Sholtz informed one of her clients, a New York-based energy trading firm called A.G. Clean Air, that then-Mobil Corporation (now ExxonMobil) needed to purchase about $17.5 million in RECLAIM credits to operate in the L.A. Basin. Mobil indeed had an option contract with her to acquire those credits, and if A.G. sold them to the oil titan through her, it could make a bundle, perhaps $5 million, depending on credit prices. But when A.G. couldn't buy enough credits to complete the Mobil transaction itself, Sholtz discovered that credits from her own company that she needed to use had been committed elsewhere by an employee while she was out ill. She had a dilemma: come clean or try to fix the muddle herself.

To trick A.G. into believing she could still consummate the deal for credits, Sholtz staged an elaborate act, court records show. From November 2000 to April 2002, she emailed and faxed fraudulent sales documents to A.G., including phony invoices showing, Mobil owed her about $16 million when in fact it did not under the option contract. In more artifice, she emailed A.G. officials "falsified" correspondence between her and a Mobil executive that she was impersonating. The fakery was intended to buy her time until she could unload A.G.'s credits to someone else besides Mobil and pay A.G. what it could have made with the oil company if the original deal could have been completed. Eventually, A.G. caught on to the stonewalling, technically known as "lulling," demanding to be paid in full. By then, authorities were onto her. A.G. and Mobil declined comment for this story.

AN EASY FIX

Sholtz asserts, as she has in court documents, that the initial federal charges against her were overblown, and in this regard she has a point. Contrary to early media accounts and government reports about her, she never trafficked in counterfeit credits because there weren't any.

Her downfall, she insisted in interviews and in her plea agreement, traced from her entanglements with a smooth-talking Texas financier named Jimmy Keller. He was on Sholtz's payroll from 1998 to 2000 before she fired him, and Sholtz said she last spoke with Keller in 2002. (One of her ex-cohorts said he died several years ago.) Sholtz said it was Keller who committed the credits that could have stopped her prosecution by encumbering them in a phony, high-yield investment scheme involving bank notes. It took her about eight months to reconstruct what had happened. When she had, though, RECLAIM credit prices had plunged, diminishing the money she had to throw at the problem. "I wasn't panicked–I was angry," Sholtz said. "I should have just said, 'I will find a way out,' and admit I messed up. I could have sold my part of the company and learned a big lesson. But I thought nobody would have traded with us anymore or that A.G. might have forced us to sell the company to them and fire our employees. I didn't have the courage or maturity to ask for help."

Because AQMD regulators were blind originally to what had transpired, Sholtz continued barreling forward. Among other actions, she solicited money from new investors to pay off existing ones in a Ponzi-type scheme, Howard Grobstein, the court appointed bankruptcy trustee, wrote in filed documents. In another instance, she blamed the destruction of the World Trade Centers during the 9/11 terrorist attacks for missing deal paperwork. Sholtz disputes that she misled as many people as some have charged, and said she felt demonized by a few of the accusations against her. "There's been so much misinformation, it's astounding," she said. "Some people really didn't want to know the truth. They just wanted to blame me without looking at themselves or their associates."

Nonetheless, in February 2001, while still misleading A.G., Sholtz insisted the Netherlands government test its own nitrogen-oxide emissions trading program. Months later, she tried playing white knight when RECLAIM credit prices soared during the California electricity crisis by offering to stabilize trading through a centralized auction similar to hers. Governor Gray Davis had ordered power plants statewide to generate electricity however they could, even from high-polluting machinery. Traders and speculators from Texas to New York seized the opportunity, hoarding credits to sell at huge markups to utilities frantically buying more than their allotment. With RECLAIM approaching meltdown, district brass temporarily pulled utilities from the market. They also spurned Sholtz's rescue plan.

The next year, her two promising companies flopped into bankruptcy. What she hoped would be a reorganization plan ossified into dissolution. It got messier. Individual investors claimed losing retirement accounts, college funds, and nest eggs in the collapse. Multi-million dollar settlements were cut with two large energy entities, Calpine and Intergen. The Bradbury mansion was sold. Where she was once hailed as brilliant, foresighted and charming, she was now characterized as dishonest and, according to one official, "manipulative." Just as that was occurring, questions arose about her Ph.D. cited in stories, the Netherlands, and elsewhere. As the *Weekly* reported, she had no doctorate because she had not completed her dissertation at Washington University. Sholtz said that a colleague had introduced her at a public function as "Dr. Anne Sholtz" and since she was close to earning her advanced degree, she let the lie stand. "That would have been so easy to fix," she said, "but, again, it required a level of maturity that I didn't have."

GAMING THE SYSTEM

EPA AGENTS ARRESTED HER at a Monrovia gym in 2004. The theatrics of it, Sholtz suspected, were meant to intimidate her. "I was handcuffed and outside there were guys with big guns," she recalled. "They wanted to embarrass me. Did they think I was going to flee in my Spandex?" The incarceration of a niche green celebrity chummy with AQMD brass at the Metropolitan Detention Center rattled others, too. Inside local environmental and regulatory circles, feelings of betrayal, fury, and anguish erupted.

She would eventually be indicted on six federal counts stemming from the A.G.-Mobil transaction. One knowledgeable source, said Sholtz lucked out, because federal investigators had turned over to the Justice Department enough evidence for more than eighty counts. Charges filed, the white collar case seemed to turn invisible, as if the region's virulent smog—still the unhealthiest in the nation for ozone and particulate matter—had devoured it. Four years lapsed from her 2004 arrest to her 2008 sentencing, and even then her punishment warranted no Justice Department press release.

The two prosecutors handling the case, Assistant U.S. Attorneys Joseph Johns and Dorothy Kim, have steadfastly refused comment beyond Johns saying last year it was a calculated gamble to have Sholtz plead guilty to a single count. Adding to the mystery in *United States v. Anne Sholtz*, many of the key court documents, the transcript of her sentencing hearing among them, remain quarantined by judicial order. Justice Department spokesman Thom Mrozek said one reason is that her case involves "under seal filings" that might signal ongoing investigations into other areas. Wayne Nastri, the EPA's West Coast administrator, was virtually the only significant suit to speak up. In a January 2008 letter to Judge Collins, Nastri recommended that she hand Sholtz a message-sending sentence. "Environmental regulatory programs which utilize market mechanisms," Nastri wrote, "will fail if the integrity of such programs can be seriously compromised."

At the April 2008 sentencing hearing, which caught many off guard because of the case's frequent delays, Sholtz wept and foretold of family harm if she were given hard time. But what mattered to Collins, according to numerous people present that day, was that Sholtz's companies had paid A.G. so it actually turned a profit in its trade dealings with her over time, in spite of her misleading actions. (Sholtz estimates that amount at $28 million.) Alluding to that and other factors, Collins stunned the Justice Department, EPA, and some of Sholtz's victimized investors by giving her a skimpy sentence: one year of home detention as part of her five years of probation, plus a conditional ban on AQMD emissions trading.

In a surreal coda to one of the bigger cases of cap-and-trade criminality, Collins chided prosecutors for their strategy while praising Sholtz's defense attorney, Richard Callahan of Pasadena. Even so, environmentalists and others say it is incumbent on regulators to learn from Sholtz's gaming so it is not repeated on the bigger carbon stage. "We definitely see [this] fraud as a cautionary tale for the state thirty-five and the country as we move toward greenhouse gas regulations and potential market mechanisms," said Bill Magavern, director of Sierra Club California. "In discussions about it, I've brought up the fact that there has been outright criminal fraud and I find that most people don't know about it."

OPERATION BALD-HEADED EAGLE

THUMB THROUGH THE FEDERAL government's case file on Sholtz and you would think she had confined her ambitions to smoggy

Southern California. The felony that torpedoed her career, after all, involved Torrance refiner ExxonMobil Corporation. What you would never glean from the available prosecution documents was Sholtz's involvement in a spectacular and alarming international venture–one intersecting the worlds of espionage, foreign policy, environmental markets, and con-artistry–in the years before authorities were chasing her. All of that has been buried until now. A months-long *Pasadena Weekly* investigation, based on business records, operational memos, wire transfers, invoices, résumés, and other documents scooped up by federal and bankruptcy officials and obtained by the paper, coupled with Sholtz's own rendition of events, tells part of this bizarre story of cap-and-trade money gone sideways into areas it was never intended to occupy.

Peel back to 1998. After losing about $1.7 million in soured deals in the AQMD's smog cap-and-trade program when a credit buyers' check bounced, Sholtz said that Keller confided to her about an opportunity to dig her way out. The seemingly well-connected financier and dealmaker she had hired that year told her that not only could she recoup her losses and then some but simultaneously serve her country. The U.S. Government, he said, farmed out contracts to private firms for an extraordinary purpose: returning to federal coffers some of the government bonds, gold, cash, and other valuable items distributed to America's allies, in some cases going decades back. Whether they were first allocated as foreign aid, secret payments, or other forms of funding from Washington, D.C. was not evident.

Keller, according to Sholtz, explained that once the booty was returned to the U.S., they could be converted into high-yield securities able to generate revenue. Contractors involved in this so-called repatriation or extraction effort could use the interest from the securities for their own businesses and charitable purposes before delivering the items back to the U.S. Treasury. Sholtz said Keller introduced her in Las Vegas to a cadre of men supposedly able to pull off these sensitive extractions. Many of them had CIA and military special forces backgrounds, and she said Keller told her it was "normal business" to employ them. "He said, 'You're special, the government has been watching you.' I fell for it hook, line and sinker."

Sholtz wasn't exactly dispassionate about the older Keller in those days. In fact, she was in a romantic relationship with him, impressed by his smarts, interests, and charms. "He swept me off my feet," Sholtz said. "He had that Southern air about him." So, during the same summer the Monica Lewinsky scandal exploded, Sholtz, then thirty-three, launched a money-retrieval mission dubbed Operation Bald-Headed Eagle. Its specific target was a pallet of boxes stashed near the Philippine capital of Manila allegedly containing $20 million in mid-1930s U.S. Federal Reserve notes, plus German bonds, platinum bars, and other commodities of mysterious origin and undisclosed value. Based on her correspondence, Sholtz seemed transfixed by it all.

With the money she expected to rake in, Sholtz said she hoped to pave over the financial hole she claimed Keller created for her, re-capitalize her companies and support local philanthropies. To accomplish this trifecta, she founded a "charitable trust" supposedly blessed by the United Nations to take initial possession of the goods, memos show. Sholtz said one of the lawyers assisting her set up Gold Ray Ltd., which was chartered in the British West Indies. Technically, her companies, Automated Credit Exchange and its parent, EonXchange, were not part of Gold Ray. Like the Iran-Contra scandal of the late-1980s, Operation Bald-Headed Eagle married profit to American foreign policy. In the place of the enterprising, buck-toothed Colonel as its shot-caller, it was an entrepreneurial economist who seemed to fancy herself as an Olivia North.

Mission financing was not quite as daring as selling arms for hostages, but it was dicey, nonetheless. According to a September 14th, 2004, memo by Kathy Phelps, the lawyer for the court-appointed trustee overseeing Sholtz's bankruptcy proceedings, an outwardly normal series of RECLAIM trades actually was Sholtz misappropriating roughly 500,000 credits owned by clients Chevron Corporation, Mobil, and oil-and-gas producer Aera Energy, which she then sold to power maker Southern California Edison for $1,913,162. In a June 18th, 1998 letter from Sholtz to Edison, Sholtz instructed the utility to pay that amount to a Florida attorney assisting her with Eagle.

Phelps, approached about her memo entitled "EonXchange—analysis of stolen credits," said she and the bankruptcy trustee handed over evidence about Eagle to the government because it wasn't their focus. Even so, Phelps wondered if the losses Sholtz incurred from Eagle were a reason why she initiated some of the financial improprieties later alleged. "The depth of what [she] was involved in was extensive," Phelps said. Shown Phelps' memo, Sholtz adamantly denied the RECLAIM credits sold to Edison were stolen but conceded she lacked the records to pinpoint where they had originated. "The money we made from the Edison deal was our money!" Sholtz added. "We just sold [Edison] credits we got stuck with from another transaction. It wasn't some grand scheme."

The paper trail suggests otherwise. Within days of receiving the windfall from the Edison transaction, it became the down payment on her plan to ferry former U.S. aid from the Philippines, records show. At its core, Eagle involved retrieving the treasure in a meticulously choreographed, special-access transfer from a holding company near Clark International Airport outside of Manila and flying it 7,400 miles to McCarran International Airport in Las Vegas without the usual inspections.

An aviation outfit on Imperial Highway in El Segundo that called itself Air America Holdings, Inc. agreed to transport the goods on an executive Boeing 707. Sholtz negotiated with the firm's president, who claimed to have been a veteran CIA pilot for the agency's Air America charter airline, which gained notoriety as an American paramilitary asset during the Vietnam War. The airline later disbanded.

This pilot, in a missive on a conspiracy-focused website, said that after Vietnam ended the CIA formed a new, covert airline under his last name. With the agency's assistance, he flew missions from 1974 to 1988, delivering arms to Asia, the Middle East, even the Soviet Union. By the late-1980s, he said he shut the charter down because he believed CIA operations were harming U.S. interests. Two years later, he asserted the Justice Department charged him with wire fraud to "silence and discredit" him. The book, *Drugging America: A Trojan Horse*, also captured his story. The pilot, whose name and others the *Weekly* is withholding because none of them were charged for their participation in Eagle, did not return phone calls seeking comment.

EAGLE LANDS (SORTA)

SHOLTZ SAID THIS PILOT not only told her he was still associated with the CIA; he instructed her on what to write in operational documents. Whether you believe her insistence she was merely the front, and not a ringleader, this was no standard mission. Members of her Eagle team declared holding "diplomatic immunity" and other high-level governmental protections freeing the 707 from customs, immigration, and security scrutiny, Gold Ray letters signed by Sholtz stressed repeatedly.

The team itself was no less formidable. A retired U.S. Army lieutenant colonel with fourteen years in U.S. Special Forces and a Philippine colonel were two of the point men. Another, the overseas lawyer representing the Philippine company maintaining the booty, was once connected to Philippine President Ferdinand Marcos' administration, several knowledgeable sources said. Sholtz recalled meeting this lawyer to discuss Eagle in Sri Lanka, where she said he told her the loot was given to Marcos' people by U.S. authorities who supported them. Marcos was deposed in 1986. Emails and calls to the Philippines embassy about the colonel and to the Philippine Bar Association about the lawyer went unreturned.

Sholtz and Air America Holdings settled on a $200,000 fee for the chartered 707 to make the three-leg trip that would take it from Los Angeles International Airport to the Philippines and finally to Las Vegas, invoices show. On June 26th, 1998, the pilot warranted in a short memo to Sholtz that their aircraft would not face the usual restrictions and protocols landing in Las Vegas, implying Nevada airport personnel were in on the caper and that they had lined up a protected spot to unload the plane's cargo. "This is to certify that entry into and departure from the drop off point of the merchandise has been cleared and traditional formalities for the personnel and merchandise will not be observed," the pilot wrote. No government body, in other words, was going to be hassling them about the contents of the 707's belly.

But three weeks later, Eagle had yet to lift off. The jet they intended to use had experienced "severe mechanical malfunctions," the pilot wrote in a "sincere" apology to Sholtz. "Obtaining an alternate aircraft is not as simple as telephoning a [typical] charter service," he said in a July 13th letter. "The only aircraft we can utilize must meet rather narrow parameters of ownership, nationality, crew requirements and most importantly range." As an alternative, the pilot suggested switching to an older, slower, propeller-driven DC-6 or another Boeing 707 standing by in London. Sholtz would only have to pay $25,000 more for the round trips. "Air America also owns a C-130 but this aircraft is considered too high profile for this mission, and is too expensive to operate," the pilot wrote. "We therefore have discontinued its use."

Despite the hiccups and apparent pressure that Sholtz felt to hasten the mission, her plan still retained its VIP access in and out of international airports. The retired lieutenant colonel working with the ex-CIA pilot, she wrote July 17th, had "full diplomatic papers" that conferred on him "full diplomatic immunity," a flag, "which may have been code for something else" and an inspections clearance-pass alternatively called the "raincoat" or "rain repellent." All she needed from her Manila contacts was confirmation, preferably in writing, that everything was synced in the Philippines, she said in a July 22nd memo. "We prefer the [plane's] tail number not be recorded, but we have been able to alter this as a strict requirement, and we can allow it be recorded... The most important verification is that the diplomatic flight will be able to skip customs and proceed strictly to the hangar" to load the merchandise and related equipment. Air America Holdings, she added, was ready to take off within seventy-two hours of payment.

Asked why she believed Washington would condone such furtive actions when the Air Force could simply dispatch its own C-130 to collect the pallets, Sholtz responded: "I wasn't looking at the mechanics. We were meeting real people who were supposedly working with the U.S. Government. We needed to help our country. I was starry-eyed, thinking this is going to be fantastic! You don't think something this big could not be true." Guy Bailey, a Miami attorney who represented Sholtz on Eagle before a falling out, remembered her recounting the same story as the documents paint. "She said she was in some sort of contractual arrangement with the CIA and the Treasury Department to go retrieve currency, gold, or something from the Philippines," Bailey told the *Weekly*. Bailey said that as far as he knew, the 707 arrived in the Philippines, waited a week there to collect the goods and left with an empty cargo hold for unexplained reasons.

Sholtz said she has heard that version and another one where the booty was returned to the U.S., and everybody profited but her because she had been swindled. By mid-summer 1998, Sholtz said Eagle team members would not answer her questions, then her phone calls. It was as if they had vanished. "I don't know what happened. Sometimes it depends on the day," she said. "I thought they'd chosen us to do this great work, and it was so flattering and if you have any narcissism, it's 'Oh boy.' Nobody said it was illegal. Now I'm thinking there has to be a conspiracy."

NO PRESSURE

WHILE IT SEEMS LIKELY Eagle was little more than a Nigerian-type scam on Sholtz, the fact that RECLAIM money was alleged to have helped finance it infuses it with relevance in understanding how well authorities have policed cap-and-trades heretofore. There is also the issue of Washington's awareness of former—or phony—spies and soldiers portraying themselves as agents on government-sanctioned missions. If something like Eagle would deliver gold bars into a U.S. airport un-checked, what else could be brought into the country?

For its part, the CIA denied involvement with Eagle and its participants. "These individuals, to my knowledge, neither have, nor have had any affiliation with the agency," said Agency Spokesman Paul Gimigliano. "We're not part of this tale." State Department Spokeswoman Laura Tischler said diplomatic officials knew nothing about Eagle, either. She did note it is illegal to claim diplomatic immunity if it is not officially conferred. The Treasury Department never answered the *Weekly*'s inquiries. In New York, the UN Office of Legal Affairs found no evidence after searching its records that the organization was affiliated with Sholtz or Gold Ray. A UN Official said the organization does not typically approve private charities, and says it is illegal to misuse the UN's name.

Meanwhile, back in Los Angeles, the silence over Eagle today is crushing. All three companies allegedly fleeced of their RECLAIM credits to help finance the scheme—Chevron, Mobil, and Aera—

refused comment or never returned calls. Edison Spokesman Steve Conroy would only say the utility was reviewing the matter after the *Weekly*'s inquiries.

In spite of ample documentation and a four year investigation, the U.S. Attorney's Office never charged Sholtz, Keller or their associates with a potential array of felonies stemming from alleged misuse of smog credit money or the extraction scheme. One natural question that arises is whether the U.S. Intelligence Community or other federal officials pressed the Justice Department not to prosecute Eagle for unstated reasons, and whether that prompted the record-sealing and prosecutorial silence. Justice Department spokesman Thom Mrozek rejected the notion of external arm-twisting. In fact, his only elaboration on the entire Sholtz matter was that his office "has never been influenced by political pressure" from outside.

For all the Department of Justice's explanations, EPA officials were disappointed Eagle was not prosecuted or fleshed out by the FBI and others. In a statement to the *Weekly*, the EPA said: "[We] investigated this fraudulent scheme because companies and individuals must legally and accurately trade air pollution credits if cap-and-trade programs are to succeed and air emissions are to be actually reduced." The agency had known about the offshore ventures for years. In 2004, Ronald Modjeski, the EPA criminal investigative agent assigned the case, filed an affidavit confirming Sholtz's deal making for federal reserve notes, currency, gold, and other financial instruments for "large amounts of money." The EPA refused to allow Modjeski, who spent nearly 4,000 man hours investigating Sholtz, to be interviewed.

HOOKY SPOOKY

In hindsight, Sholtz said that she believes Keller and the others on the Eagle team targeted her all along. They probably knew from research that her maternal grandfather, David Sholtz, had been governor of Florida during the 1930s, and decided to appeal to her public service instinct, she added. Soon after she fired Keller in 2000, Sholtz said the tone of their relationship changed. She claimed that he began placing threatening phone calls describing what she was wearing, her location and how he didn't plan on serving any jail time to intimidate her from testifying about him. In Pasadena in 2002, Sholtz said another Eagle participant tried frightening her with the warning: "You know people disappear all the time." She refused to identify him. "I told the U.S. Attorney during my prosecution that there's this whole world where people are roped into thinking they are working with the CIA and military personnel or [the National Security Agency] and they didn't seem interested. I got scammed, but so do a lot of people and they're too embarrassed to talk about it."

After Eagle fizzled, Sholtz did not lose her appetite for cloak-and-dagger currency repatriation. Just months later, in February 1999, she set her sights on the western coast of Africa, documents and interviews indicate. This time, Sholtz hired Dale Toler, a former combat pilot with an intelligence background who was now CEO of a Virginia electronics-technology company. His assignment: to haul back $35 million in U.S. currency supposedly squirreled away in Ghana. A mission report about the venture, prepared by the squad acting on Sholtz's behalf, said the U.S. Treasury Department suspected beforehand that the U.S. cash the Africans contended holding was "potentially fraudulent." Even so, the report said, "preliminary arrangements were also made with United States Customs officials for a prearranged arrival point" should the "recovery" be successful. The millions at the center of it had originally been appropriated for Sierra Leone, a small, mineral-rich, war-torn country west of Ghana.

The trip to extract the $35 million for Sholtz formally kicked off when her squad's lead agent met a burly, bespectacled doctor who had represented himself as Ghana's security chief at the Golden Tulip hotel in the capital city of Accra. (Toler, in an interview with the *Weekly*, confirmed he was there without letting on whether he was the negotiating agent.) Detective work soon confirmed the Ghanaian had lied about the position he supposedly held, but he knew plenty about the $35 million. The agent drove with him in a black Dodge Dakota pickup for about forty-five minutes to a private, walled residential compound topped with shards of glass for a discussion on how the money would be transferred. Security personnel concerned about the agent's safety tailed the pickup as long as they could.

Inside the property, the Ghanaian told the agent he required $80,000 for his cut to arrange the movement of the U.S. currency to the Accra airport for its repatriation to America. "Not so fast," the agent said. Under the original agreement, the Ghanaian was to receive his commission after the transfer. The Ghanaian said his terms had changed: he needed early compensation to pay others involved. For an hour, the two men squabbled back and forth over logistics and promises to no avail. Afterwards, the Ghanaian drove Sholtz's representative back to the Golden Tulip hotel in a circuitous route so the agent would be unable to retrace where he had been.

A few hours later, during a night meeting at the Kata International Hotel, the two tried reviving the negotiations. Sholtz's agent insisted on seeing the $35 million with his own eyes; his counterpart demanded $10,000 for the privilege. After being arm-twisted further, the Ghanaian agreed to the inspection. The next day he picked up the agent at the Golden Tulip and took him to a different walled compound. At a picnic table inside, the agent was shown stacks of what appeared to be American currency "five wide and two across," the mission report said. They money was wrapped in thick plastic and stored in a small, metal box. When the agent tried touching the currency, he was warned he was not allowed to by one of the Ghanaian's associates. The associate tried delicately unsealing a packet to show him it was genuine, only to clumsily reveal ordinary paper with the dimensions of U.S. dollars tucked under the real ones.

Realizing his own vulnerability in the midst of a flimsy con, the agent pretended he was satisfied and requested to be driven back to the Golden Tulip by the Ghanaian's associates. The car took a long, winding path in the dark until the agent determined they were headed in the opposite way of the hotel and maybe to someplace from where he would never return alive. When traffic slowed, the agent jumped out of the car and "evaded" the men, the mission report said, in what might have been a scene out of an espionage flick. From solicitation to dangled loot, the whole setup was a "scam," the report concluded.

Sholtz estimated she lost more than $125,000 of her own money on the failed excursion. There is no indication RECLAIM credits were involved. Toler said one of the chief reasons he agreed to go, despite suspecting beforehand the $35 million was bogus, was that Sholtz herself was planning to make the trip, and that she likely would have been either kidnapped for ransom or killed by the Africans. (Sholtz acknowledged she had intended to go.) Toler, overall, blamed Keller for whipping up Sholtz, who he described as dishonest and gullible. "Much of this [currency repatriation] is fantasy," Toler added. But Sholtz "believed there was money in the Philippines and Ghana, even though she had been advised by me it didn't exist. It was her greed. People made a lot of money off her. I've seen over the years folks who think the world revolves around a deal." Toler said that Keller died in the Bahamas a few years ago; this may explain why the feds have had difficulty saying whether they ever charged him.

In October 1992, about five years before the Ghana operation, a congressional probe into international bank fraud suggested that Toler's firm, a now defunct Virginia machine-tool company called RD&D, was part of an alleged, clandestine effort quarterbacked by the CIA to arm the Iraqi military and curry favor with Saddam Hussein's government. A federal prosecutor appearing before a Senate intelligence committee testified that Toler's company was not a CIA front, but wouldn't respond when asked if Toler had worked for the U.S. National Security Administration, which conducts global eavesdropping operations. Whatever his background, Sholtz said she was stunned at Toler's negative comments about her. Sholtz said that Toler in 2002 tried to locate money she contends that Keller had "stolen" from her. "Toler said we were the victims, and now he's changing his story," Sholtz said. "I'm speechless."

Also involved in the Ghana operation, records and interviews show, was the Jedburgh Group, a Lake Mary, Florida-based firm that provides intelligence, security and financial services to industry and governments worldwide. Former U.S. Intelligence and Military Officers work for Jedburgh. By far the best known is retired U.S. Major General John Singlaub, a decorated military officer involved with the CIA's predecessor agency, the Korean War, and American counterinsurgency efforts. In the late-1980s, he was connected to the Iran-Contra scandal and ultra-right-wing, anti-communist groups in Central America.

Jedburgh executive David Keith Freeman confirmed to the *Weekly* that his company was a client of Sholtz's "for a short time a very long time ago," and said it helped evaluate the mission's "potential for recovery." He refused further comment about Ghana and other work the firm provided for Sholtz, citing client confidentiality rules. Freeman did say the practice of people posing as former or current U.S. Intelligence Officers in financial scams is fairly widespread and known in the industry as "hooky spooky," he said. "It's the frog and the scorpion."

Roughly six months later after the Ghana operation debacle, in November 1999, with authorities still unaware of what had occurred, Sholtz was not a marked smog credit broker, by any means. She was an invitee to a major climate change conference at the United Nations as a member of the Emissions Marketing Association, records show.

IT COMES AND GOES

SO WHY WEREN'T THESE activities in the Justice Department's crosshairs if they wanted to send a message about tainting cap-and-trades as the regulatory milieu shifts toward them? Furthermore, even if there are legitimate ex-spies and soldiers traveling around the globe for someone like Sholtz, shouldn't there be some transparency? USC Law School Professor Rebecca Lonergan, who worked in the U.S. Attorney's Los Angeles office for sixteen years, said prosecutors probably made a judgment call based on what they could prove in court, what evidence they could gather overseas, the intricacies of her different schemes and other factors. "When you have a person like [Sholtz] one of the difficulties is sifting through the mass of seemingly exculpatory evidence," Lonegran said. "You have a person who would make a great movie living as a con artist but you have to find out the individual schemes. Criminal prosecutors simply can't charge a person with being a fraudster."

True as that may be, there is still interest. Larry Neal, deputy Republican staff director for the House Energy and Commerce Committee, said Congressmen Barton and Walden believe it is important to remove the veil of secrecy over the Sholtz matter to follow where it leads. "We haven't seen allegations on currency repatriation scams, but it is our aim to gather all facts surrounding the Sholtz case, regardless of what they entail," Neal wrote via email. "It has been more than a year since the sentencing and there's still no public justification for all the judicial [secrecy]. After all, the case was about an Anne Sholtz cap-and-trade scam, not an al Qaeda terrorism cell."

For his part, AQMD Executive Director Barry Wallerstein both refused an interview about Sholtz and forbade anyone at the air district from commenting for this story. (His feelings about Sholtz aside, Wallerstein is said to be upset about a book on the iconic Los Angeles smog crisis this writer co-authored with a former AQMD staffer.) But that does not mean he's not talking. In a seven-page letter to Representative Henry Waxman who chairs the House's Energy and Commerce Committee, Wallerstein portrayed the RECLAIM cap-and-trade as virtually bulletproof to criminality. In this letter, prompted by congressional interest in Sholtz, Wallerstein ticked off the AQMD's robust computer database that checks the availability and ownership of credits, well-scrutinized trade registration forms and a three-person trade approval team. "The safeguards...have been successful in preventing any fraudulent trades from ever being registered," Wallerstein concluded.

Yet considering the breadth of Sholtz's activities, questions about whether RECLAIM bankrolled attempted asset-repatriation ventures, much less speculators' profiteering of the market during the 2001-02 electricity crisis, there are obviously cracks in the machine. Would stamping the credits with identification numbers and developing methods to police their ownership history in real time have helped? "What this points up is that there had to have been a failure in the design," said EPA Senior Counsel Allan Zabel. "It's ridiculous if people can get away with this sort of stuff. The system must be sufficiently designed so that somebody trying to do it would trigger a red flag that brings in investigative interest."

In answering some of Barton and Walden's questions about cap-and-trade fraud, the EPA said its criminal investigative agents meet with AQMD officials weekly. As of June, though, the EPA reported it had no criminal cases with filed charges involving emissions trading crimes—anywhere. But the story does not end there. Between the time of her arrest and the date of her sentencing,

Sholtz tried softening her punishment. In 2005, she testified in the trial of a con man who stole about $4.5 million from an Idaho businessman in a wire fraud case that she knew about from her financial dealings. More provocatively, she offered to spill about sensitive subjects closer to home.

On April 9th, 2005, her lawyer, Richard Callahan, emailed the U.S. Attorney's Office a two-page letter entitled "Areas of Possible Cooperation for Anne Sholtz." Callahan wrote that his client would share "credible firsthand information" on four different subjects if it would help Sholtz's plea agreement. Sholtz, Callahan wrote, knew about a "major U.S. bank" that was engaged in money laundering, check kiting, manipulation of subpoenaed documents, and even murder. In a direct reference to the Eagle scheme and others, Callahan said Sholtz had details about "fraud, money laundering [and] wire fraud by people claiming to work for the U.S. government...in the 'extraction of assets' overseas..."

Sholtz's last tipoff was a humdinger. Callahan said that she had knowledge of "repeated and flagrant violations" inside the air district's RECLAIM program that resulted in retribution—and threats of more of it—against potential whistleblowers, and the release of over one million excess pounds of nitrogen oxide when AQMD personnel could have offset it. By 2007, RECLAIM had transacted about forty million pounds of air pollution credits, reports show, so one million pounds in unauthorized discharges would be no small addition. Sholtz, Callahan said, also knew about "manipulation of data [or presenting it in a misleading fashion] to choose projects that would lead to personal gain for (AQMD) Board Members..." This document was the only one in which Sholtz declined comment. It is not evident if any of her tips sparked arrests or investigations because there have been no publicly revealed inquiries into RECLAIM since Sholtz's arrest. A district spokesperson asked for comment referred back to Wallerstein's gag order.

If all this seems like a crippling, humiliating and tragic slide for someone who might have ascended to legend of the Green Economy, Sholtz said she has largely put it behind her as she moves towards new horizons that she aimed to keep private. She is not sure if she will re-approach the cap-and-trade world again if she is allowed to broker. "The RECLAIM business was exciting," Sholtz said, her eyebrows arching. "Being able to do a transaction, solve a problem, make software do new things, help the environment. The money just comes in and it goes."

LA Weekly *News Editor Jill Stewart contributed to this story*

SCAFFOLDING MAN AND MACHINE

Few incidents can compare to the tragedies that occurred and the ensuing public dramas that played out after the day the Colorado Street Bridge nearly fell apart.

—*Pasadena Weekly*, September 18th, 2003

JUST PAST QUITTING TIME on Friday August 1st, 1913, soot-caked construction workers pouring concrete into the highest arch of the future Colorado Street Bridge heard a bloodcurdling snap. Something that wasn't supposed to had torn loose. Hovering 150 feet above the Arroyo Seco, a lush view all around, the men felt their boots tremble. Seconds later, the walkway below them dissolved and a colleague hollered, "Jump!"

By the ungodly rumble, it was as if the entire structure was collapsing.

Actually, only a minor section on the San Rafael side had, but it packed a devastating wallop. When the mold for the top of span number nine buckled, it created a thunderous pancaking action that snatched three workers–and almost eight more–in a violent, plunging mass. Hundreds of tons of wet concrete, scaffolding, man, and machine came crashing onto the floor of the valley, kicking up dust and pandemonium where there had been nifty organization before.

The boom ricocheted through the gorge, into the undulating, green hills of Busch Gardens, off the Vista Del Arroyo Hotel and toward the storefronts along Colorado Boulevard. Burly carpenters and concrete men rushed toward the cloudy pile. Above them, scaffolding shaken loose by the jarring, dangled precariously. A lookout was later stationed to monitor what might else plummet.

Within half an hour, hundreds of townsfolk drawn by the concussive sound had hurried into the Arroyo Seco to rubberneck or volunteer assistance. On this dusky Friday, the parlors and clinking shops could wait, and police sweated to work crowd control. Businessmen asked what had gone wrong. Women sobbed. Those closest to the accident perimeter could see one of the gruesome results: John Visco, an Italian-born carpenter with an infant at home, had died instantly. If his broken neck hadn't killed him, his crushed skull had.

James "C.J." Johnson, a native Missourian who earned his pay stubs raking concrete through the forms, was still breathing. The devout were convinced his survival transcended dumb luck. They believed it was a God-given miracle. The timbers that had swept off the twenty-eight year old married man from his perch had cushioned his thump and then crisscrossed over him so he was not struck by falling wreckage. It took twenty minutes to dig him out. Transported by ambulance to Marengo Avenue Hospital, he was one torn-up fellow. Doctors said his arm was mangled, he would probably lose an eye and that he had suffered head trauma and internal bleeding.

UP TO HIS NECK

THE SOLE PASADENAN AMONG the casualties was a wire technician identified as Harry Collins of Delacey Street. He had been buried alive underneath an estimated twelve feet of soupy concrete and muck. Groaning in pain, consumed in darkness, he begged for someone, anyone to help him.

Groveling was not required. While one group attended Johnson, another focused on Collins. Led by the shift foreman, people grabbed crowbars, jacks, saws, and axes to extricate him from what one observer called "the death pile." Space was cramped, and the rescue party winnowed to eight men. After three or four hours, the last part digging by lantern, they had made real progress. A *Los Angeles Times* reporter on scene said the men "burrowed into the heap like prairie dogs, sawing their way as they went." When Collins whimpered he could not last, a chum reassured him he could. "Never mind, old man," he said. "We'll have you out soon."

Upon reaching him through a makeshift hole, the rescuers found their victim covered up to his neck in hardening concrete that he moaned was stinging his eyes. He was in unbearable pain. R.H. Newcomb, an area physician who had come to assist, begged to do something to numb the man's suffering. So, a rope was tied around Newcomb, and he was lowered into the hole by a jury-rigged hoist. The doctor gave Collins a sleep-inducing hypodermic shot right into the forehead because that was only part of him exposed. Eventually he was carried to Pasadena Hospital in critical condition.

ALL CLEAR

THE RESCUE IN THE gorge was as dramatic as the collapse was shocking. A buzz pierced the 30,000-plus-town of eccentrics and scions, housewives and haberdashers. In-the-know company men tried pedaling the bright side to the most shaken. Had the top of the arch fallen an hour earlier instead of at knock-off time, a dozen men might have perished. See, it could have been worse.

As it were, charges of the Mercereau Bridge & Construction Company, the job contractor, recounted white-knuckled escapes that made for vivid reading. The competing newspapers were going at it to play up the drama, but going at it without riling the status quo.

One worker told of the experience that almost splattered him in the dirt. He had been preparing to climb down the superstructure to grab some chow at the mess-tent when the scaffolding snapped and the floor beneath him literally vanished. About to drop, he threw his arms around a steel brace jutting from one of the dried forms and hung mid-air until he could whip his torso over a beam. A co-worker and his relative who swung right next to him used the same escape: they grabbed strips of reinforcing metal rebar in the concrete and held on for dear life. Apparent Hispanics, their last name was the same as the street—Colorado. Once they pulled themselves up, they shimmied down the bridge and helped yank out Collins.

During the next several days, general disbelief and puzzlement about the collapse gelled to fuzzy anger about the cause. Muttering aloud, average folks asked how all hell had broken loose with no warning from safety inspectors and no inkling of prior trouble? The previous fourteen months of construction had seen nothing much go wrong. Sure, the grunts earned crackerjack wages—$2 to $4.50 a day, in part because of the hazards—but they had trusted the engineers to return them to their families intact.

For the brain trust of the Colorado Street Bridge, another question dominated. Would the $234,000 project be delayed past its expected October premiere date? Schedules and reputations were at stake. If completed, this would be the tallest concrete overpass of its kind anyplace in the world and certainly the finest in Southern California. It would be a legend from birth.

A post-accident inspection squelched that uncertainty.

"From my observations this morning, I can say there is no injury to the arch of the bridge, although it had a very severe test," proclaimed City Councilmember and Public Works Commissioner T.D. Allin. "The opening of the bridge probably will be delayed [just] thirty days. If there is traffic over it by Thanksgiving, I will be satisfied."

SUICIDE BRIDGE

Come December 13th, it will be exactly ninety years since the Colorado Street Bridge's ceremonial ribbons were cut and the praise gushed. Ninety years since the bridge was first lionized for its breathtaking arches, dreamy curve and goblet lampposts. Functionally, its opening gave Pasadena an automotive gateway to reach Los Angeles, the cowtown metropolis with all the banks. Equally important, it provided access to the region's most stylish suburb.

Forget that redolent New Year's Day parade. Pasadenans were bananas about their motorcars before Henry Ford was a name-brand icon. With an estimated 5,000 cars in 1913, many owned by East Coast magnates with vacation estates here, there were more tailpipes per capita in the Crown City than anyplace in America. At the Huntington Hotel, where luxury came standard, the garage had room for 150 cars. (To keep the hired help rested—and segregated from their class-conscious masters—there was sleeping quarters for forty chauffeurs.)

The car culture exploded in ensuing years. The bridge was nearly detonated. Government engineers classified it obsolete before it hit adolescence. What traffic wear-and-tear did not undermine, structural questions and eroding floodwaters from the Devil's Gate area nearly accomplished. The state wanted it dismantled in 1935. And 1951. And 1977. Finally a decade ago, a $27.3 million overhaul spearheaded by a local preservation group wrapped up, ensuring the span would not be tomorrow's trivia stumper. It rests today protected on the National Register of Historic Places.

The bridge's aesthetic shimmer certainly stirred the imagination. Creative types have worn out pens and paintbrushes trying to capture the soul of the 1,468 foot long viaduct. Elegant and functional, a hearty endorsement of man's capacity to tame nature with geometrical élan, there is a singular magnetism about it that still rivets the eye.

Less celebrated, though just as enduring among the masses, the bridge has also nurtured a macabre alter ego its prim designers never asked for. Well over a hundred people have killed themselves by leaping from "Suicide Bridge," roughly a third of them during the Great Depression. One of the first jumpers was the ill wife of a Los Angeles tie-maker. One of the last may have been a guilt-ridden freshman bible student from the now-closed Worldwide Church of God.

Not surprisingly, the urban mythology that has flowered around bridge-related deaths has fostered ghost stories and cultish twaddle. A pervasive rumor was that an immigrant construction worker lost his balance and tumbled into a drying concrete forms. According to legend, the foreman did not notice the man's absence until it was too late, and his body was left there entombed. Betrayed in life, the worker's spirit supposedly has haunted the bridge from the netherworld, beckoning the lost and dejected to join him. Researchers who have combed into this story have concluded it was a campfire tale fanned in the dark alleys of the Internet.

Little interest, conversely, has been devoted to the events of August 1st, 1913. There has been almost nothing written in depth about the incident that took the lives of three, possibly four men since the calamity itself. It is a throwaway line in coffee-table books, an historical afterthought in a city giddy about its nostalgia.

But thumb through the old newspaper accounts and one might conclude the forebears of the Colorado Street Bridge wanted people to forget. The span had been a hard sell even if had been a practical one.

ONE MAN'S DREAM

BEFORE THE BRIDGE WAS up, crossing the Arroyo had been a sweaty, unreliable affair that bogged down horses, buggies and crank-started cars. After 1892, the roads descending toward the only east-west crossing over the streambed, the privately owned Scoville Bridge, were winding and prone to mudslides. People got hurt, an indeterminate number killed, on the zigzagging passage from Orange Grove Boulevard, site of Millionaire Row, to the rugged hills of Annandale and San Rafael.

Even so, it was not the politicians or the growing car industry agitating for a street-level conduit. It was the chief of Pasadena's Board of Trade, forerunner of the Chamber of Commerce. Edwin Sorver, a curly-haired, East Coast transplant, was the young go-getter who ran the group. He craved big progress, and could stomach righteous battles. For a city trying to flourish beyond being an address for blue bloods and health resorts, the basics were required. It needed its own water supply, its own electricity free of Edison's grip and, naturally, freedom of movement.

Well, Sorver's bridge vision was polarizing. One band of citizens was spitting-mad about the cost. Effected homeowners along the Arroyo were upset too about its eyesore potential. NIMBYism in a pocket watch world was not much different than NIMBYism in the digital one.

But Sorver and his minions stumped exhaustively. They ran pro-bridge ads, printed posters and guided naysayers on tours. "Modern roads, not horse trails!" was the campaign slogan. Case made for them, Pasadena voters overwhelming approved a $100,000 bond measure to pay for a fair chunk of it. The county and the three cities involved (Pasadena, L.A. and the now-defunct town of San Rafael) chipped in the balance.

Construction had gone well. The only serious commotion had predated it. For chief designer, Sorver had handpicked John Alexander Low Waddell, a decorated, globetrotting Kansas City engineer with a passing resemblance to Teddy Roosevelt. Waddell, known for lift bridges, devised the eleven-arch superstructure that stands today. Its proposed budget just happened to be $6,000 over budget. When Sorver pressed him to shave expenses, the proud Waddell said he already had, and he knew his business better than some booster.

Feeling squeezed, Sorver went around Waddell. He consulted with the man who had built three L.A.-area beach piers, a handsome contractor named John Drake Mercereau. He did some technical thinking and suggested the unorthodox. Mercereau concluded they could save the money by curving the eastern side of the bridge fifty degrees to take advantage of firmer substrate than where Waddell's foundations would have been sunk. It would make the roadway longer but less complicated. Sorver agreed happily. Waddell did not. He went ape, lampooning the idea as unsound engineering, yet still stayed on board.

This was not just any roadbed; the Colorado Street Bridge was national news, and its state-of-the-art assemblage fascinated both the gentry and commoners.

Forty to seventy workers employed by Mercereau hammered, poured and sawed at any one shift. Horse-drawn wagons schlepped timbers for scaffolding and the forms down the Arroyo. Sand and gravel were brought in by truck and later mixed with cement by a gasoline-powered turbine. The resulting concrete slurry was then poured directly into receiving hoppers, like steel dump cars, running on a specially designed tramway where the road would eventually be. It was not efficient to blend ingredients on the ground and have to pulley it up fifteen stories when you could mix it directly over the forms. This was not the 1800s. Gravity and machines were allies.

BUT NOT ALWAYS

Visco and Johnson had been on the track near one of the hoppers when the rumbling began at 5:00 p.m. Collins, a concrete finisher, was in the center of scaffolding nearby. The men who escaped had been on the edge of it. One accident theory floated was that somebody had goofed by forgetting to set the brake on one of the dump-cars. The rolling bin might have accidentally struck a post holding the arch's wooden cast in place. When it gave way, it sent the dump-car, the scaffolding and all those tons of liquid concrete hurtling downward in a lethal avalanche.

Nobody knew for sure. At the dawn of the Progressive Era in California politics, there were no industrial workplace investigators or worker's compensation funds. Personal injury lawyers did not skulk around, at least not just yet. And muckracking journalism was only emerging. (The progenitor of it, writer Upton Sinclair, relocated to the Pasadena good life in 1915.)

Neither were there any leadership declarations about getting to the bottom of the incident. Sorver, Mercereau, and Waddell said zero publicly. The same went for Mayor Richard Lee Metcalf and the rest of the Pasadena City Council. At the two Council meetings following the accident, the top city business was a citizen protest about flat-wheel trolley cars and denial of a Maple Street sidewalk extension. The members of the County Board of Supervisors who traveled to the accident site on August 2nd to inspect it stayed mum, too.

Officially, the compelling news was the cost to repair the lost arch and scaffolding: $1,500. The safety worry was about the rickety scaffolding that had not dropped. What already had fallen seemed incidental.

Completing the bridge was the benchmark. Construction also was a dirty, dangerous profession that claimed thousands of lives every year in post-Industrial America. You cannot judge any of it by today's standards, but you can wonder.

"There was a more haphazard approach to these issues then," explained state historian Kevin Starr. "The temptation is to imply a conspiracy [by the politicians], which can be true, but it can also be that it just didn't register on the radar screen."

Did the cities and the companies at least send back-door condolences to the victim's families? Was there a moment a silence? A check cut? A memorial plaque? All these years later, it is the mystery stitched through the bloodstains.

"To the extent city fathers saw this as a potential [hurdle] to their great dream, they wanted it to keep it moving like George

Ellery trying to get the telescope up to Mount Wilson," said Sue Mossman, Executive Director of Pasadena Heritage, the preservation outfit that has championed the bridge. "When you look at the magnitude of the project and the way it was built basically by hand, the probability there'd be an accident was pretty high... And, this bridge was fairly controversial."

WHIMSY AND DESPAIR

If there was a face to the tragedy, it was Visco's. A *Pasadena Daily News* article published August 4th characterized the family's loss as one of "clean-minded aspiration cut short by 'fate.'"

Visco had emigrated to the U.S. as a child. He was not much for mingling or chitchat about Woodrow Wilson and his League of Nations or pennant races. He wanted to assimilate, enrolling himself in a night course to learn English. Carpentry was his trade but he poured concrete for Mr. Mercereau.

In 1912 he married a pretty, olive-skinned woman who had come to the states from Mazatlán, Mexico. Visco was Juana Rojas' third husband. Her first had died, her second had run off and she had to work in a San Diego laundry to support her two kids. When she married Visco, they set up house on Wilde Street, southwest of downtown L.A. In summer of 1913, three weeks before she would be widowed again, Juana delivered Visco's son, John, Jr.

Nobody from the city or the company came in person to inform her about the accident at first. A neighbor of hers, a carpenter who happened to have read a story about it, took on that duty around sunrise on August 2nd. He rapped on the door and looked so pale that Juana asked if he was sick. No, the neighbor told her. It was John who had been hurt.

"Oh," she said, "I know he is dead."

Later that afternoon a Mercereau representative dropped by, offering to help. Juana was said to be frantic. Then she refused to believe her husband was gone.

Two generations later, the vestiges of Juana's grief remain in her granddaughter's creaky memories. Pasadena Police Commander Marilyn Diaz, whose paternal grandfather was Juana's second husband, has tried reconstructing what happened in the aftermath of Visco's gory fall. His son, John, Jr., turned out like the dad he never really knew—self-taught, determined, Diaz said. He was a Culver City fireman before he went into the trunk footlocker business with Diaz's father.

Twice widowed, Juana died before World War II.

"It leaves me a little bit wistful," said Diaz, a thirty year department veteran who runs the field operations division. "I think about when this occurred, the police never went out and notified my grandmother. Almost a hundred years later, the Pasadena Police Department has changed. We have tremendous support for victim's families, whether it involves a gang member or anybody else. We want to show dignity. It's a different time."

Scant personal information was revealed about the other two fatalities. Collins, who had come to Pasadena just four months earlier from Camden, New Jersey, was wounded head-to-toe and at one point had nine nurses treating him, plus Dr. Newcomb. They had to scrape dried concrete off him, and it was almost impossible without hurting him more. Collins died of infections from his wounds on August 10th, wounds which would be easily treatable today with antibiotics. He left behind a five year old son. Johnson, the concrete raker, expired from his wounds as well.

On August 4th, 1913 the tough questions started flying. A coroner's jury, a citizen's panel summoned to investigate and deliberate on certain fatalities like a specialized grand jury, gathered at the Turner-and-Stevens funeral parlor on North Raymond Avenue.

A Mercereau vice president named F.W. Proctor testified early on. He admitted he still was puzzled. The only scenario he could think of was that the mold for the top of the arch, otherwise known as false work, had probably broken because it had been improperly over-weighted. When it snapped, the concrete burst through the rows of scaffolding, taking Collins, Johnson, and Visco with it.

"Something gave way," Proctor said. "Nobody knows what... It's one of those things that makes a man wonder how much he knows after all."

"Was there any inspection of the work as it proceeded?" he was asked.

"The City of Pasadena has an engineer on the job," Proctor piped up.

Before more could be learned, City Coroner Calvin Hartwell abruptly ended this line of inquiry. He told the jury that the section of the arch destroyed, a thirty foot by sixty foot frame, was outside Pasadena boundaries, in the minutely inhabited city of San Rafael. Thus, Pasadena's responsibility was nullified. Officials from the city across the gorge were never trotted before the jury. (San Rafael, which includes what is now the Linda Vista area and land west of the bridge, was mainly farmland run by two families. It was annexed by Pasadena in 1914.)

Coroner jury member F.F. Berry was dissatisfied with what he heard. Based on newspaper accounts from the time, he bore down on the foreman of the carpenters, one John Galloway. Had the false work been inspected? Berry asked. Yes, Galloway said. They always checked for signs of weight-bearing strain. Okay, Berry continued, were there any safety precautions (in this, the age before safety harnesses)? Galloway replied there were ropes workers could grab, but he did not seem to understand the gist of the question.

In the end, the jury's verdict was a stale one absent of personal blame, but the message was potent. "Visco's death," the jury wrote, "was the result of a fracture of the skull caused by faulty construction of the false work of the Colorado Street Bridge which fell August 1."

Judgment made, the impaneled group was dismissed. No charges were ever brought.

Hollywood, though, understood a dramatic story when it saw one. A week after the boom in the Arroyo, a script had already been written to depict it as a silent movie. The Lubin Company shot the "moving picture play" using the bridge and the city's Union National Bank as backdrops. Spectators watched the filming. The storyline involved a promising young architect who falls in love with the bank president's daughter. Through wiles or connections, the architect lands a "very important" bridge contract. Then the bridge collapses.

A *Pasadena Star-News* writer who refused to give away the entire plot said it would be "sufficiently interesting" to locals if the picture ever made the movie palaces in town. It is unclear if this ever did.

Four months later, bands and bunting infused the Colorado Street Bridge dedication with an electric, carnival atmosphere.

Among other pols, the chairman of the county Board of Supervisors spoke and drew "gasps of amazement" from the large crowd. There were already 40,000 cars in the county, he said, and every one of them eventually would be traversing the bridge.

Mercereau didn't make the celebration: she had been killed in a car accident inspecting a damn he built in Ventura County. Waddell did not attend either, and there was ripe speculation he was still upset about the revision to his design. Whether another pall hung over him or the others no one can say today.

To read how dozens of people ninety years ago risked their own lives to try and rescue two men in the shadow of a wobbled colossus with tons of scaffolding teetering above them is a remarkable ode to heart. One eyewitness said there was, "probably no greater act of heroism ever performed in the city." To read how the responsible were let off the hook is a darker trip backwards.

Special thanks to the staff of the Pasadena Public Library, the Pasadena Museum of History, Pasadena Heritage and Ray Dashner.

THE FULL EMPLOYMENT ACT FOR SPIES

Peace breaking out around globe encourages spies.
—Los Angeles Business Journal, July 9th, 1990

IN THE SIX YEARS since Richard Miller waddled into espionage fame by trading FBI secrets for a trench coat, $65,000, and the sexual favors of a KGB agent, U.S.-Soviet relations got downright friendly.

But not friendly enough to put spying out of business, even in Los Angeles where the world of espionage mingles oddly with smog, traffic, and glitz. Experts say it is a golden irony of glasnost that as the Cold War was swept away in Europe, spying has heated up—especially in the Southland, where liberal Hollywood producers have portrayed communism as a romantic alternative to capitalism.

"It's not a question if the KGB is in Southern California, it's a question of how many are there," asserted former CIA officer George Carver. It doesn't take a Kremlinologist to figure out why.

For decades, the Pentagon has directed billions of dollars in defense contracts to the likes of Lockheed, Northrop, Rockwell, and Hughes, all based in Los Angeles. The result, in the words of Los Angeles FBI Chief Lawrence Lawler, is that "Southern California is the most target-rich area in terms of technology in the U.S. The Soviets know that well."

Indeed, much of America's military arsenal was designed or built in Los Angeles—from nuclear-tipped missiles and eavesdropping satellites, to battle-ready jets and Star Wars gear. Encircling that sprawling weapons assembly line are a host of military bases like the Long Beach Naval Shipyard, Riverside's March Air Force Base, and the Air Force's Special Projects Office in El Segundo. Even Rand Corporation, the think tank that has honed some of

America's greatest defense minds, sits unobtrusively under the palm trees in Santa Monica.

That has made Southern California a juicy target for Soviet espionage, even more so today as the funds for Moscow's military arsenal shrink under perostroika.

"There are a lot of Russians who have come over here since things have gotten better [between the two countries]," said Zola Zlobinski, an émigré from Kiev who has been in America since 1976. "Most of them just want a better life, but some of them look suspicious and ask a lot of questions like the KGB does."

Zlobinski has reason to be dubious. Her father gave convincted KGB agent Svetlana Ogorodnikov $10,000 to deliver to his brother to Russia before the spy case erupted. But Ogorodnikov, the woman who seduced Miller, never carried out her end of the bargain. "My mother almost got into a fight with her because of that," Zola said.

The Miller spy scandal proved typical East-West hubs of espionage–Moscow, Washington, Berlin, and Vienna–do not have a monopoly on spies. And Hollywood's idea that KGB and CIA agents only snoop around in the cold with trench coats on, like the $675 Burberry number Svetlana gave her FBI lover, was laughable.

So was the Miller case, to a point.

Likened to an overweight Inspector Clouseau of *Pink Panther* fame, Miller became the first FBI agent ever charged with espionage, though he claimed he was only trying to revive his sagging career by infiltrating the KGB. His first trial ended in a mistrial in 1985, but he was convicted during the second trial for giving Ogorodnikov a secret FBI manual on U.S. espionage goals.

Miller, now fifty-two, appealed his conviction and begins a third trial next month.

The first two trials shocked Angelenos, more accustomed to hearing about movie-star gossip or the newest kind of frozen yogurt than stories fit for a John Le Carré thriller. Revelations about secret dinners in Mischa's Russian restaurant and meetings between KGB agents and undercover FBI agents from Los Angeles International Airport to Marina del Rey titillated the city.

But, intelligence experts, say, the Miller case was sensationalized by the press, and cloaked a more sophisticated KGB penetration of Los Angeles.

The Soviets, say the FBI, launched West Coast espionage operations from two primary spots: their consulate in San Francisco and their embassy in Mexico City. The KGB has been buoyed by its success in California's high-tech haven, Silicon Valley, which Carver says the KGB wanted to make into "an extension of the Soviet industrial base."

Fifteen years ago Andrew Daulton Lee and his friend Christopher Boyce, an employee at TRW's El Segundo facility, were convicted of selling a top-secret satellite manual to the Soviets, enabling Moscow to learn of U.S. intelligence gathering and missile-tracking methods. That case later became the inspiration for the movie *The Falcon and the Snowman.*

Hughes Aircraft Company also had a run-in with espionage in 1981. Hughes employee William Holden Bell was recruited by a Polish intelligence officer, acting as a proxy for the KGB, and traded data on secret radar systems, air-to-air missiles, and NATO defense secrets for the bargain-basement price of $110,000.

And Northrop, which probably fears congressional budget cutters as much as the KGB, had one of its employees caught in an FBI sting for trying to sell sensitive stealth technology.

(Even John Walker, Jr., who gave the KGB a wealth of material on cruise missiles, U.S. war plans, and even the codes for launching nuclear missiles, was stationed for a time in San Diego.)

The FBI and CIA, which maintains a field office in West Los Angeles, is now concerned that the thousands of unemployed defense workers will give the Soviets more than maps of the city's freeway system. It's a quandary: The same global changes that have accelerated prospects for world peace have spurred espionage opportunities between former adversaries.

"The biggest problem is all the openness that comes from peace breaking out," the FBI's Lawler said. "One might say, 'We are all friends and don't worry about spying,' when in fact additional information allows them to spy even more. Added to that are the defense layoffs here. The Soviets could try to get to a disgruntled employee or somebody that needs money. Rosey the Riveter won't give away defense secrets, but an unemployed corporate vice president could."

That prospect has defense contractors on their toes.

"In Southern California, we have seen the Soviets use three espionage methods," explained the FBI's Lawler. "They collect information from trade shows and conventions and peruse annual reports and brochures. Sometimes they'll wait for a greedy American to contact them, like they did with Boyce and Bell, or they'll study organization charts and look for people with weakenesses or financial troubles. They also try to establish contact in Russian communities, like the kind we have here."

Southland aerospace contractors, who helped create Southern California's economic boom of the 1980s thanks to its favorite son, Ronald Reagan, are on the defensive.

At Hughes Aircraft Company, where radars for the F-18 and F-14 were built and the Maverick and Phoenix conventional missiles are made, security is being stepped up. A special video tells workers how the KGB and other "hostile intelligence agencies" work, even now.

"The whole defense industry is of a common mindset: intelligence activity has not decreased, it's increased," exclaimed Hughes Vice President of Security George Best, a former FBI agent. "They [the Soviets] still want NATO defense plans but they are also after western industrial technology that might allow them to leapfrog others—commercial satellites, fiber optics, advanced computers. We go to great lengths to thwart the KGB because it's become so much easier for them to move from East to West."

While the KGB no doubt knows Los Angeles as well as many native Southlanders, many are concerned that America's allies are the spies of the future.

Japan, whose aggressive businessmen have bought up large chunks of prime Los Angeles real estate, may soon compete with the Soviets, Germans, and British for the industrial parts and economic secrets that some hope will make Los Angeles the gateway to the Pacific.

Just two weeks ago, U.S. Customs Agents arrested a Los Angeles engineer for trying to sell four Japanese companies Star Wars computer software.

Is Atlantic Richfield or Pacific Enterprises or MGM/UA the next target instead of Northrop's B-2 plant in Pico Rivera? Some say yes.

"In the future you'll see more industrial spying between the United States and its allies as we move move away from the Cold War," said USC Assistant Professor of International Relations Alex Hybel. "That's not to say the KGB isn't still working in Los Angeles. Even a friend, like the Soviets now seem to be now, can always turn out to be a bad enemy again."

THE VICODIN THIEVES

An open house leaves valuables at risk—even the contents of your medicine cabinet.
—*Los Angeles Times*, March 19th, 2006

DANELL ADAMS FELT CONFIDENT she had locked away temptation as she readied her ocean-view Laguna Beach home last year for an open house.

Knowing that thieves sometimes posed as potential home buyers, she locked her jewelry in a safe and hid her keepsakes and electronics. It was only later that Adams realized that her mistake was not thinking cynically enough—and she is a thirty-three year veteran of the city's police force.

Sometime during the open house, three prescription medications—a painkiller, a muscle relaxant, and a sleep aid—were taken from her master bathroom. Adams had left the vials beside the sink to remind herself to take the pills she needed after back surgery.

"It was a little thing you don't think about," said Adams, a supervising detective. "It was like, 'How easy was that?' Then it alarmed me. That was some pretty heavy-duty medication."

Other home sellers also have discovered that public showings of their properties lightened their medicine cabinets.

Although prescription drug thefts may not come to mind as owners prep their homes for an open house, they occur frequently enough that agents routinely advise clients to stash away pharmaceuticals along with heirloom brooches, iPods, and Rolexes. Websites run by brokerages and government agencies across the nation post similar warnings.

When someone attending an open house or a yard sale lingers in the bathroom, they actually may be "pharming"—cadging pills for resale or their own addiction, according to Tom Riley, a spokesman for the White House Office of Drug Control Policy.

"It's a much more common phenomenon than people realize," Riley said. "We hear anecdotes about it all the time, and it's probably underreported because people consider the content of their medicine cabinet private. Plus, they don't want to seem stupid" for having left medications in easy reach.

Criminals' favorite targets appear to be multi-million dollar homes swarming with visitors during Sunday open houses, when owners are often away. No statistics are kept on the most commonly swiped prescriptions, but real estate agents and local police report that painkillers such as Vicodin and Oxycontin and tranquilizers have gone missing. One broker reported migraine medicine stolen from a Bel-Air client.

Crooks frequently work in pairs using a distract-and-conquer scheme, in which one asks the agent questions while the other hunts for loot. The ploy is a reason why many agents work in pairs. If a house is split-level, an agent stays on the ground floor to welcome attendees while the other goes upstairs, watching visitors for suspicious behavior.

"If we have ten, twenty, thirty people in an open house, it's hard to control them all the time," said Vince Malta, president of the California Association of Realtors.

Coldwell Banker agent Mary Lu Tuthill once had a Brentwood client who discovered her Ritalin missing following an open house. In another incident, Tuthill's partner observed a woman rummaging through a homeowner's master bathroom medicine cabinet. Before they kicked her out, the two agents persuaded the woman to empty her pockets. She had not stolen anything–yet.

Of course, thieves have snatched more than pills. A ring operating on the Westside a few years ago grabbed rings, watches, and laptops.

Concerns about theft and personal safety are why Tuthill today only hosts open houses with off-duty police officers on the premises. Like many of her peers, she requires prospects to furnish identification, address, broker's name, and related information before entering. "We live in desperate times," Tuthill said. "Some people are willing to take advantage."

Visitors at public open houses sometimes hesitate when asked to give out contact information, Tuthill said, because they fear agents will use it to hound them with follow-ups.

"They don't like to give out their phone number," Tuthill added. "I say the owner just likes to know who comes in their house."

Calculating how much security open houses require is tricky. Agents estimate that thefts occur less than one percent of the time, partly because veteran Realtors can sniff out fishy visitors. Still, nobody knows the true rate, because some sellers are reluctant to disclose sensitive medical issues to police that could later be made public in a crime report.

Stolen pharmaceuticals fuel a profitable trade. A one dollar pill under subsidized healthcare can fetch multiple times that amount on the black market, according to Adams and other police. Riley, of the White House's drug control office, said stolen prescription drugs are the "one segment of the drug trade" that is still growing.

John Aaroe, President of Prudential California Reality, which represents properties from Santa Barbara to the Coachella Valley, said he has noticed that trend reflected at open houses during the last five years.

"The most obvious problem we have is with prescription drugs being taken," Aaroe said. "People are surprised. We all think our house could be burglarized or damaged. We don't think our prescription drugs are of interest to anybody else."

Agents and brokerages are typically not liable for stolen property.

The local Bonnie and Clyde of open house thievery was a polished young couple who over the course of a year hit more than fifty upscale homes as far north as Beverly Hills and as far south as Laguna Niguel. They rolled up in a black Jaguar and chic garb to create the impression that they were serious buyers.

Los Angeles Police Detective Steve Bucher, who tracked the couple before arresting them in South Pasadena in September 2003, said the pair mainly took jewelry—including a $35,000 watch—but did take a few pill containers. Quick with a turnaround, the couple could rob an open house in the morning and have the best items in a pawnshop or jewelry store by the afternoon. If need be, they impersonated brokers and broke into jewelry boxes, stealing goods in excess of $200,000.

Dewey West and Kathy Engelhardt pled guilty to numerous counts of residential burglary, Bucher said. A Superior Court judge sentenced West to sixteen years under California's three-strikes law. He escaped from the Pitchess Detention Center in Castaic, but police soon re-apprehended him.

Engelhardt never appeared to begin her four year sentence; there are outstanding warrants for her.

"Real estate agents were very aware of the ring," Bucher added. "It got through their whole network."

Adams, for her part, remains in disbelief that somebody took medicine from her home.

She said her Realtor followed up by alerting the agents representing prospective buyers who had been there that a crime had taken place.

"But there were so many people who came through," Adams said. "It's a lesson learned."

STATE AS SLUMLORD

About a hundred homes acquired for the Long Beach Freeway extension aren't in shape to be rented. Agency defends maintenance.

—*Los Angeles Times*, April 26th, 1995

As THE FIGHT OVER the Long Beach Freeway extension drags into its fourth decade, scores of homes the state has acquired in the road's pathway have been allowed to degenerate, fall vacant and become vandalized, records show.

Despite legal provisions requiring the state to maintain its properties, the *Times* found that more than a hundred homes, including many valuable landmark houses, are so decrepit they can no longer be rented out, blighting what were once well-kept neighborhoods and depriving government coffers of rental income and property tax revenue.

Many of the more than 600 houses the state has accumulated are now surplus due to a change in the freeway route years ago. Their total value is about $27 million, but state officials have taken no steps to sell them.

Eventually, the state needs to acquire about 1,000 more properties in the path of the 6.2-mile freeway spur running from Alhambra to the Foothill Freeway in Pasadena. The $1.4 billion construction job is not expected to begin for at least another decade.

Top officials at the state Department of Transportation who manage the housing say they are doing a good job, despite a lean budget.

"Basically the homes that we own are in pretty good condition...compared to our neighbors," said Jack Hallin, interim director of the Caltrans office in Los Angeles. But others at the agency disagree.

"Negligence, ignorance and wastefulness" have characterized the agency's care of historic homes, one planner wrote last year.

In frustration, some neighbors have dug into their own pockets to make repairs after Caltrans failed to renovate uninhabitable houses that attract vagrants and crime. Tenants have sometimes sued. One collected $15,000 after she was injured when a waterlogged ceiling that she had complained about crashed down on her head.

"They are worse than slumlords," said attorney Chris Sutton, who represents several tenants who have sued Caltrans.

A *Times* review of agency records and property files shows that:

* Nearly a quarter of the Caltrans houses are uninhabitable or vacant, in spite of a 1973 federal court order requiring the state to make its "best efforts" to maintain the properties.

* Caltrans has failed to sell off 110 homes that have been surplus, in most cases since 1986, even though state law requires the agency to sell excess land. State highway funds are now so tight that Caltrans is planning to lay off about 300 employees here.

* Despite strict national guidelines requiring that historic landmarks be carefully preserved, many of the agency's sixty-nine vintage homes have deteriorated badly. More than a dozen are rotting and vacant.

* The agency has poorly managed its maintenance budget and hired firms accused of overbilling and shoddy repair work.

* Five Caltrans employees and three other state workers rent freeway houses, with some of them often delinquent in paying rent. Three relatives of ex-local Caltrans director Jerry Baxter have also lived in or tried to rent houses. One property rented by a Baxter relative received about $28,000 in repairs, while other nearby homes deteriorated.

Baxter, who left the agency last year for a top post at the Metropolitan Transportation Authority, declined to be interviewed. Auditors reported preliminarily that his relatives received no special treatment, but the matter remains under review. Officials said privacy rules barred them from disclosing the state employees' rental arrangements.

Caltrans Director James van Loben Sels told the *Times* last week that he is dissatisfied with management at the Los Angeles office and would like to see the agency get out of the housing business.

In Los Angeles, Hallin and his aides acknowledged that some historic homes have decayed and promised to pump $3.5 million into renovations soon. They said that scores of the 610 Caltrans homes are unoccupied and need repairs, but that no laws had been broken.

Critics argue that the agency's substandard properties violate a 1973 court order requiring Caltrans to use its "best efforts" to maintain its properties and rent them out to "prevent vacant structures from becoming public health and safety hazards." The injunction was secured by South Pasadena and public interest groups trying to stop freeway construction and impose stronger environmental controls.

Antonio Rossmann, legal counsel for South Pasadena, said the pattern of neglect documented by the *Times* shows that the agency has breached the court order. "That Caltrans has systematically broken the injunction transcends legal compliance, it becomes a public disgrace," he said.

Caltrans collects millions of dollars a year by renting the houses for $300 to $2,300 a month. Most of this money has been plowed into other Caltrans operations, officials said. While $5 million was collected by Caltrans from homes in Los Angeles and Ventura counties last year, only about $1.8 million was allocated for their maintenance.

Along the proposed Long Beach Freeway extension, no rent was collected on a quarter of the Caltrans properties because they are vacant. Records show that 106 of the 157 vacant homes are uninhabitable.

Two boarded-up houses in the 2000 block of Berkshire Avenue in South Pasadena have long been community eyesores and together need $125,000 in repairs, according to Caltrans' estimate last year.

One is a Spanish-style bungalow with buckled floors, collapsed ceiling and blistering paint that has been empty for a decade. Arson fires have hit twice during the seventeen years Caltrans has owned it, records show. The other house, vacant at least seven years, is riddled by dry rot and termites.

Typically, complaints to local health and building officials go nowhere, because Caltrans, like other state agencies, is exempt from compliance with local regulations.

If Caltrans' properties were not exempt, "they'd have bundles of violations," South Pasadena City Manager Kenneth Farfsing said.

There has been a smattering of violations issued against Caltrans' properties for various problems such as sewage backups and fire dangers, records show.

Generally, unhappy citizens have just one place to turn, Caltrans.

Neighbors, city officials, and the local assemblyman have written at least fourteen letters since 1990 beseeching Caltrans to restore the Berkshire Avenue houses.

The agency agreed a year ago to begin major repairs soon. But the houses remain untouched.

Joe Boyd, Caltrans Deputy Director in Los Angeles, told the *Times* that work would not begin until next month. "Some of the things we said were going to come true, didn't," he said.

Fed up with the state's inaction, neighbors in some cases made repairs on their own. South Pasadena resident Philip Stocker said he spent $6,000 fixing up a neighboring Caltrans home. "I gave up on complaining," he said.

In Pasadena, homeowner's associations and preservationists have battled nearly twenty-five years to force Caltrans to maintain its vintage houses located just a block away from upscale Orange Grove Boulevard, documents show.

"Their record is deplorable," said Claire Bogaard, former director of Pasadena Heritage. "Year after year, they've promised action and yet they've done nothing."

Caltrans owns sixty-nine homes that are listed with the National Register of Historic Places or are candidates for landmark status because of their age and design significance. Federal and state laws prohibit neglect of these properties and require that repairs meet strict guidelines.

Once architectural gems, many houses are now empty caverns with rotting wood, buckling floors, waterlogged plaster, rat infestations and scattered trash. Fifteen are unrentable, records show. Some have been vacant for almost a decade.

In one Craftsman-style home in Pasadena, the front door is unlocked. Vagrants, using candles for light, have left burn spots on the floors and fouled toilets that are not working.

A few doors away on St. John Avenue, a vacant ninety-eight year old house with a weather-beaten facade and shattered windows has been stripped of its antique hardware and fixtures.

Caltrans environmental planner Ronald Kosinski last year itemized extensive repairs needed at the eight historic homes most heavily damaged by the agency's neglect, vandalism or careless workers. He warned colleagues to rethink their "penny-wise, pounds-foolish" policy that has "alienated...communities and put Caltrans on the defensive."

Upon learning of the decay, Elizabeth Merritt at the National Trust for Historic Preservation, said, "I'm really appalled. We knew there was a problem, but nothing this bad."

Meanwhile, residents in working-class El Sereno have been complaining since the 1980s about uneven upkeep of Caltrans property, rent hikes, pest infestations and empty houses.

In the 3000 block of Sheffield Avenue, ten Caltrans homes recently were either boarded up or vacant. One was a crash pad, with gang tags adorning the walls. The air reeked of refuse and urine. Out back, mattresses were piled high in an open garage with exposed electrical wires.

Caltrans officials said most of their homes are in good repair and tenants overall are satisfied. But they said budgetary constraints limit the repairs they can undertake.

"The [historic] houses are older. They really need a lot of work," said Caltrans property chief Theo Walker in Los Angeles. "But if you have x dollars in your budget, you can only do certain things."

Records show that the agency is sitting on $27 million worth of homes that became surplus years ago when the proposed freeway was rerouted to spare downtown South Pasadena and other historic enclaves. Yet a state law passed in 1979 requires the state to sell off excess residential property.

"They should sell the excess homes and pour the money into the remaining ones," Pasadena activist Lorna Moore said.

Caltrans officials said it is premature to sell them because the proposed freeway route has not yet won federal approval. They said the old path, which the state transportation commission has officially rescinded, might be resurrected someday. They also noted that sale proceeds would go to the state general fund, and not necessarily into renovations.

The *Times* reviewed hundreds of internal Caltrans records showing that officials often have been slow to make repairs, paid uneven attention to properties and made questionable expenditures on certain homes.

Boyd said there may be an occasional expenditure that "didn't make sense," but said that overall the maintenance program is managed wisely.

In several instances, the *Times* visited vacant and deteriorated homes with crystal-clear swimming pools that had been regularly maintained. In another case, records show the agency paid a contractor an hourly rate of $23.50 to water a lawn.

Instead of repairing or replacing the roof on an El Sereno property recently, Caltrans paid more than $800 both in 1993 and 1994 to cover it with a tarp, records show.

Meanwhile, Eustace Cox, a disabled engineer, said a plastic tarp has covered his leaky roof in Pasadena for the last two years because Caltrans officials told him that there was no money for non-emergency repairs. "They said all the homes will be refurbished [someday], but they've said that for years," Cox said.

While many homes have decayed, records show that Caltrans invested nearly $28,000 in one Pasadena house during a three year period, including almost $15,000 for interior paint and floor refinishing. Caltrans auditors found that one of the tenants was a relative of Baxter, the former Caltrans official.

Auditors concluded that Baxter's relative received no special treatment, nor did his children who lived in or tried to rent freeway houses on two other occasions.

Baxter's daughter briefly rented a home a decade ago. Last year, Baxter personally asked for a list of vacant Caltrans homes in Pasadena and went with his son to pick out a place. When he discovered that the only one he wanted was claimed, Baxter was agitated, recalled Caltrans rental agent Billye Tate.

Jim Drago, Caltrans chief spokesman, said he believed that Baxter's efforts on his son's behalf were ill-advised but not illegal. "It's fair to say it's inappropriate," he said.

Criticism has been leveled against other Caltrans officials directly in charge of maintaining the freeway homes, according to audit reports.

Acting on allegations from a whistle-blower in 1991, auditors concluded that officials overpaid contractors doing yard and lot of cleanup work, approved checks for repairs before the jobs were started, and paid for work that had to be redone.

They overspent their budget by about twenty-five percent three years in a row, for a total of $3 million in overruns, records show. Part of this was caused by a $600,000 expenditure to re-sod lawns—a job that auditors determined was not properly supervised and was awarded without competitive bidding.

In another matter, auditors are reviewing the bills that Vipel Construction of Buena Park has submitted to Caltrans during the last three years to determine if the company "submitted altered receipts to support their invoices," according to an auditor's confidential report.

Vipel President Joseph Thankachen said he was unaware of any review and said there are no billing improprieties.

Caltrans officials acknowledged some oversight troubles, and said a new computer system has helped correct billing and scheduling problems.

Auditors also have investigated allegations that some contractors curried favor with Caltrans property officials or received favorable treatment.

Auditors inquiring into accusations that Caltrans employees had received "gifts and services" from contractors were not able to substantiate that any presents had changed hands. Sources, however, told the *Times* that they have seen colleagues accept gift baskets, food, alcohol, and a watch.

Caltrans rental agent Daniel Soroky recalled that he was offered a gold coin several years ago by an executive of a company that contracts with Caltrans.

"I was flabbergasted. It was the size of a quarter," said Soroky, who did not accept the coin. "I didn't think it was appropriate."

For tenants, the quality of repair jobs by Caltrans contractors has sparked many complaints, records, and interviews show.

Doug Hoover, a former Caltrans rental agent who was transferred two years ago to another division, recalled phone calls from numerous tenants upset by shabby or incomplete repairs.

"You could tell many of the contractors didn't have the faintest idea what they were doing," Hoover said. "But the ones that got all the complaints kept being invited to bid again... What makes me so frustrated was that this was our tax dollars going down the drain."

Lyn Miller, who rents a historic house in Pasadena, complained in a letter to Caltrans about an electrician who knocked out electrical service to half of the house, as well as another repair firm that installed an unvented water heater that emitted "lethal fumes."

Another tenant, Harry Nickelson, is suing Caltrans for $512,000 in damages, alleging that contractors Caltrans hired in 1993 improperly removed his apartment's asbestos-containing flooring and contaminated his possessions.

The South Coast Air Quality Management District has slapped Caltrans and two of its contractors with notices of violation for failure to follow state regulations for handling and disposing of asbestos in this case.

The asbestos incident was not Nickelson's only brush with botched repair work.

Exterminators hired to eliminate rats from his current rental used poison and traps that killed the rats inside the walls but left a horrible stench, he said.

Then, during the storms this winter, he said the roof leaked so much that a six by eight foot swath of plaster came loose from the living room ceiling.

Looking at the bright side, Nickelson noted that Caltrans did dispatch a plumber to fix a few things.

"They fixed the faucet drips and my dishwasher while the roof was leaking like a sieve," he said. "When I take people into the house, I have to apologize."

Co-written with Richard Winton

THE MYSTERY MILLION

Why would a U.S. Congressman from Oklahoma come to L.A. to raise money? Perhaps because he holds the purse strings to critical federal transportation dollars.

—*LA CityBeat*, March 10th, 2005

HIGH UP IN A downtown skyscraper, inside the white-linen world of Bunker Hill's City Club, the campaign checks were being scribbled next to the scrambled eggs and coffee. It was an eclectic bunch that had assembled, north county conservatives and stiff management types milling around with dapper lobbyists, but they were united by their purpose on the morning of May 28th, 2004. The guests had come to raise money for the man of the hour—a congressman from America's former Dust Bowl whose face few had ever seen before.

Ernest Istook (R-Oklahoma) had just granted the MTA what it had long coveted: federal subsidies to pay for roughly half the cost of an $898 million light rail line through East Los Angeles. Just eight days earlier, Istook had been openly skeptical that the line deserved federal funds in a lean budget year, and as chairman of the House Transportation Appropriations Committee his opinion was decisive. His continued resistance meant delays, uncertainty, and a sense of frittered opportunity.

Those anxieties would soon melt. After his L.A. fact-finding trip and talks with some of Southern California's House Members, Istook's reservations about the trolley changed to an official blessing. And he jetted home richer than he had come. A series of California fundraisers, including the Bunker Hill affair, had fattened his campaign war chest by about $25,000.

Nobody questioned the timing of Istook's flip-flop, perhaps because few outside the area's clubby transit world had pieced it together, or perhaps because out-of-state representatives are continually raising money here. The congressman's approval for the extension of the Gold Line into East L.A. is what got the headlines, not the fact the Metropolitan Transportation Authority CEO Roger Snoble had attended the City Club event, or that it was cohosted by one of the agency's former executives, Arthur Sohikian.

If this is business as usual in L.A., it has become a crowded marketplace. For the last year, Angelenos have been deluged with reports about pay-to-play investigations into former aides, commissioners, and public relations confidantes of Mayor Jim Hahn. His opponents in the mayoral race have seized on the FBI and District Attorney inquiries as proof that influence peddling cuts through City Hall. Meanwhile, people like Istook—little-known congressmen with plum committee jobs—tend not to attract much attention for the campaign dough they scoop up here.

Istook declined to be interviewed for this story. His campaign manager did not return phone calls.

Because of his power over the purse strings, the Oklahoman was not a man the MTA could ignore. Los Angeles' reputation for rail expenditures had been sullied by multi-million dollar miscues during Metro Rail's subway construction in the 1990s. Since then, Southern California's fractious congressional delegation had not had much luck corralling funds for big-ticket projects from a reluctant Bush administration. New York, Boston, and Philadelphia—old-money, rail-dependent cities just a hop from Washington, D.C.—took advantage. The death of longtime Los Angeles Representative Julian Dixon, considered the go-to man to get the region federal bucks, did not help.

But thanks to Istook, things were looking suddenly sunnier. On May 26th, two days before his City Club event, Istook announced he was withdrawing his opposition to the six-mile extension of the Gold Line, which is set to run from Union Station to Atlantic Boulevard by late 2009. (Istook also had been out here in April, when he inspected the proposed right-of-way by helicopter.) The MTA, he wrote, had soothed his concerns about the extension's cost-effectiveness and pruned back its first year funding request from $80 million to $60 million. It was not a guarantee the money would always be there, he cautioned, but "significant progress" had been made toward laying track.

His okay meant that the MTA could sign a construction contract against a looming deadline that might have added $100 million to the project's overall price tag. Istook's role was so hyped there were whispers—unfounded, it turned out—that Governor Arnold Schwarzenegger might pop his head into the fundraiser. An Istook congressional colleague, Howard P. "Buck" McKeon (R-Santa Clarita) did attend.

Snoble was not available for comment on this story, MTA spokesman Ed Scannell said. According to Scannell, Snoble and the agency's government relations chief, Gary Clark, were at the City Club strictly for logistical reasons. After the event, they were taking Istook on a tour of the preliminary work being done on the line before the congressman rushed to catch a flight.

State and in-house regulations prohibit MTA employees from soliciting or directing any campaign contribution of more than $10 from any company, consultant, legal firm, or vendor seeking work with the agency.

Snoble "was not a contributor and had nothing to do with setting up" the event, Scannell said. "We have very strict guidelines we live by... Certainly, given Istook's limited amount of time and the fact we are talking about a major project, [Snoble] would have been remiss not to talk to him."

So, what was the agency's role at the City Club? According to one attendee: "MTA participated in the sense they were there respectfully, and did the tour and briefing afterwards. But I don't think it was the fundraiser that changed [Istook's] mind. My sense was that Istook got religion on the issue and [asked], 'By the way, how much money can I raise?'"

THE MYSTERY MILLION

MARK PISANO, EXECUTIVE DIRECTOR of the Southern California Association of Governments (SCAG), the southland's regional planning body, said Istook needed assurances the East L.A. line met tough new White House performance standards. With Congress facing

$30-40 billion in similar requests and only a fraction of that to spend, the sales job had to be impressive. "He wasn't convinced that the East L.A. line was one of the projects worth funding," Pisano said. "We agreed with his premise on performance but disagreed that the East L.A. line didn't meet it."

Sohikian, MTA's government-relations manager until 1997 and now a political consultant with real estate and transit clients, said Istook had been voicing his qualms about the line with federal officials for months before he came to L.A. Sohikian also said the transit industry typically takes it upon themselves to show their support when an important politician comes to town. Istook back then was toying with a 2004 U.S. Senate run.

"The more we can do to educate members to bring funds to L.A., the better," Sohikian said.

One lobbyist, who spoke on the condition his name not be used, said the MTA is more involved than it lets on. He said they informally encourage firms who do business with it to contribute to visiting House and Senate members with a big say on projects.

"The arm twisting is very subtle," the lobbyist said. "It's couched in terms of the public good. It doesn't say the congressman wants to see you on this list."

Pisano and Istook required no introductions. Almost exactly one year earlier, in 2003, Istook had trekked to Southern California to hear about gridlock-cutting rail projects in L.A. and Orange County, the case for magnetic levitation trains, and the danger of the area falling out of compliance with federal Clean Air standards. A fundraiser was thrown for him at the City Club, this time over cocktails and hors d'oeuvres and fewer people than would attend the May 2004 soirée.

Istook received $27,750 from California sources during the second quarter of 2003, campaign records show. Companies headquartered out of state but with large L.A. presences also ponied up. Among his 2003 and 2004 California donors with MTA ties were Sohikian, Nick Patsaouras, Northrop-Grumman Corporation, Parsons Corporation, Bechtel, and the law firm of O'Melveny & Myers.

"It was nothing spectacular, no big money," said Patsaouras, an ex-MTA board member, of the 2003 event. Istook is "a decision-maker allocating transportation money, and we've had fund-raisers like this as long as I can remember. We're not virgins."

The then-seven term congressman certainly remembered Pisano.

Sometime after his 2003 trip, Pisano briefed Istook about a sticky situation closer to Pisano's home base. A December 2001 Caltrans audit of SCAG's books uncovered problems with its management and accounting. Auditors had, in particular, red-flagged SCAG's handling of a design-engineering contract to improve traffic flow on State Route 71 in a hot-growth section of the Inland Empire. San Bernardino and Riverside counties had been at each other's throat over the bottleneck there since the early 1990s, and part of SCAG's mission is to settle internecine feuds.

Caltrans examiners questioned SCAG about how the $947,921 contract with Omaha-based HDR was structured and where the proper documentation was. When no satisfactory answers came back, Caltrans notified the Federal Highway Administration that SCAG was "a high-risk recipient" for money out of Washington, D.C.–a major blow.

"We thought the audit displayed a somewhat surprising and large number of deficiencies in the way they were running the agency from an organization and project-management standpoint," said Brian Smith, Caltrans Deputy Director for Modal Programs. "It's a matter of documentation, of where's the beef? We haven't had to declare other agencies like them as a high-risk recipient. We are obviously dealing with federal money."

The Federal Highway Administration docked the nearly $1 million from its payments to California and slapped that unwanted "high-risk" label on SCAG. Caltrans, through which all federal transit money flows, could have stripped the money out of SCAG, but did not want to cripple the organization financially. The SCAG board huddled in closed session debating its options, including whether to sue Caltrans over the money. The audit report also hit the papers with an embarrassing thud, as word spread that SCAG had bounced some employees' paychecks, lost money on a business venture, and overused purchase orders. None of the bad publicity, though, mentioned the HDR contract.

Pisano appealed the ruling to U.S. Department of Transportation officials, noting that SCAG had implemented a number of reforms to clean up contracting and administrative procedures; even Caltrans acknowledges that now. When the department wouldn't bend, Pisano lobbied some of California's congressional delegation and then members of the House Transportation Subcommittee, including then-chairman Istook.

"I didn't think the [punishment] was commensurate with the finding," Pisano said in a series of interviews. "There were no improprieties, just incorrect procedures we needed to tighten. There was nothing Caltrans found we hadn't found ourselves."

This issue, which Pisano hopes will soon be resolved with a clearance audit by Caltrans, does raise a question: Why would a congressman from America's heartland, a committee chair already knee-deep in sectarian disputes about Amtrak subsidies and anti-terrorism rail security, care about a convoluted contract squabble in the suburban outskirts of a state half a continent away?

Micah Leydors, Istook's deputy chief of staff, said it was the principle. Her boss was sympathetic to Pisano's argument that federal officials were being inflexible about releasing the money. An effort to settle it with a legislative fix failed, so Istook instead inserted a $1 million appropriation in the 2004-2005 federal transit bill signed by President Bush to reimburse the state and relieve the heat on SCAG. People suspicious of it have nicknamed the appropriation "the mystery million."

Leydors, though, said there was nothing mysterious about it. "What was presented to us was that it was a small infraction, and [SCAG] was getting the death penalty for jaywalking," she said.

Pisano was adamant he did nothing to aid Istook with his Southern California money-raising, though he conceded he knew an event had been planned for him in Santa Clarita. Likewise, several MTA officials admitted they knew in advance about Istook's City Club event in 2004.

"Everyone who comes through here has a fundraiser," said Pisano. "I never contributed to Istook."

"We're just not that type of agency," Pisano added. "We don't have contractors and vendors."

Istook, a lawyer by training and Texan by birth, is described as a religious conservative who got his start in Congress after terms on a city council and the state legislature. His home office is in Oklahoma City, which was hit by domestic terrorism when the Murrah Federal Building was blown up in 1995. Considered hard-nosed about spending, he no longer chairs the House Transportation Subcommittee that he led in 2003 and 2004. Today, he is Vice Chairman of the Homeland Security Appropriations Subcommittee.

GREASING THE SKIDS

Critics say humbug to mitigation efforts.
—*Los Angeles Daily News*, September 24th, 1995

DURING THE HOLIDAY SEASON last year, the Metropolitan Transportation Authority brought a Yuletide bonanza to Hollywood Boulevard–and a goody bag that could have filled a Winnebago-sized sleigh.

There was a full-size Santa's Village embellished with elves, imported mountain snow and turkey giveaways. Strolling carolers belted out Christmas favorites while flickering lights and 650 Douglas Fir wreaths adorned the background.

But Santa and his flourishes did not come cheap: The checkbook cheer cost taxpayers about $400,000, MTA records show.

A onetime outpouring for a blighted town trying to recapture its old glory?

Hardly.

The Christmas largess was just one sliver of the $2.1 million the agency has expended since fall 1993 to cushion the impacts of subway construction on businesses and residents throughout the world-famous thoroughfare.

Of that, about half the money, or slightly more than $1 million, financed such items as cocktail parties, holiday festivities, banners and free magazines, according to records obtained by the *Daily News*.

Critics of the so-called Hollywood Construction Impact Program, including several MTA board members, say those expenditures were a frivolous waste of taxpayer money that have done little to assist property owners and others inconvenienced by Metro Rail tunneling.

Besides the holiday trimmings, they cite the $25,000 the agency dished out for a star-studded cocktail party and $166,000 for temporary, mural-splashed construction fencing. Likewise, an outdoor eating festival planned for next weekend is getting $20,000.

An additional $14 million in the program has been set aside for future programs before Red Line cars rumble under the boulevard in three years.

"It's an outrageous and unreasonable expenditure of public money," said Nick Patsaouras, an MTA board member and San Fernando Valley businessman. "Mitigation measures are supposed to relate to construction impacts, not Santa's Village and advertising."

Added longtime area activist Robert Nudelman: "It's another MTA disaster in Hollywood."

Franklin White, the MTA's Chief Executive Officer, would not comment.

His aides said the program is being retooled to emphasize more nuts-and-bolts community programs linked to transportation, including better signage and cleanup programs.

"The spirit of the program is great, but some of the particulars need to be re-evaluated, and that's what we are doing," said MTA spokeswoman Andrea Greene. "The bottom line is that Metro Rail will be the catalyst for the rejuvenation of Hollywood."

A lot of the rejuvenation has been necessary because of the MTA project.

In August 1994, Red Line digging caused parts of the boulevard to sink up to nine inches. Structural damage from that mishap and others prompted 1,100 area property owners to sue the MTA with claims exceeding $1.5 billion.

Ten months later, tunneling work halted when a mammoth sinkhole near a Metro Rail staging area opened up the street and aggravated festering wounds about subway building in urbanized Los Angeles. A few weeks after the chasm appeared, investigators raided the contractor's field offices, and the MTA pulled the company off the job.

Approved by the transit agency three years ago, the impact program was designed to help Hollywood Boulevard businesses and others grapple with less spectacular public works hassles—poor storefront access, traffic snarls, equipment noise, and crime. Showcasing the area was also a goal.

Even so, preventing a repeat of the horror stories experienced by downtown merchants who lost their customers, and sometimes their livelihoods, to subway barricades and other obstacles remained paramount, transit officials said.

As proof of their efforts in Hollywood, subway officials point to several expenditures they claim have eased tunneling headaches.

Records show that the MTA has paid roughly $456,000 to a pair of private security firms that patrol Hollywood station-building areas, $330,000 for trolleys to ferry people around traffic bottlenecks, and $75,000 to clean streets, parking meters and other utilities soiled by construction. An unspecified amount has financed "Open for Business" signs for companies located near heavy construction.

But critics insist the MTA has not done nearly enough to offset the adverse impacts of construction.

In an interview, Hollywood Councilwoman Jackie Goldberg upbraided the transit authority for refusing to release promised funding and largely misspending what they did subsidize.

Among other problems, she said, a $90,000 MTA street-lighting effort never materialized because it was so costly. Poor marketing, she and others said, killed the trolleys after only a few months of operation.

"And the Christmas party was a disaster, with a lot of money spent at the last minute," Goldberg said. This program has "probably been the biggest frustration, other than the sinkhole, in my council life. I've thought they wanted to spend as little as possible so they can spend it on other things."

Transit officials dispute that contention, saying the area's fragmented politics and their own vast bureaucracy torpedoed the efforts. Many of the contracts, they add, were not competitively bid, because the goal was to get the work done as quickly as possible.

Said the MTA's Greene: "What is extremely frustrating to us is that the merchants, politicians, and residents backed these efforts at the time and then they turn around and attack us for doing what they asked for. First the agency is criticized for spending too much and then for too little. We have to work as a team."

Under the original plans, the MTA was going to award mitigation funds at a $4 million-a-year clip, meaning an additional $6 million should already have been spent. Greene attributed most of the delays to "differences of opinions" within the community over what projects to back.

No similar mitigation account has been created for Metro Rail's San Fernando Valley leg because city officials haven't sought it, Greene added.

Meanwhile, Hollywood activists believe any goodwill the MTA once had has turned to resentment because of the costly marketing programs that don't adequately target struggling shop owners and residents. They said they have unsuccessfully lobbied for better signs, soundproofing and low-interest loans.

Instead, critics argue, the money has flowed to organizations they say are politically connected, pointing to the nonprofit Hollywood Arts Council. Records show it has four MTA contracts, including a summer banner program and holiday promotional magazine valued at $102,000.

Oscar Arslanian, an executive member of the arts group, was also a member of a special citizens committee that submitted recommendations on how the mitigation account was to be parceled out.

"The MTA has bought friends and influence using this mitigation money—it's a payoff to the who's who of Hollywood. But it hasn't helped the merchants," said Doreet Hakman, the outspoken owner of the Boulevard's Snow White Coffee Shop. "Not one penny went to alleviate their hardship."

Arslanian said out of "conscience" he never would have voted on MTA Art Council contracts, and that much of the group's transit funding went for efforts that predated Red Line tunneling. He also noted the citizens panel was ultimately disbanded by Goldberg because it was making so little headway.

Nonetheless, organizations that are, or have been been, the target of government investigations have also landed MTA community money, records indicate.

The Hollywood Chamber of Commerce, a longtime subway champion, received roughly $100,000 in contracts that financed a newsletter, Christmas lights and an Adopt-A-Block cleaning program. Three years ago, the booster group settled a lengthy state investigation alleging it had misappropriated $700,000 in royalties earmarked for maintenance of the landmark Hollywood sign and Walk of Fame.

Leron Gubler, the chamber's executive director, said he believes the proposed changes in the subway construction impact plan represent a step in the right direction.

Gubler and Goldberg said they back proposals to revamp the mitigation plan though it is still to be approved by the MTA board. The proposal would downplay holiday and marketing events and beef up free parking, sidewalk repairs, cleaning, advertising, signage and economic development.

Gubler sees light at the end of the tunnel. "I'm actually encouraged things will happen properly" he said. "The time for mitigation is now."

In the hopes of softening the impact of Metro Rail construction under Hollywood Boulevard, the Metropolitan Transportation Authority has spent $2.1 million out of a $16 million account on a host of various programs and events.

DEATH ON THE TARMAC

Military altered details surrounding son's death.
—*San Gabriel Valley Tribune*, October 2nd, 1994

SAL AND MARGE CAMPISI find themselves gazing a lot these days at the crisp portrait resting on the living room television set.

The picture, tucked inside a simple, U.S. Air Force frame, is of a determined looking thirty year old in military fatigues. It's John, the couple's oldest son.

With U.S. forces now in Haiti, the Campisis can hardly believe four years have passed since their son became the first American casualty of the Persian Gulf War. The picture, however, reminds them of something equally wrenching: the three-year battle they have waged with the Pentagon to learn how he really died.

Keep in mind the Air Force Staff Sergeant from West Covina wasn't a victim of an Iraqi missile or bullet. He was killed when a maintenance truck struck him on a darkened airport runway in Saudi Arabia. After changing their story several times, the government concluded John contributed to his death by sleeping in a hazardous spot.

His father, a veteran of the Korean War, still gets enraged when he hears that explanation. Based on the records he has struggled to get, Campisi is convinced it was Air Force brass who faltered, not his son. Not only that, he has proof his critically wounded son remained on the runway more than an hour before an ambulance arrived. Once it came, he was not even taken to an American military hospital.

"They goofed up and didn't want the public to know, so they stonewalled us," said Campisi, sixty-one, a supervisor at Vita-Pakt Citrus Corporation in Covina. "I worry the parents of kids who may die in Haiti might never find out what happened. I never expected to feel that way."

Parked in the driveway of their four bedroom Evanwood Street home is a U.S.-built car with an American flag bumper sticker. Sal and Marge still fly the flag on July 4th. They remember backing the Vietnam War when everyone was against it, and dressing their kids in Navy costumes on Halloween.

At the time John died, two of his three brothers were serving in the Navy, one on a nuclear attack submarine.

Today, Campisi says, John's death has made him wary of U.S. missions abroad and more sympathetic to prisoner-of-war activists. Unlike the three generations of family members who joined the service, Matt Campisi, John's twenty-three year old brother, says he will not join.

"We feel betrayed," he said.

The West Covina air man was used to travel.

After graduating from Edgewood High School in West Covina, he spent the next eleven years moving between routine assignments in Mississippi, Arizona, Victorville, South Korea, the Philippines, and Nebraska.

John, an electronics specialist assigned to maintain highflying reconnaissance planes, was among the first soldiers dispatched to Saudi Arabia during the U.S. military build-up there.

It was his last mission.

On August 12th, 1990—five months before Western forces began prying Saddam Hussein's outmatched troops from Kuwait—Sal and Marge Campisi were rattled out of bed by a 3:00 A.M. phone call. It was John's wife, Charlene, telling them John had died in some freak accident.

"It was like a stab in the heart," Sal Campisi said.

John's death was big news. His funeral in Rowland Heights, complete with military honors, drew 300 people and led the local news. He was a son, a husband, a father of four young children who had given his life in the post-Cold War world.

But what really happened to him could not fit neatly into a sound bite.

The Air Force initially said John died while on break at 5:00 A.M., as he was lying on a concrete runway in Riyadh used by American warplanes. A maintenance truck made a U-turn and ran over him, shattering his torso. After the collision, the Air Force said he was rushed to an unnamed military hospital.

His family bought that explanation until officials at Offutt Air Force Base in Nebraska, where John was last stationed, refused to turn over his autopsy report. Angry that they wouldn't release the document, his widow threatened a lawsuit and the report materialized.

Jaws dropped when the family read it: John had not been taken to a U.S. medical facility at all. He was treated at a Saudi Arabian one.

"It really sent my antenna up," Campisi said. "I'm listening to President Bush telling us on TV about all the medical care we have in place and we find out they didn't have a U.S. hospital there yet."

From then on, Campisi began calling the Pentagon regularly during his lunch breaks, but what he learned was contradictory. One official gave the original line. Another said John had been struck by a plane. Someone else said he had fallen asleep under a truck.

Frustrated, the family began pursuing the Air Force's official accident report.

"I remember an argument with this one major," Campisi recalled. He said, "Everyone else whose son or daughter was killed has been satisfied with our explanations. Why aren't you?' Another guy said we were "ghouls."

Next, they called their congressman, U.S. Representative David Dreier, a Covina Republican, who hand-delivered a letter from the family to the White House. Bush wrote back, saying John's injuries were so severe American surgeons could not save him.

Campisi had better luck calling staff Sargeant. Jerry McKinney, who saw the incident and is now out of the service. According to McKinney, the truck hit John when he was smoking a cigarette in a designated "safe zone"—a place trucks aren't supposed to be. Medical help, he added, was delayed because the ambulance had to pass through security checkpoints.

But it was not until early last year that the family's persistence paid off. They finally got the accident report under the Freedom of Information Act.

Investigators had concluded that John's supervisor had erred by allowing aircraft personnel to rest in a poorly lit area between spy planes and the runway, the report said. Moreover, the truck driver was negligent by not checking to see whether people were in his path, the report said.

The most surprising item in the report reveals that the incident occurred at 4:11 A.M.—forty-five minutes earlier than initial reports—meaning it took sixty-five minutes to transport him to a Saudi Arabian military hospital, Sal Campisi concluded. The report also said John had exercised "poor judgment" by sleeping near the flight line.

"John was no dummy who would lay out somewhere that would be dangerous," Marge Campisi said. Her "kids should know that."

Still, the family says, they feel vindicated. Inconsistencies between the autopsy and the accident report, they say, show the Pentagon badly managed the runway area and covered up their mistakes later.

"I just hope in Haiti they don't repeat them," Campisi said.

Air Force Lieutenant Colonel Mike Gannon last week said the service stands by the accident report and denies there was any cover up. He noted John's death came in the early days of an operation involving 500,000 American soldiers and that U.S. military hospitals were in place by early September 1990.

"We don't discourage people from getting information," Gannon said. "Obviously [Sal] feels differently."

But it was Campisi's frustration with the military that sent a father searching for information on his son's death in unlikely places.

In January 1991, Campisi called KABC radio talk show host Michael Jackson who had then-Vice President Dan Quayle as a guest and disputed Quayle's contention that the U.S. had state-of-the-art hospitals in Saudi Arabia. "A guy at the show said Quayle was spitting BBs he was so mad afterward," Campisi said.

A year later he called the show again, this time to speak with Desert Storm commander General Norman Schwarzkopf. His advice: keep squeezing the military for information.

While in Nebraska in 1992, Campisi met Lieutenant Colonel David Wolfe, John's old boss. Wolfe told him he had written a complete account of the accident and that his superiors had altered it to spread the blame around.

"But he said, 'You'll never get the truth, and if you repeat this conversation I'll deny it.'" Campisi said.

Wolfe is no longer in the service. The Pentagon refused to give out his phone number.

Today, two years later, Campisi wants to put it behind him and is looking for closure.

He savors family get-togethers like never before and visits the cemetery regularly. His wife has immersed herself in her sales job and cries watching news broadcasts about soldiers killed in the line of duty.

Late last month, on a humid runway at Nebraska's Offutt Field, a $4.8 million dormitory was dedicated in John's name.

"My son was doing his job and was a victim of an accident that shouldn't have happened," Campisi said. "If the military had told the truth I would have let this go."

DROWNING WITH EYES ON HIM

Father seeks answers to son's drowning.

—*San Gabriel Valley Tribune*, August 27th, 1994

FOR NEARLY HALF HIS son's life, Gary Chan dreamed of hugging his boy tightly.

Two hundred miles and a family dispute had separated the pair for four years, leaving them more like strangers than relatives. Not until Steven Chan was hospitalized four years later did he finally reach out for his father's arms. After that, they were practically inseparable.

"He went wherever I went," said Chan, thirty-seven. "He'd wait at the door for me to get home."

After July 6th, it was Steven who never arrived home.

The newfound father-son bond was broken forever that day when Steven drowned in the shallow end of a Charter Oak High School swimming pool being used by a Covina YMCA summer day camp program. Three lifeguards were on duty on that July morning, police reports show. Since then, new information has come to light regarding conditions at the pool a week before the drowning and the ratio of lifeguards to children.

During the nearly two months that have passed, Chan has found solace through his faith in God, but the shaken father does not have peace. Not until he knows all the facts. Chan has hired a private investigator to pursue the missing pieces to a tragedy that took his only child.

"I feel cheated," Chan said. "I just got to know my son and now he's gone."

When his second-grade classes at Badillo Elementary School ended in June, Steven was not thrilled with the idea of going to day camp. He had other ideas for spending his summer. But he changed his mind after hearing about planned trips to Disneyland and other amusement parks.

On Steven's second day of camp, his father drove him to the Charter Oak pool at 7:00 A.M. Uneasy because his boy could not swim, Gary Chan said he asked to speak to the group leader, but could not locate him.

"I said, I'd like to leave a note saying he didn't know how to swim,'" said Chan. "A lady whose name I didn't get told me it wasn't necessary!"

Later that day, Gary Chan—a probate attorney and former accountant—was eating lunch at a Glendale steak house with some colleagues when his pager vibrated. The readout displayed his office phone number and the digits 911. Probably an anxious client, he remembered thinking.

When he called his office, the secretary told him the Covina YMCA wanted him to phone them right away. Frantic and out of change for another call, Chan, dressed in a business suit, ran back to his high-rise office, grabbed the phone and called the YMCA.

"They said there was an emergency and that my son was at the hospital," Chan recalled. "I asked them what was going on and they said they couldn't say anything. I was totally panicked."

Soon he was on the freeway, breaking the speed limit, stopping just long enough to pick up his mother. Once inside San Dimas Community Hospital, they were told to wait in an area near the emergency room. Finally, a somber doctor walked in and dispensed the unthinkable message: Steven was dead.

"He said he was sorry but they weren't able to revive him," Chan said.

He comforted his mother and then walked to the emergency room where he saw Steven's small body on a steel hospital table, clad in his swimming suit.

"I've seen death before with my dad but I looked and couldn't believe it," Chan said. "I ran outside to the parking lot to catch my breath and hold my emotions back."

For Chan, mornings are the worst. That's when Steven would roust his dad out of bed and plunk himself in front of the television to watch *Power Rangers*.

Now, as Chan tries to keep to his morning routine, he has his faith and the passing time to comfort him.

"I was numbed and shocked at first, but after we buried him, it's a little better," Chan said. "I know he's in heaven."

Adding to his grief is the nagging uncertainty of not knowing exactly what happened the day his son died. Both the Los Angeles County Coroner's Office and the Covina Police Department have ruled the drowning an accident.

That has not satisfied him. Driven to find some answers, Chan hired attorney Stanley Shure, who hired a private investigator. The YMCA also hired a private investigator, but employees and officials with the Covina branch have repeatedly declined to discuss the incident. All calls have been referred to attorney Mike Fox.

Fox said no one has been disciplined and the drowning has not led to any change in policy.

Meanwhile, officials with the California Department of Social Services, which regulates daycare centers, briefly looked into the accident before realizing it took place at a day camp program exempt from state licensing.

Day camps differ from regular daycare programs because they generally involve excursions, social services attorney James Simon said. Had the YMCA camp been a daycare center, at least one adult would have had to be present for every six children, he said.

As it was, thirty of the sixty children in the two pools when Steven drowned were from the YMCA day camp. Three counselors were also there along with the lifeguards, Fox said.

After learning of the drowning, the county health department made a routine investigation into the condition of the pool and found it satisfactory, said Robert Daetwiler, an environmental health specialist.

Police say Steven was last seen alive playing with other non-swimmers in the shallow end of the Charter Oak High swimming pool, which is next to the diving pool. He and another eight year old Covina boy were playing a game by holding their breath under water, police said.

Yet when the eight year old came up for air, he noticed Steven hadn't, police said.

Within minutes, the boy and a nearby girl helped drag Steven to the side of the pool, police reports show. Lifeguards then plucked the sixty-five-pound child from the water and began CPR.

Gary Chan said he is confounded by the image of his son playing underwater games. Steven hated to have his head in water, even to rinse out shampoo.

"That's what I can't reconcile," he said. "I don't know if we'll ever know what happened."

Shure, Chan's attorney, says he suspects that supervision was inadequate because the police report said one of the lifeguards was putting equipment away at the time Steven drowned. YMCA attorney Fox disagreed.

"The lifeguard was cleaning the deep pool, but he went and put the equipment away and was, in fact, there at the shallow pool when it opened," Fox said.

Shortly before Steven's death, Sally Anne DeWitt, twenty-seven, of Covina, a former lifeguard with the city of Alhambra, took her own son to the Charter Oak pool.

What she saw led her to call the Covina YMCA and then write a cautionary letter to the Covina police. In the letter, she outlined what she said were concerns that only four lifeguards were on duty June 28th to watch some 200 children. She said lifeguards were not wearing uniforms or rotating positions to help sharpen concentration.

"I became very concerned with the safety of the pool...I know how fast an accident can happen," DeWitt wrote to police after she did not receive a return phone call from Covina YMCA Director Ed Kopszywa, she told police.

The letter led police to question Kopszywa, who said there were 191 swimmers and four lifeguards on duty June 28th. In documents obtained by this newspaper, Kopszywa told police the organization has set a standard of one lifeguard for every fifty swimmers. Kopszywa declined to comment on the letter, but Fox said the ratio of children to adults is actually judged by whatever is safe under the circumstances. And the supervision on June 28th was sufficient, he added.

"All told there were four lifeguards and probably thirteen to fifteen counselors walking back and forth on the deck," Fox said.

Keith Cunningham, the aquatics director for the Pasadena YMCA, said his lifeguards rotate as frequently as every five minutes if the pool is crowded.

Cunningham said his lifeguards do not wear uniforms and that it is up to individual YMCAs whether to use them.

She tries to find answers to his son's death, Chan—who after the incident resigned from his position as a board member with the Burbank YMCA—spends a lot of time reminiscing. He remembers the joy he and his wife, Vivian, felt when their only child was born healthy November 1st 1986.

Their euphoria began to fade after they brought their newborn back home to Alhambra. Vivian Chan returned to her accounting job and the couple had a hard time deciding on daycare arrangements, Chan said.

Chan suggested hiring a nanny. But fears about Steven's exposure to germs from a nanny or other children led the couple to ask Gary Chan's fifty year old mother to tend to the infant.

Grandmother Sue Chan reluctantly agreed, and Steven was sent to live with her and his grandfather in El Centro, east of San Diego, where the family owned a grocery store, Gary Chan said.

"It was hard," Sue Chan recalled. "But I took care of him."

On weekends and holidays both parents visited, though Gary Chan made the trips more often, Sue Chan said.

Vivian Chan, Steven's mother, declined several requests for interviews.

In 1989 Sue Chan's husband, Henry, died of a heart attack and his widow moved to Covina. Steven was now geographically closer to his parents, who then lived in Thousand Oaks. But emotionally, "he remained distant," Gary Chan said. He would cling to his grandmother and offer only courtesy hugs to his dad. "We were still kind of strangers," Chan said.

They became more than that one night in 1990 at Queen of the Valley Hospital in West Covina, as Gary Chan watched his small son battle pneumonia.

Chan kept a round-the-clock vigil in Steven's room. On the third evening, Steven had a frightening reaction to some medication. Eager to do something, Gary Chan reached to adjust Steven's oxygen mask.

As he did, Steven reached out too, and hugged his dad as tightly as he could. "We really started our relationship there," Chan said.

Two years later, Chan separated from his wife and moved into the Covina home with Sue Chan and Steven. During the next two years, the father and son traveled everywhere together, sharing picnics, shopping excursions, treats at McDonald's and trips to a Monterey Park church.

"It was always daddy this, daddy that. He loved his daddy," Sue Chan said.

Co-written with Bill Heatherman

Part Two

DAN QUIXOTE

Outsider turned coalition builder turned political pariah, Daniel Arguello finds himself in the center of Alhambra's most explosive scandal.

—*Pasadena Weekly,* December 8th, 2005

MORE TIMES THAN HE can count, Daniel Arguello has begun his day massaging his achy right leg, the one ripped to pulp in Vietnam thirty-seven years ago, and doing what others might judge absurd. He thanks it for courage in life's darker moments.

When at eighteen he overheard an Army nurse poormouth his chances to walk again, the high school dropout from East Los Angeles grunted and grimaced through a long rehab until he actually could jog without wishing someone would put him out of his misery. The comeback power of that rebuilt limb later steadied him through a job market that distrusted his skin color, then the psychic wreckage of burying a son.

It even withstood the backlash of helping nail one of Alhambra's favorite sons at the same juncture Arguello's foes were assailing his scruples. Freakish timing or mere payback, he would never be the same. Ever since August 2004, when he wore a secret recording device that county prosecutors used to indict former councilman and school board member Parker Williams in a money-for-vote sting operation, creepy things had been happening to the then-Vice Mayor. Strangers had popped up at City Hall and his favorite Pasadena lunch spot inquiring about Arguello's whereabouts. Anonymous calls to his lawyer had warned that, "Dan should be very, very careful." Those unsolved incidents and a few others brought him police protection.

Late one Tuesday evening this spring, outside one of the Main Street clubs he frequents, Arguello, fifty-eight, sensed eyes tracking him again. Was it intimidation? Was it someone looking for dirt to smear his credibility as star witness in the Williams trial?

Whatever it was, Arguello decided he was done peering into the shadows. So he leaned on that gimpy leg once more, walking home on it for a mile, instead of driving his orange Saab. Paging Oliver Stone.

"I'd lived worried long enough" Arguello said. "I was fed up. I was thinking that night, 'If you're following me, come and get it!' So I walked... Not that I'm fast."

POLITICS IS A BATTLE

OVERTAKING HIM CERTAINLY IS easier than pigeonholing him as a deserving martyr or crafty opportunist. After two terms on the Council, Arguello has no signature policy that jumps out, and little statewide cachet. His top achievement may be prodding a city Establishment known for ferociously protecting its own.

Trim and single, with feathery salt-and-pepper hair that draws comparisons to a Latino Richard Gere, Arguello has a playboy reputation that he knows irks his more straitlaced enemies. He admits doing his best thinking in the wee hours with a scotch in hand and Miles Davis on the stereo. Affable and droll, popular with shopkeepers and gadflies, he also is a book hound with a passion for British Literature.

None of which says much about the sunny fatalism washing through a guy who seems to tread cautiously around destiny's cliffs without canceling the hike.

"Some people say I still have a Cholo gait. They say, 'Get a haircut and a better walk!' What they don't know is that I keep my hair long because half my peers have lost theirs. What they don't know is that I walk like this to cover up my limp."

Don't expect his council colleagues to lend him a cane. While tempers have cooled between their respective factions, 2006 may prove explosive. The District Attorney's case against Williams could peel back how small, land-oriented cities like Alhambra truly operate, and what money can buy if a familiar figure serves it up.

"I know who Parker is–I don't think there's anybody who hasn't been touched by the good things he's done," current Mayor Steve Placido said. "So to see someone or two people involved in bribery, I don't think that casts a favorable light on the city. Unfortunately, the facts that we know are mostly through the papers, and I'm not sure the papers knows that much."

Williams, sixty-eight, a gaunt-faced man respected for his decades of civic involvement, declined comment for this story. Since his indictment, he has remained visible around town, telling friends he made a stupid mistake, one source said. Indicted with him was Frank Liu, seventy-two, his business partner on the senior-housing project that Williams allegedly offered $2,500, then $25,000 to Arguello to support.

Richard Hirsh, Williams' defense attorney, would not discuss strategy except to say that Arguello's character would be an issue at trial. No date has been set.

What likely motivated Hirsh's client? Leverage.

Last spring, Arguello nearly accomplished what no one else ever had in this city pinched between the San Gabriel Mountains and the Valley's southern rim. He nearly toppled Alhambra's white Council majority with his own Latino clique after the city's most legendary Anglo councilman, Talmadge Burke, died.

The irony was undeniable, the bigger metaphor obvious. It would happen in Los Angeles with Antonio Villaraigosa's milestone 2005 mayoral election as it already happened here. Latinos whose ancestors once hoed the fields wanted a place at the table. Arguello likened it to India rising up against its British Viceroys.

Williams, however, was not as much interested in history as he was in counting council votes–three out of five being the magic number–for his city-subsidized development. Too bad he didn't wait until after the November 2004 election, a mudslinging contest that seemed more like a big-money congressional race than small-town campaigning.

Arguello, first elected in 1998 and re-elected in 2002, wasn't running himself, but his influence was, and it got walloped. His entire slate of council and school board candidates all went down in flames to Establishment-backed figures.

The reconstituted council majority, quarterbacked by the clean-cut and cunning Paul Talbot, pounced vengefully. It took away the Buick LeSabre that Arguello was allowed to use in his rotation as mayor amid uninvestigated charges that he drove it to strip clubs and bars. His plum committee posts were yanked next.

The venom usually did not cascade out at council meetings; that was left for the insanity of election season, or whispers to reporters or in private tirades. But if you watched closely, the desired impression that all was well was purely cosmetic.

At one tense council meeting, Arguello challenged the community activist who accused him of misusing the city car to show his evidence. There was silence.

Rene Nava, a onetime Arguello supporter, was not as quiet when he ran against him. He lashed Arguello for dirty campaigning when Arguello accused him of stalking a woman. The messy charges hit the papers, and later the legal docket.

Can't you feel the love?

"Before Dan Arguello came along, there never was hardball politics here," Talbot, forty-four, remarked. "It was much more collegial. Dan's style is old school L.A. where you fought for every inch of ground. We had a team-building session in January where Dan said, 'Politics is a battle.' We said, 'No, it's community service.'"

Community, as you will see, is a rather elastic term in Alhambra.

Now on the losing end of a 4-1 majority, Arguello has had a simple enough objective—staying relevant. He shows up to meetings often as the least liked fellow in the room. He plays soft-voiced devil's advocate when there is an opening. He birddogs officials he contends are fast tracking the $400 million redevelopment juggernaut that spruced up downtown and is now heading west.

Probably not surprisingly, Arguello himself wants to head north. Last month, he announced his second bid for the state Assembly seat occupied by fellow Democrat Judy Chu. Arguello said he is not so much fleeing his hometown as he is chasing Sacramento in his longtime quest to be a state lawmaker. The folks who hope he stumbles to a better-funded opponent chirp that Arguello better not act as if his council job is "the consolation prize" if he loses the race for the 49th District.

Still, it was Williams, the former Chamber of Commerce president known for his workout fanaticism and general exuberance, who sullied Alhambra's good name, right?

You might not know it from Alhambra's leadership, which never publicly denounced his alleged graft. Some leaders, in fact, privately suggest that Arguello was so inherently venal that he practically emailed Williams he was for sale.

Bureaucrats do not seem to be sweating the headlines, either. This fall, the Williams-Liu project was forwarded to Alhambra's planning commission for consideration before Arguello's appointees on the panel tossed it. The development now sits in limbo.

City Manager Julio Fuentes, who declined comment for this story, said in a statement the city had "no authority" to halt a project review if the applicant had submitted the proper paperwork and fees. The neighboring city of Montebello took a different tact after Williams and Liu were arrested: they scrubbed a condominium project they were proposing.

Then again, there's no place like Alhambra.

POWERFUL FRIENDS

THE BEDROOM COMMUNITY OF 86,000 has your standard-issue car dealerships, dated neighborhoods, and institutional stucco. Its redeveloped downtown, a compact version of Old Pasadena fringed with clubs, art-deco neon and ethnic beauty shops, teems on weekends. The $25 million facelift there looks like money well spent.

Yet reputations, as Arguello will remind you, can be hard to shake. Eccentric music producer Phil Spector, now on trial for the 2003 shooting death of an actress at his Alhambra mansion, once commented, somewhat quizzically, that his adopted city, "is a hick town where there is no place to go that you shouldn't."

At 102 years old, Alhambra is one of the region's municipal old-timers. This longevity, observers suggest, has accounted for a virtually permanent white incumbency on the council, even as its constituency became minority-majority. Alhambra was once fairly split among white families with generational roots here and Latino empty-nesters who relocated from East L.A.

Today, Asians, particularly immigrants from China and the poorer Far East nations, comprise nearly half the population. Latinos represent about one-third. Whites make up most of the dwindling balance. No Chinese-American has ever been on the council, though Japanese-American Gary Yamauchi was elected last year.

All this, however, was static in the Shakespearean-like melodrama in which somebody as controversial as Dan Arguello tried outlasting somebody as entrenched as Parker Williams.

If the paradox doesn't wow you, the trampled friendships may. The same people who today wince at Arguello's name are precisely the ones who groomed him for office.

In 1998, he was a comer: a self-deprecating moderate with a Purple Heart, an easy smile, and a living room everybody who mattered had stood in.

Talbot, who runs a State Farm Insurance agency with his wife, not only re-named Arguello to a commission post that Arguello used to create a following, he also raised campaign money for him—and, of course, insured him personally. School Board Member and ex-councilwoman Barbara Messina, now one of Arguello's most braying critics, dished out counsel. Typical of small towns, their kids were friends.

These insiders had something else in common: real estate. It has been the coin of the realm here since Benjamin Wilson, the city's founder, settled a farming empire stretching from Riverside to the Westside twenty years before the Civil War.

That tradition lived on. Williams, once in recycling and economic development, jumped into developing. Talbot owned a piece of a First Street business a few blocks from the $20 million Edward Cinema complex downtown. Councilman Mark Paulson, a career realtor, managed and rented property nearby. Even one of the city's famous old police chiefs was an ex-real estate man.

It gets better. Paulson sold Williams and Liu the land they needed for their now-infamous housing project. Before that, Paulson sold Arguello the right house for launching his campaign.

Given those strands, few were prepared when Arguello and fellow Councilman Efron Moreno started poking into city contracts and practices. Why, they asked, did Alhambra's longtime outside law firm, Burke, Williams & Sorenson, never have to bid? The firm has netted $8.8 million from Alhambra in the last five years.

The chasm among former friends cracked wide in 2003, when Talbot proposed election changes that would have limited individual contributions to $2,500 and created a runoff system. He said it was fairness. Moreno and Arguello labeled it an Establishment power grab fueled partly by anti-Hispanic prejudices.

"I came on here because I wanted a change," Moreno, thirty-nine, said. "I didn't like this good old boy thing where the machine expects you to pay your dues through the chamber, the Rotary Club and so forth... I remember asking [Talbot] why he was not supporting Dan in his last reelection. He said, 'I'm afraid you're [also] secretly supporting a Hispanic woman candidate and somehow the three of you will get along better and fire the city manager and the city attorney and you'll turn Alhambra into South Gate.' It was like, man, how dare you?"

South Gate is anathema around municipal water-coolers these days. The small community outside downtown L.A. nearly went bankrupt after its former city manager, Albert Robles, was convicted of bribery in a case that cost taxpayers $12 million.

Talbot disputed using the word "Hispanic" in his conversation with Moreno. He also asked how he could hold a racial grudge when a slew of city staffers, including the long-serving Fuentes, are of Mexican descent. So are two candidates he endorsed last year.

"My comment about South Gate was not about race. It was about cronyism" by Arguello's camp, he said. "I'm a Eucharistic minister giving people communion and I know people in the church have read quotes that I'm racist. It's painful. In America, nothing is worse than being stamped a child molester or a racist."

Because of that and other discord, Talbot said that while he remains cordial to Arguello, "there is no real relationship."

YOU GOTTA WONDER

ALHAMBRA'S OLD GUARD WAS strafed in the weeks leading up to the November 2004 election by a Moreno mailer titled *The Greedy Bunch.*" It took swipes at the likes of Williams, Messina, and then-Alhambra Education Foundation President Steve Perry. Perry, a former city police officer and school board member, was fired from both jobs after getting caught stealing $30,000 from the city's police association when he was in charge of it in 1992.

"These," Moreno said, "are the people running the city."

The Establishment answered. Rumors floated that Moreno was tied to the Mexican Mafia. He would lose in a tight race.

Doubts also wrapped around Arguello, an auditor at Pacifica Services, a connected Pasadena-based project-management and consulting firm. A buzz grew that he had steered towing, golf course, lobbying, and other contracts to associates from East L.A. This was thinly veiled code for the perceived Latino political mob run by former lawmaker and onetime-Arguello boss Richard Alatorre.

Around City Hall, acquaintances that showed up seeking work were caustically dubbed FOD (Friends of Dan.) Interestingly, most of the work they received passed on 5-0 council votes with little debate. Only the golf course deal to George Almeida was rescinded for slipshod performance.

"Dan's priorities were not to advance the priorities of Alhambra but to advance those of Dan Arguello," said Barbara Messina, whose husband was defeated by him in the 2002 election. "I've talked to people who knew him before I knew him and they confirmed that this is the way Dan is. He's ruthless... Yes, he can be very smooth... But if their faction would've picked up one more vote, the city would have turned into something really ugly."

Arguello acknowledges urging associates to bid in every case except the towing job, saying public contracts should be open to the general community. He believes the patronage charge hit because an "inner circle" was used to getting city work, and because he wanted a robust debate on issues, not "lovefest" rubber-stamping.

"I never told anybody they'd get a contract," he said. "I encouraged them to compete. Contract compliance is what I do for a living. I know the law."

Arguello's son, Dominic, said the rancor toward his father, the perception he is dirty or overblew the threats against him to garner sympathy, should be discounted because they were kicked up by "the same group."

"Anybody who knows my father knows the person he is," he said. "He's a man of his word."

Then there's the Alatorre factor.

Before he went to the L.A. City Council in 1985 as a raspy-voiced backroom fighter, before he pled guilty to accepting illicit funds in a scandal that also exposed a cocaine addiction, he was Alhambra's popular state assemblyman. Even after his conviction, he was so well regarded that Burke, Williams and Sorenson hired him—on Arguello's recommendation—for $50,000 to advise the city on litigation aimed at completing the long-delayed 710 Freeway extension. Rock-ribbed support for the roadway is ideological sacrament here.

Yet in 2002, Alatorre watched his name trashed in order to club Arguello.

"My observation, and I am on the outside looking in, is that Alhambra has been a very entrenched city led by a handful of people and that anybody who wants to challenge that becomes an enemy," Alatorre said. "They should give Dan credit for being honest, but sometimes you wonder who was offered the bribe."

THROUGH THE PAIN

THE MAN IN THE middle stabs gingerly at his Caesar Salad as he retells the prophecy.

It was just after his triumphant reelection in 2002, and the iconic Talmadge Burke was congratulating him. Burke, for those who have lived out of the country, was Alhambra's thirteen-time councilman. With fifty-one years in office, he was California's longest-serving elected official, a legend who fought the railroads and remembered the old smudge pots, not to mention being a property owner himself. Well-wishers lavished him with endless parties and twenty-plus buildings in his name. When he died in February 2004 in his mid-eighties, the town lost its eternal grandfather.

But back in 2002, Burke, a lifelong Republican, had a story for Arguello. It was how Alhambra's Establishment guarded the kingdom. When 1970s-era Councilman Mike Rubino tried shaking down an ambulance company operator, the city elders, Burke said, made sure the person he sought the bribe from was an undercover police officer. Rubino was prosecuted for his act and was forced to resign in the end.

"Talmadge basically warned me," Arguello said with a nervous smile. "Eighteen months later, it came true. Paul Talbot had done such a good job telling the old Establishment that I was a sleazebag that people started believing it. The *Pasadena Star-News* wrote about me and the towing contract. People started believing the myth, and Parker was one of them."

If you could skip back in time, it is miraculous Arguello was around to hear that tale.

He was raised in the East L.A. neighborhood of Boyle Heights to working-class parents that he joked didn't "beat him enough" because he turned out so levelheaded. Needing pocket money, he worked as a busboy and as a milkman. Those graveyard shifts crimped his senior year studies at Roosevelt High School and he dropped out.

Eddie Martinez, one of Arguello's commission appointees, grew up next door. The teenage Dan he remembers was not a rabble-rouser screaming, "Viva La Raza!"

"He was [just] self confident and good with the girls," Martinez said.

Then he was drafted.

The Army welcomed recruits, Arguello recalled, with a "lousy" steak sandwich at its Olympic Boulevard induction center before busing them to Fort Ord, near Monterey, for basic training. In Louisiana, where Arguello completed his infantry training, he learned to sidestep armadillos and coral snakes as well as Jim Crow attitudes, risky for an olive-skinned recruit with black friends.

It would get scarier. On his helicopter ride into Vietnam, Arguello gazed down on a magnificent countryside he instinctually knew America (and he) did not belong. The Army stationed him with the twenty-fifth Infantry near Cuchi. Just a city kid in 1966, he barely realized the marches he was on were patrols to flush out the Viet Cong.

He felt safer when his platoon was attached to a mechanized unit. One night, though, while dozing on an armored personnel carrier, the quiet exploded with artillery and tracer bursts. His platoon had been lulled into a trap.

Boom!

"I remember being in the air and everything looking all red," he said. "Next I was on the ground, scrambling for my weapon, and I couldn't see out of one eye. I couldn't feel one of my boots, either. It'd been blown off my foot."

A Puerto Rican platoon buddy tried staunching the bleeding, but where to start? Arguello had nine acute shrapnel wounds lacing him scalp to feet.

Medics ferried him to a field hospital. A military priest came to his bedside within an hour and dispensed Last Rites. Somehow, despite the blood loss and trauma, he hung on, "fickle Catholic" that he was.

They transported him to Saigon for surgery, then to Japan for skin grafts. It was there he heard a nurse remark he was being shipped home because he would never walk on his right leg again. From Japan he went to Walter Reed Hospital, and from Walter Reed to the West Coast for painful rehabilitation next to vets who had lost eyes, legs, and arms.

"I had to live with this—seeing people missing body parts—for a year. Though I came back with a lot intact, I still lost parts, too.

"The fear of not being able to make my dreams pushed me. Small dreams: walk on two legs again, go to college. If I didn't overcome my fear, I didn't get to reach my dreams. My right leg taught me that."

The Army assigned him a grunt job at a Ford Ord weapons warehouse to finish out his tour of duty. Instead of breezing through it, he found himself facing military investigators accusing him of filching a .45-caliber handgun, purportedly to show off to chums back home. They confined him to base and assigned him a hack lawyer with a miniature hangman's noose on his desk. Arguello, then nineteen, maintained his innocence and snuck back to L.A. on weekends.

"My parents didn't know about the charge," Arguello said. "They thought I had a weekend pass. The Army was screwing me over."

Right before his tour ended in June 1968, investigators cleared Arguello. The culprit had been his drill sergeant.

BREAD WITH YOUR SOUL

More than thirty years removed from those painful memories, Arguello tried acting unfazed when Williams strode in, but his heart was pounding out of his chest. Over chicken lunches, Arguello got him to lay out the bribe, just as the D.A. instructed.

There was a dreamlike quality about it all.

Once Arguello and Williams finished their meals, they headed toward their cars for the money drop. At his Honda SUV, Williams reached in, pulled out an envelope containing $25,000—ten times the previous amount—and handed it to Arguello.

This time, deputized by the D.A., Arguello accepted it. Arguello, a believer in destiny, said he had to do what was right, whatever the Establishment thought of him playing the bait.

"At that point, I wasn't looking at what was going to happen or what people would say, because of my fear and respect of the law," he said.

"The whole thing was still like a bad movie."

At least he had his legs to boost him home.

THE LAST (LOS ANGELES) PICTURE SHOW

Previously unseen pictures of presidential candidate reignite question of what happened his last day alive.

SUDDENLY HE WAS THERE, inside a chic Lincoln Continental, spectacularly unprotected as he grinned at onlookers woozy at what dumb luck had plunked into their midst. The city of movie stars and rock gods had been expecting him, just not in the cool shadows outside of downtown's Biltmore Hotel. History had pulled a fast one. A brown-haired college student palming a metallic device when he stumbled across this scene had no intention of squandering his brush with it. With nobody cordoning him off, he edged close enough to the man-of-the-hour to read his expression.

The student's goal was to shoot.

The whole world was gnawing its cuticles watching to see if the polarizing face in the car could reproduce Camelot within any reasonable facsimile. Of course, the mob despised him, the political left was torn over him and Wall Street and the Kremlin harbored their own sharp opinions. But, as the college kid discovered in the year of the Tet Offensive and LSD-mixed Kool-Aid, the guy behind the excitement was mortal—a floppy-haired man weary around the eyes, facing backwards in the rear seat of somebody's chrome-and-leather luxury sedan. Robert Francis Kennedy might have wanted to take a whiz or grab a Phillipe's French Dip nearby if not for his excursion in the filtered sunlight near Fifth Street and Grand Avenue.

RFK, an adventurer, the first to dive into frigid waters and an armchair philosopher apt to quote the ancient Greeks, was achingly aware of his vulnerability to assassins by the time he had arrived here for the 1968 California primary. Outwardly, the New York Senator and former U.S. Attorney General in his older brother's administration ridiculed his fear of being murdered as tiny compared to his determination to achieve a higher good. Even so, palpable threats made him flinch, if not more fatalistic where the public could not see. "Everybody," one insider explained, "remembered Dallas."

But did anyone learn from it where it counted? The young man with the camera—my older brother, Paul Jacobs—was able to get within about a dozen feet of the next potential leader of the free world until, finally, a staffer shooed him away. The resulting two photographs from a borrowed Nikon Nikorrmat 35mm camera caught RFK in unscripted poses, and not just any, either. Because Paul likely took them hours before infamy doubled down in the kitchen of the sprawling, Myron Hunt-designed Ambassador Hotel, he unknowingly had on film a pair of the last privately captured photos of the second Kennedy to die on the job.

In grainy black and white, there he is fist-pumping wellwishers, including a woman in a polka dot scarf, while a couple of men with small movie cameras film from the driver's side. A curious fellow in a fedora, sunglasses, and a patterned shirt observes the action, and a bespectacled aide in the front passenger seat is caught mouth agape communicating with someone outside his door. In a more intimate photo, there he is again seated sideways with an absorbed expression and his hair parted in that hard, Ivy League sweep. To his right is the regal, brick façade of the Biltmore, L.A.'s VIP address that had hosted under its Italian-like cathedral ceilings Academy Award ceremonies, Jack Kennedy during the 1960 Democratic National Convention, and the Beatles (via helipad) four years later. To the left are the Central Library and the office towers of Figueroa Street.

This, however, is the sadly noble tale about the scar fate rolled over, not geography. Examine both photos carefully and you will notice a mark on RFK's head that might mean more than anything or anyone in the frames. The misshapen, dime-sized blemish high up on the right side of his forehead, in fact, might have spared him from a killer's bullet had the injury that caused it kept him away from the Ambassador. My brother had his own life-or-death component here, one connected to the figure in the Lincoln, which was probably light blue like the L.A. sky before chronic smog painted it taupe grit. By providence, he was bumping into the man perhaps best able to end the unpopular war that Jack greenlit under the anti-communist domino theory. A war that Paul and his chums were convinced could very well get them killed in olive green military uniforms within a year or so of college graduation.

At the time their brief encounter occurred, my twenty-one year old brother with Dustin Hoffmans *Graduate*-esque hair and a boy-next-door mug was a part-time statistician for L.A. County's Probation Department—when he wasn't taking his senior year classes at USC and getting used to life as a newly married man with tremors about the humid jungles of Southeast Asia in his head. As usual, after quitting time, he walked up from Temple Street to the west side of the Biltmore, where his then wife picked him up in their egg white VW Bug. This Tuesday was different. Paul, dumbfounded he could get within a football first down of Kennedy, clicked away, dwelling less on his subject's political iconography than his rendezvous with celebrity, as if he had lucked into a long elevator ride with Elvis.

Unintentionally exposing the safety of a presidential candidate whose own brother was executed was the last thing Paul contemplated. Yet, the camera he carried with him as an amateur shutterbug could have been a pistol; and that open, unprotected sedan—named after the slavery-abolishing president himself shot in the head 103 years earlier—another Kennedy casket. RFK's entourage had already relived that parallel after firecrackers exploded next to the motorcade as it passed through San Francisco's Chinatown during a campaign rally a few days earlier. Ethel, Kennedy's pregnant wife, flung herself to the bottom of the car upon hearing the bursts. Though her husband had continued waving and smiling defiantly, a *Newsweek* columnist traveling with him noticed what others missed. The candidate's knees buckled.

Such came with the territory only he could occupy. On a barnstorming tour of California the day before the primary on Tuesday, June 4th, 1968—where he was contesting Minnesota Senator Eugene McCarthy and Vice President Hubert Humphrey for the

Democratic Party's presidential nomination after Lyndon Johnson declined to seek reelection—the junior Kennedy was everywhere. On the Monday before, he had flown from L.A. to the Bay Area, returned south to Watts and Long Beach, and then continued on to San Diego. Hitting those three big media markets for the news cycle required 1,200 miles worth of travel in thirteen hours.

Big crowds whooped for him, even if not everyone was beguiled with his candidacy or his promise to bring peace to Vietnam and comfort to the disenfranchised. "How 'bout your brother? Who killed your brother?" someone shouted. RFK, who was the third youngest of nine children, faltered in his speeches that day. A journalist with him said he acted "spaced-out," his mind someplace else. "I don't feel good," he acknowledged to an aide, a rare admission for a man who had been surviving on four hours of shuteye with nary a gripe. A campaign volunteer meeting him later that day likened his handshake to a noodle. RFK was acting withdrawn and mousy when his persona needed to be outsized and embracing.

At his last stop in San Diego, where 3,000 supporters turned out to hear him at the El Cortez Hotel, he was unable to finish his remarks on the first stab. He had to sit down on the stage before an aide took him to a bathroom, where he vomited. Returning to the audience, he tried completing his speech, wrapping up with a favorite proverb by George Bernard Shaw: "Some men see things as they are, and ask why? I dream of things that never were, and ask, why not?" On the plane back to L.A. near midnight, the candidate shriveled in near-exhaustion. Ethel admonished the nosy reporters on board to leave him be. People meeting him for the first time then were struck by how aged he looked, his youthful face slightly wrinkled, brown-blond hair graying, blue eyes staring from a gaunt skull typical for an old man, not one forty-two. Was this really the leader who liked ending his day on the hustings with a bowl of chocolate ice cream and a Heineken?

Besides the enormity of what he was attempting, RFK was also stricken by the possibility that he had neglected his own family. In April, police in Hickory Hill, Indiana had apprehended David, one of his eleven children, for throwing rocks at passing motorists. A child psychologist that RFK queried about the behavior suggested the boy was hurling objects at people he didn't know because he could not lob them at someone he did. Like his Dad. Kennedy, thus, saw the upside of defeat. "If I lose," he said, "I'll go home and raise the next generation of Kennedy's." Probably thinking along those lines, he took the six of his kids with him in California to Disneyland the Sunday before his Monday dash up and down the state ahead of primary balloting.

Something else that was neglected, appallingly, was his safety from madmen. Presidential candidates back then, even ones named Kennedy, traveled without U.S. Secret Service protection. Equally absent was assistance from the Los Angeles Police Department, one of whose officers ticketed RFK's motorcade for running a red light. Sam Yorty, the city's feisty, attention-loving Republican mayor who had supported JFK over Nixon in 1960, considered the younger Kennedy a radical. An East Coast subversive. Rather than all professionals, RFK's bodyguards sometimes were celebrity athletes like Roosevelt Grier, the husky former-tackle for the Los Angeles Rams, and Olympic decathlete Rafer Johnson. In South Central, an activist group called the Sons of Watts watched out for him only a few months after a lone gunman had taken out Martin Luther King, Jr. in Memphis. Why not ask the Hells Angels, as the Rolling Stones would do with deadly consequences at the Altamont in Northern California the next year, to guard his flank?

RFK should not have had to worry about any of it because it was hard enough being in the shadow of Jack—the war hero turned thirty-fifth president, America's glamour-boy-in-chief, hand tucked stylishly in suit coat, a bedroom-eyed, political natural whether behind a podium or tossing out one liners with Hyannis Port drollness. Robert, for much of his life, had been a tag-a-long bringing up the rear of a privileged New England family committed to public service (and private enjoyments). After Lee Harvey Oswald and/or others murdered his older brother that autumn day in Texas, RFK, then U.S. Attorney General, surrendered himself to existential grief, to questioning God with brooding indignation. But having battled the Mafia, J. Edgar Hoover, bullwhip segregationists, and the nuclearizing Soviets in his mid-thirties, he knew he had something to offer a divided country despite withstanding character attacks on him as an opportunist hanging ten on his family's magic brand. In a way, RFK was harder to dissect than Jack, and tougher to promote. It wasn't just the superficial—the semi-buck teeth, the reedy voice, and what one writer called a "shy gawkiness"—but a spirit co-opted by innocent hope and raw cunning difficult to express on a bumper sticker.

When Robert needed California peace, he often headed toward the setting sun. In May, he had spent time at the Malibu beach home of John Frankenheimer, who had risen from actor to cameraman to director for such classics as the Birdman of Alcatraz and the Cold War mind-control thriller, The Manchurian Candidate. Out there with him on that visit were Shirley MacLaine, her brother Warren Beatty, actress Jean Seaberg and her novelist husband, Romain Gary. Comfortable on the coast, RFK returned with some of his family to Frankenheimer's place on June 3rd, the night before the primary. Observing Robert's bone-weary appearance, Frankenheimer let his guest and his wife stay in the master bedroom.

The next morning broke gray and chilly in a soupy, seasonal mist that Angelenos call June Gloom. If RFK was about to assume pole position over the two other Democrats by winning California, he needed a breather following nearly three months of nonstop campaign activity as a late-entering candidate. He spent a good part of what would end up his last conscious day sleeping in, playing with his kids in the choppy water, and sunning once the fog burned off. Transistor radios hyped the election before moving on to traffic and Dodgers pitcher Don Drysdale's bid for a sixth shutout. Rumors of George Harrison's rental home off the Sunset Strip, on a street called Blue Jay Way, stayed off the airwaves.

On this same day was an incident that history stupendously has never zoomed in on in the post-mortems of the next numbing hours. While swimming outside the director's house, his son David was knocked off his feet by a crashing breaker and sucked beneath the waterline by California's notorious undertow. Near him, RFK dove under to rescue his boy, pulling him to the surface. Both emerged from the saltwater bruised and scraped from being thrust onto the rocky ocean floor. The elder Kennedy, in fact, now sported a noticeable abrasion on his forehead mere hours before he might appear on national television. His terrified son was so grateful for his father's nimble reflexes that he promised him he would return the favor when he could.

Sometime later, the sapped presidential candidate got horizontal, falling asleep on two poolside chairs as Frankenheimer's guests gnoshed from a buffet. One attendee studied RFK's limp body and parted lips dreading that he was not breathing. Once awake, Kennedy suggested skipping his own election night celebration at the Ambassador Hotel. Just hang there. Defy convention. Family, friends, and others could watch the primary results trickle in from Malibu. The media could travel out, too. By mid-afternoon, after exit polls showed him ahead of McCarthy in the California race, the notion of being a no-show at his own fete crumbled. Around 6:00 P.M., Frankenheimer, who was collecting footage for a campaign documentary and providing television and film footage for RFK, daubed his forehead blemish with theatrical makeup so he would not appear like he had taken a hard Frisbee off the noggin.

The thirty-eight year old director then drove RFK, outfitted in a handsome, blue pinstriped suit, to the event about an hour east. Some accounts suggest that Frankenheimer, who had a passing resemblance to actor Leslie Nielsen, ferried him in his Rolls Royce Silver Shadow. A tantalizing online clip about the journey narrated by Fred Dutton, RFK's campaign director, though, was filmed from a powder blue convertible identical to what my brother photographed. Whatever car was used, Frankenheimer pressed the accelerator like "a bat out of hell that night...carried away" in the moment, Dutton said. Hollywood and Washington were never more incestuous than the day before the inevitable unthinkable. Frankenheimer, all the same, was berating himself for inviting over to RFK's Malibu sendoff a batch of distracting showbiz types, among them Roman Polanski, director of the upcoming Rosemary's Baby, his stunning wife, Sharon Tate, and future Walt Disney Corporation President Frank Wells. Cursing his decision-making, Frankenheimer drove past the Vermont Avenue turnoff, entangling himself in the traffic of the Harbor Freeway Interchange too far east. "Take it easy, John," his passenger told him kindly. "Life is too short."

In his suite at Mid-Wilshire's Ambassador, an Establishment stomping ground in the experimental sixties, Kennedy found more celebrities—Milton Berle, George Plimpton, Budd Schulberg, John Glenn—in boisterous, party mode. Did RFK hear the news? He had cinched four out of five state primaries, giving him crucial tailwind needed to make him the Democratic nominee if California later fell into his column. RFK took nothing for granted whatever others' excitement about his chances, edgy that McCarthy, the so-called peace candidate, might stymie him from a dominating victory in his home state of New York. Still, there was a difference in him from hours earlier when he had pined to remain in Malibu. At the hotel, he acted unshackled, giddy, marginally cheeky, observers noted. He smoked a cigar in the hallway and quoted Lord Tweedsmuir about politics being an "honorable adventure."

"I feel now for the first time that I've shaken off the shadow of my brother," he told Kenny O'Donnell, his other campaign manager, in a phone call that evening. "I feel like I made it on my own."

Everyone by now knows the bloodshed that prevented him from striding into the Oval Office. Just after midnight, after winning the all-important California primary, Kennedy appeared in the muggy, raucous hotel ballroom of the Ambassador. "We are a great country, an unselfish country, and a compassionate country..." he told supporters. "Now it's on to Chicago, and let's win there."

"We want Bobby! We want Bobby!" the crowd chanted back.

En route to a victory party already underway at The Factory—a nightspot owned by Pierre Salinger, Sammy Davis, Jr., and other liberal glitterati—RFK was led through the hotel kitchen. Some of his aides had psychedelic garb with them for the revelry. Just as their boss turned around to scout for his wife, a Palestinian-born drifter supposedly angry with Kennedy's recent pro-Israel comments fired a snub-nosed .22 caliber Iver-Johnson cadet revolver. One bullet caught Kennedy behind the right ear. He fell backward onto the concrete floor with a hole in his head. Grier, Johnson, and faithful bodyguard Bill Barry wrestled with the shooter—twenty-four year old Sirhan Sirhan—to make him drop the pistol. Somehow in the chaos Sirhan squirmed away and got his weapon again until he was subdued with hands around his throat. "Don't kill him!" hollered Jesse "Big Daddy" Unruh, speaker of the California legislature, from the top of a serving table. "We want him alive," meaning not executed before he could confess, as had happened with Jack Ruby in Dallas.

A total of thirteen bullets were fired and five others besides RFK were struck, none lethally. "Is everybody else all right?" Robert Kennedy asked Ethel as she caressed him on the kitchen floor. He passed out from there, never to wake again. He was pronounced dead at 1:44 A.M. the next day. Hearing the news early the following morning, Paul felt a chill dash up his spine and blood vacate his stomach. Not only had he seen RFK from through the lens of his camera the previous day, he had voted for him, too. Later, Kennedy's body traveled by funeral train, just like Lincoln's cortege, with tens of thousands of people lined up along the tracks to bid farewell.

Endorse or denounce his politics all you want, bathe in his family's mystique or harpoon it; one can still argue, even mawkishly, that with RFK's final breath in a local hospital went America's fleeting hope to redeem itself before its decade of disenchantment in the 1970s, before Nixon and his Watergate burglars, before Vietnam bled into deadly misadventure, before hyper-partisanship transmogrified into our fetid national state of being.

In the years that passed after his assassination, conspiracy theories twirled just as they had after Dallas, with some persuaded the mob or other conspirators engineered it. Could there have been a second gunman in the Ambassador kitchen that evening? Could the obscure Sirhan Sirhan have been a mind-controlled patsy planted to distract attention from the real assassin? Could the CIA have been involved, still livid with how the Kennedy's treated the agency after the Bay of Pigs fiasco? Could another group have done it? How else to explain bullet trajectories that make little sense, skeptics asked? Sirhan's lawyers in March 2012 officially contended their client did not discharge any of the bullets that killed RFK, no matter official conclusions to the contrary. In January 2012, in a strange compacting of time, Robert Kennedy, Jr. revealed his father's belief that Oswald did not act alone in assassinating John F. Kennedy and that the Warren Commission report that settled on the single-gunman theory was a "shoddy piece of craftsmanship." RFK, said his son, even felt "some guilt" that his efforts against organized crime might have incited the mafia to put the hit on JFK.

SHUTTERSPEED

I WAS A RASCALLY seven year old kid from distant, older parents living in the Pasadena foothills, not far from where Sirhan Sirhan resided, when the Ambassador's floor ran red. My bedtime came after prime time Batman ended. Paul was fifteen years older than me, meaning I idolized everything about him, from his insouciant popularity and brown MG sports car that he drove too recklessly to his waterskiing feats. In 1969, the draft tapped him, and he was sent to Ford Ord in Monterey for Army training before a likely deployment to Vietnam. At first, it seemed like a dream come true, as television romanticized war and made heroes and villains absolute to a junior G.I. Joe like me. Before long, I had a military buzz-cut to imitate Paul and my own itchy Army jacket. The sergeant high on Paul's leadership potential showered me with comic books, mess hall donuts, and niceness on one trip to Ford Ord.

Later, after the Army had Paul for some months, my intoxication with heroic combat began sobering. Every night, it seemed, the news showed the wounded being ferried to helicopters followed by kill numbers. Grownups openly bickered about whether Vietnam was worth the blood sacrifice. Back up to Ford Ord on another visit, the military staked a chain-link fence to separate adults from children to reduce their chances of contracting meningitis that had infected the base. I could only touch the brother I missed so tremendously through small, diamond-shaped squares in a cold fence. For some reason, my little-kid mind equated that distance with a more permanent one, where Paul returned dead from Vietnam in a body bag and my own joy was embalmed for good with him.

Safe to say that after serving his country, Paul survived. Decades later, when I became a writer, he emailed me the black-and-white photographs and explained the gut-wrenching timing behind them. I had no idea of their value. Busy with other projects, I let them stagnate on my hard drive for couple of years. Finally, with his permission, I posted them online, where bloggers, Kennedy experts and the *Los Angeles Times* made them an Internet sensation. The poignancy of them was undeniable. People tried deciphering who was driving the Lincoln and the Brylcreemed men in it. Was it a young John Kerry, Timothy Wirth? And what was the little motorcade doing outside the Biltmore on a campaign event nobody can peg?

The issue of when my brother took the pictures soon washed out other mysteries about them. Over the transom came an email from another Paul, Paul Schrade, and he was spitting BBs at the suggestion that the photos were taken mere hours before the killing at the Ambassador. Schrade at first dubbed the contention an "innocent mistake." RFK had spent the entire day of the primary in Malibu, never near downtown, he said. Case closed. Fred Dutton, he said, "confirmed it." As time went on the leonine-haired Schrade grew more livid with me, despite my and Paul's acknowledgement that the photos might have been snapped a day or two earlier. Outsiders weighed in with a magnifying glass, examining RFK's striped tie with others he'd donned.

I hit search engines for answers and within a millisecond understood that Schrade had justification for boiling feelings on the subject. June 1968 was still his private horror. At the time, he was a United Auto Workers chief and RFK's labor campaign standing near the candidate when Sirhan opened fire. One bullet struck Schrade in the head with a jolt that he likened to being "electrocuted." A signature photo from that evening's slaughter, besides a bus boy leaning over the fallen Kennedy, was of Schrade's head resting on a blood-soaked straw campaign hat while someone fanned him with a *Newsweek* magazine featuring RFK overlaid on JFK's image. When Schrade heard Kennedy had died, someone told him Kennedy's last words. "Is everyone all right? Is Paul all right?"

Schrade, not surprisingly, lived everyday with that traumatic moment, battling depression, losing his job, and working to uncover a conspiracy he believes killed his friend less than five years after his brother was cut down. "I was so angry," Schrade told a reporter. "We should have realized it was going to happen again." He has also tried keeping RFK's flame alive as a person worth emulating. A few years ago, the $568 million Robert F. Kennedy Community Schools, a cluster of schools built on the former Ambassador site at a record cost, opened, thanks largely to Schrade's twenty-three years of work. In dedication to him, there is the Paul Schrade Library. Bullet fragments are still lodged in his skull.

My brother's pictures seemed to have rattled them. Schrade accused me of exploiting them for personal aggrandizement, of using a remote connection to a remarkable family like a fame-mongering paparazzo. When I expressed sympathy with his perspective and asked for his assistance identifying the people with RFK in the Lincoln, he terminated his communication by saying he was "disappointed" in me. Paul Schrade was not buying the timing of Paul Jacobs' pictures, maybe because he believed all the knowable facts were in about Robert's movements and pondering otherwise invited psychic vertigo.

Remembrance, not self-serving controversy, had been my intention in posting them, and yet by bringing out what had been unseen, it was as if I had waded into territory still too radioactive for outsider exploration. Another stranger with an opinion on the matter, this one from North Carolina, fortunately was more revelatory than accusatory. Dave Loughlin, a music publisher who had read about the photos online as a self-described Kennedyphile, educated me in a long, twangy voicemail that my brother's snapshots were taken June 4th because RFK's scrape from saving his son are clearly visible there and not in previous stills from the campaign. In the pre-digital era, the mark was equal to a time stamp. After I learned about Kennedy's day in Malibu, I thanked Dave as my archaeologist. That scrape was a pinpoint. Whether it was also an omen I cannot say.

So what was RFK doing on sloping Bunker Hill on primary day 1968, if that is the correct date for the photos, when he had already delivered a speech at the hotel in April? Maybe, just maybe, RFK was in downtown L.A. being filmed by Frankenheimer's people for the documentary on this most extraordinary of days on a trip his associates never knew about or forgot to mentally warehouse in their miasma of grief and regret. Maybe, just maybe, it had happened after Frankeheimer missed his turn and circled back through downtown. I can only wish with quixotic delusion that there had never been any photographs, that Kennedy had smacked his head harder into the ocean floor, requiring stitches, concussion testing, and bed rest keeping him out of peril and in line for a presidency all about binding wounds and finding common ground again. RFK could have been our painkiller, our collective Vicodin, but Los Angeles robbed us of that fairytale.

"Historians have argued...about what Kennedy might have become, just as journalists and commentators in his lifetime debated who he really was," author Evan Thomas wrote in his excellent biography, *Robert Kennedy: His Life.* "Was he the hard, bullying, McCarthyite, wiretapping, Hoffa-Castro-obsessed hater forever scowling and vowing to get his enemies? Or was he the gentle, child-loving, poetry-reading, soulful herald of a new age? None of these images is wholly right; none wholly wrong. A better way to understand him is to examine his fear. He was brave because he was afraid. His monsters were too large and close at hand to simply flee. He had to turn and fight them."

Treacherous endings were in store for many of those at Frankenheimer's Malibu compound the day before Bobby Kennedy was gunned down. Killers from Charles Manson's "Family" murdered Sharon Tate, her unborn child and four others in a Benedict Canyon house in August 1969. Nine years later, Tate's widower, Roman Polanski, fled to France after he was charged with statutory rape. Frank Wells made it to 1994, dying in a helicopter crash in his tenth year as Disney's profit-making president. Then there was David Kennedy, who had heard about his father's murder on television hours after his father had plucked him from the undertow. He perished from a drug overdose in Palm Beach, Florida in April 1984.

Frankenheimer might have taken a bullet himself had it not been decided last minute that Schrade was a better person to be on stage with RFK than a Hollywood personality. He'd been waiting in the Ambassador parking lot to whisk his friend to the victory party at The Factory until he heard a woman run out yelling, "Kennedy's been shot." The paradox could drive a man insane. RFK had left his clothes at the house of the director of The Manchurian Candidate about U.S. soldiers brainwashed to kill. "I really had a nervous breakdown after that," Frankenheimer said later. "That's when I went to France, and that's when I went to the [Cordon Bleu], because I just had to do something else with my life, and I really couldn't go near politics for a long time after that." He passed away in 2002.

My brother agonized in his own fashion, too, seeing Kennedy's face close up and then getting word hours later that Dallas and Los Angeles were synonymous now, that the Texas Book Depository and the Ambassador's Kitchen were forever joined as cushy nests for snipers. In ensuing years, Paul, a real estate executive, family man, pilot, and philanthropist, often drove to legal appointments at Fifth and Grand wondering what Kennedy was thinking as he sat in that Lincoln with monsters milling around. Nobody may ever know.

Immediately after what happened at the Ambassador, LBJ ordered the Secret Service to guard presidential candidates. By then, Kennedy's scarred forehead had been forgotten in L.A.'s last picture show.

This story is drawn from photographs, personal recollections: the book, Robert Kennedy: His Life *by Evan Thomas (Simon and Schuster, 2002); "Bobby's Last, Longest Day"* (Newsweek, *June 16th, 1968); "Robert F. Kennedy's Assassination Remembered by Paul Schrade"* (Huffington Post, *June 4th, 2011); "John Frankenheimer: Renaissance Auteur" (hollywoodinterview.blogspot); "RFK Children Speak about JFK Assassination"* (USA Today, *January 12th, 2013), "Robert Kennedy's Final Day"* (Woodstock Journal); *and* Robert Kennedy's Last Day *(budgetfilms.com).*

DROPPING SCIENCE

Chromium-6 is a known carcinogen, but the implosion of a blue-ribbon panel of scientists means we still don't know how much is safe in L.A.'s drinking water.

—*LA CityBeat,* June 3rd, 2004

THEY WERE SOME OF California's top scientists, beautiful minds every one, with stellar résumés and the research grants to prove it. Experts at tracking how industrial poisons assault the body, they had served on national health boards and written thousands of journal articles among them. Within a few years, their cachet would be polluted.

In the spring of 2001, when the national chatter was about hanging chads, these seven toxicologists and epidemiologists were asked by state officials to tackle a medical hot potato: whether chromium-6, the so-called Erin Brockovich chemical, caused cancer through drinking water. California's risk-assessment agency had proposed a Draconian crackdown on chromium-6, based largely on a patchy 1968 German study, and water agencies and industry bristled about regulatory overkill.

It was hardly an academic question. Only a few years earlier, Pacific Gas & Electric (PG&E) had paid a record $333 million for chromium discharges that sickened residents of Hinkley, the San Bernardino desert hamlet where Brockovich crusaded. Lockheed Martin Corporation forked out $60 million itself in a secret 1996 deal with residents around its former Burbank military-aircraft plant. Health problems attributed to chromium-6, known technically as hexavalent chromium, drove that settlement.

Everybody knew the odorless, yellow-green compound can cause lung and sinus-area cancers when inhaled as dust. Direct skin contact can cause tumors. But whether it bred gastrointestinal cancers, leukemia, and other disease through lifetime consumption in water had not been firmly established. Independent brainpower was needed.

Before it could even finish its work, however, the Chromate Toxicity Review Committee" was rocked by controversy, when two panelists—one man a coveted industry consultant, the other the group's liberal conscience—resigned just before their only public meeting.

The panel's report was delivered ten days before the 9/11 terrorist attacks. Experts were unfazed by its mainstream conclusion: no credible research linked chromium-6 with cancer when ingested through water. The U.S. Environmental Protection Agency (EPA) and World Health Organization, among others, had endorsed the same view. The scientists recommended the state hold steady at its existing standard, fifty parts per billion (ppb) for total chromium in water, until a national toxicology study was completed.

The news quickly reverberated where it mattered. In Sacramento, regulators tweaked policies. In Los Angeles Superior Court, PG&E's lawyers used the findings to bolster their request for summary dismissal in Hinkley follow-up cases.

Yet, six months later, the committee's pride in a job well done metastasized into confusion, and then range warfare. A lanky Westside lawyer who had worked on the Brockovich case, among others, sensed something rotten about the blue-ribbon committee's conduct. Gary Praglin dug in. Over PG&E's objections, he won what few had: judicial permission to depose members of a scientific advisory board, folks associated with it, and subpoena documents, too.

Praglin's allegations, bound up in a phonebook-sized legal brief, were at once fateful and disturbing. They ignited two State Senate hearings, and a decision by Governor Gray Davis' top environmental official to officially trash the entire report. In doing so, California's bid to have a chromium-6 standard done by January 2004, as required by law, has been shoved back several years. A legally mandated study of contaminated San Fernando Valley groundwater was waylaid as well; it is now two-and-a-half years delinquent. Then there were the dinged reputations of the scientists themselves.

Indeed, Praglin's charges seemed more like the dirty laundry from a Big Tobacco trial than a humdrum chemical review. He claimed that PG&E had "dominated the blue-ribbon panel" by embedding one former and one current consultant on the panel, and then choreographed sympathetic experts to present evidence. A trade association with inside information about the group's proceedings, he alleged, was a sham. Tales of clumsy plagiarism, leaked e-mails, fixed conclusions, and a ghostwritten Chinese study with reversed chromium-cancer results rounded out his findings. In short, he concluded the panel was rigged.

"What we have here," Praglin said recently, "is the tip of the iceberg. It was definitely undue influence. PG&E's lawyers knew that the company's consultants were involved with the blue-ribbon panel and thought they could sneak it by the judge."

PG&E denounced these claims as "baseless accusations." It swore to zero involvement with the committee's workings. Two days before the first Senate hearing, at which PG&E did not speak, its lawyers at Latham & Watkins filed an exhaustive rebuttal of every scandalous assertion. The San Francisco-based utility refused comment for this story.

Panel member Dennis Paustenbach, an Oakland toxicologist considered by activists to be overtly "industry-friendly," was the central figure in Praglin's conspiracy theory. Praglin accused him of concealing both his ties to PG&E and his efforts before and after he resigned from the committee to influence policymakers. Paustenbach, whose media consultant crowned him the "Hank Aaron of his field," has authored 200 peer-reviewed studies, taught at several universities, and once drank chromium-laced water amid public hysteria about it.

He has been caught up in other environmental dust-ups, including his 2001 role on an EPA advisory panel examining dioxin, but nothing that brought on these kinds of fireworks.

At turns angry and defiant, Paustenbach believes he was the victim of a witch-hunt by aggressive plaintiff attorneys out to make "a billion dollars" in trial awards. Paustenbach said Praglin's computer-video presentation at the Senate hearings was a cut-and-paste hatchet job of his deposition. He accurately noted that he'd informed the panel's chair of his work for PG&E, which included research and testimony during the Hinkley trial, but stressed he could be objective nonetheless.

Praglin, who works with powerhouse Los Angeles tort lawyer Thomas Girardi and Brockovich-boss Edward Masry, doesn't buy it. Paustenbach, he said, provided insufficient disclosure considering the $8.6 million he earned for his employers in chromium-related work during his career, including once sitting in a chromium-filled Jacuzzi.

"So what?" demands Paustenbach.

"I was made into a bogeyman," he said. "What did Praglin risk when he put my family, my career, my income, my home on the line? PG&E never, ever contacted me with respect to the panel. I received one phone call from them in the five years after the Brockovich case. If there was lobbying, I wasn't aware of it."

Officials with the University of California Board of Regents, who had convened the blue-ribbon panel under a contract with the state's Office of Environmental Health Hazard Assessment (OEHHA), were also angered by the Senate hearings. In a movies-come-to-life moment, Brockovich opened the hearings with fiery speech about corporate skullduggery. Deborah Ortiz (D-Sacramento), who chairs the Senate's Health and Human Services Committee, oversaw the proceedings.

Because of the outcry, the university system revamped its policies to require science advisory panel members to complete written conflict-of-interest disclosure forms based on those used by the National Academy of Science.

"Mr. Praglin took quotes of contest, flashed them up on a screen, and it was so misleading I was actually embarrassed for him," said Eric Behrens, a counsel for the University Regents. Behrens was particularly galled by how panel member Marc Schenker, a UC Davis department chair and doctor, was ripped by Praglin for having a box of PG&E litigation material in his office during the time he was on the panel. Schenker had testified his work with the utility was over by then, and whatever money PG&E had paid went into the university's pocket, not his.

"This was not a bunch of industry flacks on the panel," Behrens added. "One of the interesting things about this situation is that it's not David versus Goliath. It's two Goliaths, with PG&E on one side and the plaintiff lawyers pursuing them on the other. The university [system] was caught in the middle."

WATER SPORTS

SO WERE PEOPLE IN Southern California.

A study by the official in charge of the upper Los Angeles River, Mel Blevins, concluded that concentrated groundwater plumes of chromium-6 are moving swiftly toward production wells operated by the cities of Burbank, Glendale, and Los Angeles, as *CityBeat* reported in April. Eventually, hundreds of thousands of people may be affected as these wells are closed, and expensive imported water will have to be purchased. Blevins calls the threat, which includes a series of industrial chrome-6 hot spots registering as high as one million ppb, a "clear and present danger." Officials at the Los Angeles Department of Water and Power disagree. Cities have kept water below state standards so far by blending contaminated water with purer sources.

Medically, some believe the stomach's natural acids render most of the chemical benign; other experts say it should not be in public water at all because of its ability to enter the bloodstream and penetrate organs and tissues. Its prevalence in local aquifers traces to the region's manufacturing legacy: chrome-6 has long been utilized in chrome plating, leather tanning, welding, as a paint pigment, and as an anti-corrosive.

While Praglin's charges still rankle many, his investigation did spill sunlight on the recurring cast of players who lobby state scientists on any variety of chemical matters, usually for clients who don't want their fingerprints noticed. The standards adopted by the OEHHA can move millions of dollars from one side of a ledger sheet to the other, so there was good reason that PG&E and others would make a full-court press to oppose any reduction in the chromium-6 water threshold.

Maybe the two most fascinating players in the saga are a young, wired-in scientist named Deborah Proctor and the executive director of a trade group named John Gaston.

Proctor is a Senior Managing Scientist at Exponent Inc., a Menlo Park-based engineering and science-consulting firm traded on the NASDAQ. Paustenbach worked there when he was on the panel. PG&E, Ford, Dow Chemical, Merck & Co., and General Motors—as well as the law firms representing Lockheed and PG&E—are listed as clients on Exponent's website.

In March, Proctor petitioned the state's Air Resources Board and OEHHA to consider relaxing airborne standards for chromium-6 based on freshly published studies. Her request directly ties into water regulation, because state officials may calculate people's exposure to chromium-6 through steam inhalation during showering.

Proctor, whose records indicate was deeply involved with the blue-ribbon panel, has not responded to attempts to reach her.

"The e-mails show that Deborah Proctor leaked confidential information for PG&E's financial gain," Praglin said. "And Paustenbach is the likely source of her information."

Paustenbach responded he never disclosed anything of consequence.

If Proctor's role is still somewhat mysterious, John Gaston's is less so. Gaston is a vice president and senior consultant at CH2M Hill, a multinational engineering, construction, and technical firm with a long history in Los Angeles monitoring federally subsidized projects from Metro Rail to Superfund cleanups. During the blue-ribbon panel's deliberations, however, Gaston wore a different hat: as executive director for "the Alliance for Responsible Water Policy." In his deposition for Praglin, Gaston acknowledged that the alliance is run out of the Sacramento office of a lobbyist named Eric Newman, and lacks any board of directors or palpable infrastructure.

To Praglin, the alliance is an industry front.

On April 6th, 2001, just five days after OEHHA recommended formation of an advisory board, records show the alliance had a strategic plan ready to roll in defense of members like Honeywell and PG&E. (The utility disputes it was a member then.) Newman and Gaston urged a campaign to sway lawmakers, reporters, and regulators at OEHHA and the California Department of Health Services. They identified "experts" who felt the chemical was an overblown peril ginned-up by the media and the movie. They also proposed direct involvement in the blue-ribbon panel. "Participate in state panel's review of chromium-6," their plans said. "Influence selection of panelists..."

Newman declined comment. In his deposition, he conceded that PG&E and its lawyers paid his lobbying firm $90,000 over a fourteen-month period to bird-dog chromium regulation.

Gaston's employer, CH2M Hill, has been awarded roughly $3.7 million in contracts from the EPA to provide technical assistance on the Valley's groundwater-contamination problems, most of that in recent years, federal records show. The company's focus was to advise on filtering solvents from the water. Even so, CH2M Hill did co-sponsor a symposium on the Valley's chrome-6 pollution in January 2001. About two years earlier, the firm performed a geo-chemical analysis of the same issue.

Asked if he felt there was a conflict between his alliance work combating the proposed chrome-6 water standards and his company's efforts advising on chrome-6, Gaston said no because he does not work on L.A.-area contracts. "My bosses know. It's not a dirty little secret," he said. "Besides, I never lobbied anybody on the panel," though he admitted doing that in the legislature.

Gaston was invited to speak at the state Senate hearings, only to decide against it after seeing Praglin's PowerPoint video. "Praglin flamed me and a bunch of others as industry whores, and by the end I saw no benefit in talking about how we wanted science to prevail," he said. "I was deposed by Praglin for countless hours. He showed portions of it at the hearing. It was not a pretty sight."

Gaston, himself a former state health official, said the alliance was needed as a firewall between trial lawyers and regulators. He compared the alliance to a volunteer fire department, only activated when needed. The alliance and Gaston are currently involved with state's efforts to regulate perchlorate, a rocket-fuel booster that has contaminated former-industrial zones from Azusa to Pasadena to the Santa Susana Pass.

"When scientists and the Department of Health Services say the standard is X, we all stand up and support X," Gaston said. "It should come from fuzzy-haired people with 'ologist' after their name. But in the last ten or more years, it's become much more litigious, much more acrimonious. There is a lot of money to be made out there."

Gaston is right about that. Praglin and company are representing 900 people in the cities of Hinkley, Topock, and Kettleman with chromium health claims against PG&E. Damages in the case, which has dragged out for eight years, could be in the hundreds of millions.

Praglin was not fazed by Gaston's broadside, or murmuring by critics that he was in an unholy alliance with attention-loving politicians and left-wing activists. "Industry is taking somebody with water credentials and putting his face on the puppet," he said.

Brockovich said those strings are obvious. She said she coaxed Praglin, Ortiz, and others to scrutinize the panel, not vice versa. Praglin added it was a cold call from Ortiz that led to the hearings. Ortiz verified that.

"It's frightening to see what lengths companies will go to conceal information from the general public," Brockovich told *CityBeat*. "That panel was so corrupt it was laughable."

DEAD MICE

THE MESS DID NOT begin with the Oscar-winning Erin Brockovich, which was released in March 2000. It began in February 1999, when OEHHA proposed a 2.5 ppb limit on total chromium in drinking water. OEHHA's job was to advocate for a limit overly protective of public health. The final say would come when the Department of Health Services takes that number, factors in economics and feasibility, and establishes what is called a maximum contaminant level.

Paustenbach, records show, certainly had his say. Six months before joining the blue-ribbon panel, he met with OEHHA officials about this issue. In a follow-up letter in December 1990, he asked the agency to "reconsider its current position regarding the oral carcinogenicity of chrome-6 based on the weight of evidence."

OEHHA conceded much of their thinking was based on a German study known as Borneff. In that experiment, hundreds of mice were fed extremely high does of chrome-6-laced water. A good number of the animals developed stomach tumors, but a virus that hit the colony might have been responsible, thus muddying the results.

Blue-ribbon panel members were especially critical of the state's reliance on this study. "Except for OEHHA, other regulatory agencies attempting to analyze the risk of ingested chrome-6 have deemed this study not suitable," their report stated.

The media got into the act in August 2000, when the *Los Angeles Times* published the first in a barrage of stories about the widespread presence of chrome-6 in the Valley's groundwater. In response to those stories and public fears, Governor Gray Davis signed legislation by then-State Senator Adam Schiff for the state's health department to assess the magnitude of the Valley's chromium pollution. Roughly one year later, Davis signed a bill by Ortiz to speed up enactment of the chrome-6 contaminant level by January 1st of this year.

Driven by the panel brouhaha, however, neither of those deadlines has been met. Some have suspected the Valley report, which has been kept in a draft mode that makes it exempt from public inspection, was squelched by lobbying efforts.

But David Spath, chief of the state health department's drinking water and environmental services, insisted that was wrong. He said he has privately told officials the data indicates there is no danger to Valley residents.

"There is no political intrigue behind this," said Spath. "It may be we will just release [the assessment study]. To be honest, it's sort of an embarrassment to have a report referencing a blue-ribbon report that has been disavowed by Cal-EPA."

OEHHA Director Joan Denton said the agency realized it would take heat for leaning on the Borneff study, which is why she agreed to the formation of the blue-ribbon panel. The abandonment of its report means a final public health goal is still some ways off.

"We did take the blue-ribbon report" seriously, Denton said. "They did bring some information we didn't know about before. In the end, [as the Senate hearings ripped into the panel's actions], we were in bystander mode. It was a very visible series of events."

DO NOT EAT

UC Davis medical professor Jerold Last was selected as the chair of the blue-ribbon group, largely because of his earlier stewardship of the panel reviewing the gasoline additive MTBE. Cherry-picking scientists from a list supplied by the state and his own academic contacts, Last chose seven top-drawer scientists. One of them was John Froines, an acclaimed UCLA professor and former Chicago Seven member known for his toxic studies. Paustenbach was a second choice after another scientist declined.

Contacted by *CityBeat*, Last said there was no undue influence on the panel, and that none of the posturing around the panel affected its conclusions. Froines, he complained, was "leaking everything to OEHHA as fast as Paustenbach was leaking" to others. Mostly, Last said, he is steamed at Praglin and Ortiz. Since their hearings, he has decided against serving on future science panels. Some colleagues have stopped volunteering as well.

"It was a purely political process best exemplified by the statement by Senator Ortiz, who said we are going to totally ignore the conclusions of the science and focus on the process," Last said. "If you can't attack the science, you end up attacking the people. Based on my experience, would you feel a great deal of trust for the political system?"

Ortiz said the feeling was mutual. She explained that, according to Last's own e-mails, some material in the blue-ribbon panel report was torn almost verbatim from a Merck-funded journal article Paustenbach and Proctor penned. The article examined cancer links at chrome pollution sites in central Mexico, Scotland, and Japan.

"If [Last] felt slighted by my eleventh-hour hearing, then that is unfortunate," Ortiz said. "We are all very grateful he won't serve on future panels. He violated his obligation to be fair and objective. Am I supposed to ignore a process that appears to be rigged?"

Froines declined comment, citing his ongoing chairmanship of the State Review Board for Toxic Air Contaminants. In his Senate testimony, though, Froines expressed concerns about the panel's short time frame and its "limited" perusal of relevant literature. Of the 200 chemicals the state has reviewed, he said, chromium-6 is only second in cancer-causing potency to dioxin.

"Chromium, forgetting whether you breathe it, drink it eat it... is a carcinogen," he testified. "That's where you start from."

WAR OF THE EMAILS

READ ALL THE DOCUMENTS and one thing stands out: thrashing over a chrome-6 standard became a sort of shadow courtroom where the real sequel to Erin Brockovich was produced.

Consider April 19th, 2001, five days before Last gave panel members their workload, when the e-mails flew.

Exponent's Proctor, who somehow had the skinny on the panel's schedule, e-mailed Paustenbach saying none of the companies "want the spotlight" to state their opinions about the proposed chrome-6 standard. Later that day, Paustenbach responded to her, inviting "clients" to send studies he could share with the rest of the panel.

Frictions surfaced soon after. On April 25th, Froines e-mailed George Alexeff, OEHHA's deputy director, that the panel was "biased," that Paustenbach's conflict of interest had gone unquestioned, and that he was bolting. Last talked him out of it.

Proctor hustled, too. In mid-May, she e-mailed PG&E's attorneys at the downtown Los Angeles office at Latham & Watkins. "Because it is important that the expert panel get the best information," she wrote, "with your approval I have approached [University of Alabama scientist] Phil Cole about having Lockheed or the Alliance for Responsible Drinking Water fund him and present to the panel. Phil is most comfortable with having PG&E fund completion... I am trying to work through Dennis to get the panel to invite Phil."

Praglin later subpoenaed records showing that Cole received a check for roughly $6,500 from the alliance. Praglin also secured a ledger indicating Lockheed paid about $15,000 to have Norwegian scientist Sverre Langard travel from Oslo to Davis to attend the panel's public meeting.

Lockheed relocated from Burbank to Georgia in the early 1990s. Even before it moved, it was under federal and state groundwater and soil cleanup orders, and has built and operated extensive plants to remove solvents. Company spokesperson Gail Rymer said in response to *CityBeat* inquiries that the aerospace conglomerate is not "currently involved in tort litigation regarding chromium." Lockheed, she added, has spent in excess of $220 million on its local cleanup. Rymer acknowledged the federal government has reimbursed the company for approximately $110 million of that because of the Pentagon's control of Lockheed's Air Force Plant 14 from 1947 to 1973—one of the first times a dollar figure has been specified.

Was Lockheed involved with the alliance's efforts to sway the blue-ribbon panel? Without directly answering, Rymer said the company reserved the right to "bring good science into the debate" through an industry organization or independently.

By July 2001, the panel was splintering. Froines, whom Proctor called "so full of it," finally quit. In doing so, he expressed his "serious concerns" about the committee's functioning, but nothing directly about Paustenbach.

Nonetheless, the panel was smeared. That same month, Last received letters from two small environmental groups warning that Paustenbach had thick industry ties that should knock him off the panel. Joe Lyou of the California League of Conservation Voters Education Fund, referencing Paustenbach's work for Rockwell, PG&E, Louisiana Pacific, and others, worried—prophetically as it turned out—the conflicts would "taint the conclusions" of the panel.

Anticipating the storm, Paustenbach resigned on July 26th, before the rest of the panel voted to use him as a contributor, not a member. Paustenbach today said he regrets departing, and wonders how the activists learned so much.

"Why a week before the public hearing did these letters come in?" he asks. "At that moment, I should have said something is wrong here. That panel was a very pure panel... There's no doubt I wanted to share my scientific views after the Brockovich movie. You had the whole world thinking that if you ingest chrome-6, you get cancer."

HOLDING ON TO HUEY LONG

The maddening, populist, civil libertarian, deal-making, district-loving and just plain weird career of City Councilman Nate Holden ends July 1st, leaving behind a new political scene that can't tolerate his brand of bullish boosterism.

—*LA CityBeat,* June 26th, 2003

NATE HOLDEN, WHO HAS weathered more storms in his career than Ferdinand Magellan, looks ready to drop. Eyes bloodshot, hands limp at his side, the man legendary for knocking out one-arm pushups and puzzling zingers, slumps deep into an office chair, muttering gravelly shoptalk into the phone.

Just past lunchtime on a recent Tuesday, the shiny-domed maverick seems all of his seventy-three years, still physically imposing, still defiant, but somehow lost with no challenge at hand—except becoming private citizen Nate Holden. The public Nate Holden seems nervous about that role. By month's end, his four stints on the Los Angeles City Council and a nearly thirty-year political life that elevated him from his native Georgia to the power corridors of California politics will be dust.

If he is dreaming of tropical vacations or redeeming lost sleep, it doesn't show. What ethical hullabaloos and shifting demographic faultlines never did—bounce him from his 10th district reign—terms limits finally have. You get the sense he's disoriented about being shooed off the public stage so peacefully.

Nudged aside, Holden will have to forsake to his love of combat—a love that propelled him as a teenaged boxer, into the U.S. Army and into some singularly Nate newspaper headlines once in office. Adept with the haymaker, a recipient of punches himself for improprieties, he will jab no more. Not for his people.

"I don't have an option," he said, massaging his squiggly brow, "For all these years, I've lived and breathed this. I have to be in a frame of mind [that] there is a beginning and the end."

In Los Angeles, where council government is not the contact sport it is in Chicago and New York, Holden was like few others. He was colorful and iconoclastic, shrewd and self-destructive, outrageous and just plain out-there. The city may never see someone like him again in the age of packaged, cautious candidates always thinking past their next term limit.

Political observers are divided about his legacy. Was he Crenshaw Boulevard's Huey Long, or a poor man's Willie Brown? Was he badly misunderstood, a great political mind in a mortal skin? Or, did he fizzle out when his rival and energizer, Tom Bradley, exited the scene, and incumbency put a price tag on his idealism?

"He was like the Howard Stern of politics," said lobbyist Howard Sunkin. "He wasn't embarrassed about saying what others were afraid to. He was as shrewd as there was. [People] say 'God bless him' and 'God damn him' at the same time."

In recent years, Holden's influence waned on a new generation council. His antics marginalized him into something of a political curiosity, a flamethrower looking for a target. But he never forgot what his mentor, the late County Supervisor Kenneth Hahn taught him: fix the potholes and the rest will fix itself.

And he was never a yawn.

As Los Angeles burned in the '92 riots, Holden was the holdout vote against ousting LAPD Chief Daryl Gates because he thought the firing process had been short-circuited. Six years later he called a packed news conference to announce the Raiders were returning to the Coliseum from Oakland, which was news to team owner Al Davis.

Who can forget him branding two colleagues as "Westside Ku Klux Klansmen," or his insistence that a Valley pug dog had been skinned by sadists, and a bin of other left-field denunciations leaving onlookers asking, "Did he really say that?" All the while he exhibited a Clintonian deftness for putting himself in one seemingly impossible moral abyss after another, only to climb out and preen before his enemies, less powerful yet still intact.

L.A. should have known what they were getting. Holden had barely been representing his mid-city district a few years when then-Valley Councilman Joy Picus told him, in Holden's words, "to stop acting like the emperor."

But gag him? Please. In 1991, he proposed legislation that all restaurant workers get AIDS-tested every six months. Imagine, Holden explained to the press, that a waiter's tainted blood gets on your glass, adding, "You're dead as a donut." Instead, his proposal ended up dead, though it did provoke important debate. He is exiting office with similar flair, pushing a proposal to make every company with city business determine if they profited from slavery.

To dissect Nate Holden is, in some ways, to think of what could have been. A former aerospace engineer and state senator, he does not lack for gray matter. It is prudence that has failed him, many say.

Like one of those inflatable toys that bounce back no matter the beating, Holden lost more races than he won, defeated in bids for the assembly, Congress, the state board of equalization, and L.A. Mayor. A sly campaigner, he ran a surprisingly close race against Bradley, but could never form what might have been a formidable duo afterwards.

"After I lost, I had him down to my office for lunch," Holden recalled. "I broke down in tears. I asked him how we could work together. But his aides wouldn't let him. It was divide and conquer. Oh, what Tom and I could have done. He could have been governor without a doubt."

Holden, rhetoric aside, was no dyed-in-the-wool liberal in the mold of compatriots such as Diane Watson and Maxine Waters. Ideologically, he often went a la carte, siding with conservatives fighting a $300 million Metro Rail property tax, untrammeled redevelopment, and backing Valley secession one moment, then supporting unpopular black police chiefs and traditional civil rights issues the next. It gave some lobbyists ulcers.

In Holden's rear-view mirror, fairness and compassion were his creed. He set out to build coalitions, as Bradley did so superbly, but was often undone by, well, ignorance.

"Unfortunately," he says, "a lot of African Americans aren't very smart. They don't know the political game. Most are social reformers but are fiscally conservative."

It is comments like this that make some duck for cover and others stand up and applaud. "On paper, he doesn't look like he'd be liked by neighborhood activists, black militants, and anti-tax Republicans, but all the orphans gather around him," observed subway gadfly John Walsh. "Even when he votes the wrong way, he asks the right question. He alone single-handedly prevented the city from putting one dollar in the East L.A. subway because he realized it was a rathole. In many ways, he was like the villain in professional wrestling. He enjoyed the jeering."

Like Clinton, whose picture graces his half-emptied office, Holden hates the idea that the word "scandal" will appear in his political obituary. Being chastened does not come easy to him, including when an aide running to replace him was knocked out by disclosures he had been busted for drugs in the late-1980s. Both pitbull and victim, crusader and crucified, he does not give much quarter. Go hardball on him and expect a blast back from his pen or a thick counter complaint from Mark Geragos, one of his lawyers

So what if the media has skewered him for racy pictures with dancing girls on an Asian business trip, for putting ex-colleagues on his payroll, and a series of campaign no-nos? Sure, there were two sexual harassment suits filed, including by a former receptionist who says Holden tried forcing her to have sex with him. He was vindicated—at a cost to city taxpayers of $1.5 million.

Tool around his district, he says, and you will understand why those charges pale. The area is far better than what he inherited, with auto-body shops and mini-malls under control, national retailers lured in, patched streets, and less graffiti. He got 132 AK-47s off the street and the sale and possession of semi-automatic weapons banned. Take that.

So what if the L.A. Ethics Commission could have set up kiosk outside his office? It cited him in his final race for thirty-one violations, and those were only the latest of some 334 incidents where he accepted money beyond campaign limits. How much beyond limits? Try $165,000. Holden, though, believes the commission made him "target board" for mistakes made by his treasurer, when it should have gone after bigger fish.

"People will read about [me] in the *L.A. Times*, and yet I've been in office all these years," he says jauntily. "Who is right: the voters or the reporters?" There was "eyesore after eyesore" in the district he took over, he says. "There was white flight. Today [the whites] are moving back."

Not everybody accepts the idea that Holden's lone-wolf routine improved the public weal. "He's a character who added primarily flash but not substance," said political consultant Harvey Englander. "I don't mean to be cruel, but there won't be any libraries named after him. But he did outwit the gods."

Rick Taylor, a journeyman L.A. campaign adviser, believes the economic rejuvenation in a district badly scorched during the riots cannot be ignored.

"I think he leaves the Council doing what he wanted," said Taylor. "He's helped a lot of real people you and I will never know—not big developers, not special interests. Here's a guy who could easily not have been re-elected. He was a walking hit-piece for rival campaigns. He overcame by taking care of his base. He fixed Mr. Jones's trees."

Or Thelma Hilliard's La Cienega-area neighborhood. Holden was there time after time, helping residents get parking spaces during a county storm drain project and after the Northridge earthquake, pushing for the demolition of a crime-plagued hotel and removing graffiti lickety-split.

"He did all this with no press conference, no anything," said Hilliard, a community activist. "He just took care of his constituents. Yeah, he had a lot of notoriety, but most of us were in his corner."

His second career won't start until after a long vacation and an insider-packed sendoff tribute at Hollywood's Kodak Theatre, where the Oscars are handed out. It seems a fitting venue for a guy who could brazenly vamp before any camera, anytime.

Will he tread where other retired pols have—the lucrative lobbying business? At this, a tired Nate Holden drew up from his chair and harrumphed. "I don't like doing favors. I like twisting arms until they break. When you are a lobbyist you can't do that. But"—and a weary, toothy smile arrives—"I know how to get things done."

DEAR RIFLE

Remembering a relative's murder and the gas chamber execution of his unrepentant killer.
—Pasadena Weekly, **January 4th, 2004**

THE COSMIC TUMBLERS THAT align the universe must have required a factory re-lubing after the caskets were nailed shut. To blame the events of February 1941 and what followed on happenstance's spinning needle is just too blighting, too painful, the kind of soul-crusher that converts a devout monk into a flaming atheist. This, I tell myself, was meant to be. Had to be. Always was. The San Quentin gas chamber was inevitable from the very first handshake of the principals in the underbelly of pre-war Los Angeles. Nat Ross, a champion of second chances, needed a worker. And Maurice "Mike" Briggs wanted a job. It was no coincidence they intersected any more than the moon's gravitational orbit around the Earth.

Cotton Products Corporation, a moderate-sized rag-making factory south of Los Angeles City Hall at 1627 South Broadway, was revved up with contracts when they met in the mid-1940s at what today is a vacant lot between a red-trimmed Jack In The Box franchise and a blah, government-gray freeway overpass. Briggs, who had originally traveled to the West Coast to visit his father, seemed like a winner. In short order, he elevated himself to foreman of the washing machines. A smart aleck sort, he might have called himself the Grand Poobah of them.

The twenty-six year old newcomer with an Errol Flynn moustache and glinting smile wanted the factory women to know he was a bachelor, as well. An attractive, pouty-lipped woman named Betty Susan, then twenty-one, certainly was impressed. They flirted over textile orders, probably went on a few dates and got sweaty under the sheets. Betty deemed him such a keeper that after a brief courtship she agreed to his marriage proposal. Mrs. Maurice Briggs was pregnant mere weeks later. She quit her job in preparation for out-of-nowhere domesticity they would romanticize for their children one day.

On breaks from the grind, Nat, my great uncle, might have giggled to himself at how farfetched love stories can be, if not how ironic considering that the last film he was supposed to produce for Columbia Pictures was entitled *The Accidental Father* before zigzagging life planted him here.

Briggs, in the meantime, had never been happier. A ho-hum job had led to a spouse and a future. Then again, when had happiness stayed around him for more than a few weeks? Before the newlyweds had celebrated three months together, they began quarreling and could not stop. In their last fight, Betty accused him of cold-cocking her in the face and tearing off her garments with the promise that he was not going to leave her "with a stitch of clothing" to her name if she resisted him. Briggs, who had buried his molten temper hidden behind his hunky jaw and cigarette smoke, was tossed out of his place on South Grand Avenue in December. Nearby flophouses reserved for broken men was now where he slept.

Still, he had kept his job with a plant, which gave him hope of reclaiming Betty's heart. It was just that the woman he had swept off the plant floor was already dead-set on eliminating any trace of him. In the days after he moved out, she told him that she had lost the child in a miscarriage and, in a second whopper, had already fallen in love with another man named Gene Sperry. Briggs responded with an incredulous cluck. After he grilled her, she admitted she was still pregnant. The lie bothered him little. Over and over, he whinnied for her to take him back, promising to change his stripes and night-work schedule for the sake of their relationship. Every time she shook her head "No!" By January 1941, she had lined up a Long Beach divorce attorney. Briggs said he would go along with annulling their marriage if she kept his child, presuming she would eventually want the baby's father residing under the same roof.

Briggs, however, was losing things left and right in a city bulging with transplants like him. After he had worked shifts at Cotton Products evidently blotto, Nat had to let him go. A factory with heavy machinery and dozens of employees was no place to be sauced. A softy about people down on their luck, he soon re-hired Briggs with a probationary caveat. Briggs ignored it, coming in plastered again around February 10th. He applied for unemployment benefits cursing his need to do it.

Reuniting with Betty remained his number one obsession. Two days after Nat gave him the second heave-ho, Briggs made a Hail Mary to win her back. Please, he said. He would do anything. Anything. As before, his desperation held no truck for her. She was terminating the pregnancy for real this time. Since he had refused to help pay for the operation, she had found someone chivalrous who would. Not only was Nat a benevolent boss, he had awarded her back her old factory job so she could be her own breadwinner again.

Hearing this development, the lunatic creeper in Briggs fully took over. He contacted the Los Angeles Police Department to prevent the abortion, which in the fedora age was whispered as an illegal procedure. The department refused to entangle itself in the soap opera on Broadway. Be that way, Briggs thought. He would play detective, telling some that he believed Nat was having a fling with his girl. On a stalking trip to Cotton Products, he spied her departing with Nat in his car. He went to a Red Car bench close to her house to wait for her, seeing her return at 2:00 A.M., perhaps after visiting a back-room abortion doc. “I didn’t get a chance to talk,” Briggs said afterwards, “because she ran up the steps and locked the door in my face.”

Soon enough, he was on plant grounds again, pie-eyed, clutching a pocketknife, and hissing in Nat’s face that “he wasn’t going to be around much longer.” Nobody took the threats much more than the predictable ranting of a wife-beating, alcoholic drifter rather than a ticking time bomb. “I’m not mad at you, but am going to kill Ross,” he told his soon-to-be-ex-wife. Either on that visit or another one on Valentine’s Day, the LAPD arrested him on a seemingly minor charge. He had blown every chance afforded him to fly straight, or at minimum fly away. Why hadn’t he just stuck to his washing machines?

Ten days later, on February 24th, 1941, Briggs' divorcing spouse informed him that she was with child no more. More trickery, Briggs said. Show him proof. She did—a bloody towel used to staunch the post-procedure hemorrhaging. Briggs was floored numb, as if everything leading up to this moment was surmountable drama attached to a happily ever after. In his delusional head, it was conflicting work schedules, not his sometimes-psychotic conduct, at the root of their troubles.

Now that he knew there would be no baby, Briggs framed an incendiary exit plan by thinning out the city's population by one. The next morning he cashed his unemployment check and spent eight dollars at a Main Street pawnshop and a few bucks for accessories at another shop. Around sundown, he picked up his merchandise, strolled some blocks and stashed them near an apartment house close to the factory.

Read this next part with appreciation: It was the subplot of a destiny bitch-slap that yours truly was meant to stumble upon decades later. Just after 10:00 P.M., Briggs knocked on the side door at Cotton Products. All polite-like, he told the person who answered it that he would like a brief word with his ex-boss. Nothing heavy. Nat, who had been chatting with some floor workers as they rushed an order for Navy battleships, sighed when he heard you-know-who had reappeared. "What does he want now?" he mumbled. "I'll be back, girls."

BOOT TIPS IN THE SILT

Nat Ross, my mother's favorite uncle, already had enjoyed the sort of heartbreak-to-fame feel-good story upon which legacies are wired when Briggs asked to see him that evening. Many are crowned a wunderkind in the breathy hyperbole of our showbiz town. Few, however, lived the archetype like him. And if Nat had a fondness for men named Maurice, it might have been due to its familiar ring.

He was born in teeming San Francisco in June 1904 as the middle child of Maurice and Sonya "Dearie" Rosenberg. Seattle would have been a safer place for him. When the monster earthquake pancaked the Bay Area two years later, killing thousands and destroying more than three-quarters of the city, he barely survived it. Nat's father had to jump from the stoop of their collapsing home with his toddler-son in his arms before they were buried under tons of debris. The quick action should have been celebrated. Instead it was lost in the cold.

Despite hailing from an affluent, industrial family with a home on Nob Hill, little assistance was provided to Maurice because his relatives were livid that he had wed a commoner, pretty, plump, and vivacious as she was. Natural disasters, it turns out, can sway crystal chandeliers, just not stubborn heads from nouveau riche money beneath them. So Nat, his older sister, Rose (my maternal grandmother), her baby brother, Harold, and their parents made do. For a year, they supposedly lived in a tent in Golden Gate Park with other people made instant indigents by tectonic convulsions.

Unable to see a future there after being snubbed for emergency cash, Maurice fixed his gaze on the American Southwest, where a relative he liked had relocated to El Paso. That vision was a catalyst. The industrious, gregarious Maurice packed everybody up, got out of California and went into business with him in Texas. Within a few years, the transition was complete. Maurice had reinvented himself into a prosperous merchant selling commodities and used goods from a store.

El Paso, though within shouting distance of the Mexican Revolution across the border, brought his family money, shelter, and a driver in an age when cars were crank-started machines and men combed waxy, handlebar moustaches. Sometimes, Maurice's buddy, Francisco "Pancho" Villa, would drop by the home on Montana Street for laughs and drinks when he was not otherwise occupied on raids in places like Tierra Blanca and Chihuahua.

Maurice's second life in Texas was going aces until J.E. Mullen, a young, dark-eyed entrepreneur, breezed into the shop. Mullen was selling animal hides at a low cost. Interested? All Maurice had to do was drive with him to a clearing to inspect the hides. Four days later, in February 1915, workers trenching a ditch along the Rio Grande River discovered Maurice's boots protruding from the silt and then the mutilated, bullet-riddled corpse attached to them. My great-grandfather was thirty-six.

Identified as the leading suspect, Mullen was chased by Villa's security men by car on dusty back roads. After he gave them the slip, he fled to Juarez, Mexico, where police tracked him to a boardinghouse and arrested him. Back across the border he was sent and into the arms of El Paso detectives. Prosecutors charged Mullen, twenty-one, with murder. Pinning down his motive was something else. Why, detectives asked, would a lowlife arms dealer selling munitions to both sides of Mexico conflict bother baiting a stranger into a deadly trap. If Mullen was after Maurice's jewelry, why had he only lifted some baubles, like a gold-encrusted watch, while leaving others? Had Mullen panicked in a robbery gone wrong, or was he part of a conspiracy—one involving a personal vendetta or even Villa—to stage it that way?

The trial, sensationalized lickety-split by the newspapers as the most twisted murder case in El Paso history, was the hot ticket in town. People elbowed each other to secure courtroom seats to hear the evidential particulars. How the victim was forced to dig his own grave. Maurice's wealthy status and his macabre end at the hands of shadowy, cocky Mullen was raw titillation. One of the District Attorney's star witnesses, a fourteen year old girl among the last people to see Maurice alive, hyped interest more. Pointing at the defendant in his blue serge shirt, she said, "He left with that man [over there] and I did not see him again until his body was found."

So cosmically annihilated was she after her testimony that someone had to escort her to another city to recover. That girl was my future grandmother.

The electrifying scene ended with a guilty conviction and a sentence of thirty-five years to life, but no death penalty, for the man friends called "Red." He had been shamelessly indifferent during the proceedings, chewing gum, smoking a briar pipe, resting his legs flippantly on a chair, and he was just as detached after the verdict. He declined to appeal the ruling, saying he was "no fool," whatever that meant. His motive stayed a mystery.

UNCLE CARL'S CAMERA BOY

MAURICE'S WIDOW, SONYA, NOW had three children to care for, virtually no work experience, and not much sympathy from her husband's wealthy kin in San Francisco. The only compass point that made sense was northwest, where her older brother, actor Alexander Carr, performed on the Broadway stage with a foghorn voice. Once they arrived, Carr subsidized their living expenses in a cramped Brooklyn apartment. Even so, compared to where they had been, New York was frigid, squalid, unwelcoming and bitterly anti-Semitic. Her family's conversion to Christian Science—Rosenberg becoming Ross—only made their hardscrabble existence marginally better.

But it did not have to be this dispiriting, suggested Sonya's eldest son, Nat, now about thirteen. He was capable of bringing money home in his father's absence. Missing some school to contribute toward the rent was a noble tradeoff. Though no one knows he did it, Nat persuaded Lewis Selznick, a Russian émigré who had chartered a feature film and distribution company called World Pictures, to be his reception clerk. He parlayed that starter job to a better one with Stanley Maustbaum's theater chain. Well on his way before he could vote, he became assistant manager director of New York's Strand Theatre and from there, an East Coast film salesman for an outfit called Universal Pictures.

Come 1920, the eager beaver had switched coasts to be at Universal's 230-acre lot astride the Cahuenga Pass, where silent films, serials, and newsreels were pumped out en masse. Nat, who stood 5'8" with penetrating blue eyes, short-cropped, curly black hair, and an imagination that matched his ambition, longed to be a storyteller. In dues payment before he could get behind a camera, he became personal assistant to studio founder Carl Laemmle. Some film sites contend that Laemmle was Nat's uncle, which is news to my current generation. Others suggest there was so much nepotism in Hollywood then that Laemmle was everybody's "Uncle Carl."

Nat's vim and vigor and knack for learning things on the fly dazzled Laemmle, whether he was Nat's relation, mentor or both. In the lad he spotted executive material to be one of the Universal's first leaders. Laemmle discerned the same potential in one of Nat's early L.A. roommates, who the studio hired straight from high school. Sometimes Nat and Irving Thalberg would have supper with Nat's mother, who he had brought out from Brooklyn. After a dose of palace intrigue over the right cadre to groom, Thalberg was promoted to management while Ross bowed out. He would rather earn his stripes as a writer-director than sitting in an office.

During the Roaring Twenties, he called the shots for more than fifty Universal films, the bulk of them silent Westerns, romantic comedies and madcap sports' sendoffs. In 1922's *The Galloping Kid*, he directed cowboy star Hoot Gibson. The next year he oversaw *The Ghost Patrol*, a short written by Sinclair Lewis. His cachet rising as one of Hollywood bright young talents, Nat next oversaw episodes of the boxing series *The Leather Pushers*. In 1926's *April Fool*, about a hapless pants-presser, Nat cast himself in a role and used his uncle, Alexander Carr, as the lead. In that same year he led production of *Two Can Play* about the daughter of a wealthy financier and her two competing suitors. The heroine actress was a tortured beauty that Helena Bonham Carter could play today in a biopic. Clara Bow was Hollywood's sexualized "It Girl," and someone grateful. Nat believed in her. Three years later came his most commercial movie, 1929's *College Love*, about a university football star who took the blame for a drunken escapade the night before the big game.

Nat's storybook arc suddenly ran ashore as inspirationally as it took off. He filed for bankruptcy in July 1929. He barely escaped serious injury the next year when a team of horses frightened during filming broke loose and knocked over a fifteen foot high camera perch, sending Nat tumbling down an embankment in the hills of Killer Canyon near Universal. His life seemed to regain its buoyancy during the teeth of the Depression when he married actress-dancer Audrene Brier, who he had met while directing her in a comedy. Nat by then was actor Jack Holt's manager and a producer for Universal. Yet something soon happened, perhaps a falling out with Laemmle himself. Nat and his wife moved from Longden Avenue in Van Nuys to England to produce films for Columbia and MGM. On the eve of World War II, they came home.

Nat was now co-owner and one of the superintendents at Cotton Product with a plan in place—literally in his trouser pocket—to return to the craft that enlivened his blood. But February 24th, 1941, when Maurice Briggs rapped on the door of Cotton Products asking to speak with him, was destiny's way of ridiculing human plans while oxygenating distant generations.

LEAD DESTINY

As Nat grudgingly approached the man who had assaulted his pregnant wife, Briggs reached for something behind the door. A .25-.35 caliber Winchester rifle was in his arms. Before Nat could snatch it away, Briggs pointed the rifle at his chest and fired at his target from point-blank range. Nat screamed a ghastly scream, collapsing onto the factory floor. According to some accounts, he lay there moaning, not long for this world, when Briggs fired an insurance shot into him. The butchery had happened wordlessly.

Twenty-five employees watched the execution. Some ran with clattering shoes into the bathroom. Others fainted or shrieked. Plant worker Frank Anderson raced over to disarm the gunman, but Briggs aimed the Winchester at him with a deranged smile that implied, "Don't even think about it." Job done, Briggs tranquilly exited the property, walked two blocks to Olive and 17th Street and chucked the Winchester onto a vacant lot like it was an empty Budweiser bottle. When a passerby asked him what he was doing, Briggs, clad in a sport coat and black T-shirt, was honest. "Oh, I just killed a guy," he said. "Better call the cops." LAPD officers clapped handcuffs around him not far away. They paraded him in front of Cotton Products, too, where Briggs paused before his wife. "You won't need," he said, "to get a divorce now."

In the commotion that ensued, Ross's slaying became a tabloid feeding trough for L.A.'s dog-eat-dog newspapers. Workplace violence was rare, and this homicide sparkled with Hollywood angles, a dashingly defiant suspect and beautiful women in the center, movie noir all of it. "EX-PRODUCER OF FILMS SLAIN BY EMPLOYEE," the *Los Angeles Times* read. "NAT ROSS SLAIN BY DISCHARGED WORKER," said *Variety*. "JEALOUS HUSBAND KILLS WIFE'S BOSS," blared the *Examiner*.

"Why did I do it?" Ross was asked from the LAPD's Central Jail at the beginning of the spectacle. "Because I didn't like him. That ought to be enough." Sure, sure, but he was repentant, remorseful, the cops and media wanted to know? A human life, after all, had been deleted. "Am I sorry I did it?" Briggs famously gloated. "Yeah, I'm sorry I can't do it again! I'm ready for gas or whatever they give you in California."

His sick bravado after he was booked earned him another wicked, front-page story in the *Times*. "SUSPECT IN MAN'S KILLING QUOTED AS HAVING NO REGRET." Originally, he had planned to kill Nat with his own hands until he had decided, "it'd be too much trouble." He had wanted to shoot him ten days earlier, but had not had the money to acquire a gun and ammo. A photograph of him that accompanied one article depicted the stalky Briggs with the self-satisfied smile of a World Series winner and a face, you would swear, chiseled from a Justin Timberlake ancestor.

Briggs' motives were as one-dimensional as his sadism. Hatred. He was suspicious that his married ex-boss was having an affair with his wife after they had separated. Even if he wasn't, Briggs did not appreciate the attentions Nat showed her, nor his assistance ending the pregnancy, nor anything about him, really. Betty Susan Briggs adamantly denied she was sleeping with Nat. Brier herself was indignant at the notion her husband of five years was unfaithful. Come on. If he had wanted to philander, he knew plenty of Hollywood starlets. But he was not that sort of fella. The District Attorney concurred, saying there was "no evidence" that Nat was "in any way to blame."

Journalists and movie columnists clamored to get interviews with his widow, who soon moved to Europe. Through sobs—and probably tranquilizers—from a friend's Beverly Hills home, Brier was at a loss to explain how such a gentle soul wound up with a bullet hole in it. "He was the kindest man I ever knew—a man who helped hundreds get their start [in Hollywood] and said that there is good in everyone if only you can bring it out," Brier said. "He often remarked that violence never accomplished anything."

As events shows, my great uncle was wrong in his view about the futility of bloodshed. It had achieved his death by the same man to whom he had shown crates of compassion. It had been Nat, Brier explained, who had "pleaded" to get Briggs his job at Cotton Products, probably with the other part owner, Joseph Rosenberg, one of Nat's San Francisco relations. It had been Nat willing to bring him back until Briggs' wild, alcoholic behavior doomed him. Now this?

Briggs, still riding bravado and a dispassionate veneer, refused to testify at the coroner's inquest on February 27th, 1941. "Nothing," he said, "can incriminate me that isn't already down on paper." The District Attorney subsequently charged him with murder, malice aforethought, and remanded him to County Jail without bail. This was not his first rodeo behind bars. Not that anyone from Cotton Products had known it beforehand. As a teenager, Briggs had served time in Connecticut for felony breaking and entering and in South Carolina three years after that for felony bank robbery.

Whatever the premeditated nature of his crime, Briggs pleaded not guilty by reason of insanity so the gas chamber he had welcomed before would not book his reservation. Unsurprisingly, that sneering swagger and delight with his gory handiwork had evaporated when his trial under Los Angeles Superior Court Judge Charles W. Fricke commenced four months after the shotgun echoes.

Briggs testified that he had pulled the trigger less because he loathed the victim and more out of suicidal depression. But why had he pre-planted the rifle at Cotton Products? Why had he mowed down Nat and not himself? Briggs, the cowardly avenger, sputtered an answer. "When I definitely learned that she wasn't going to be a mother, I bought a rifle to kill myself. I remember going to the factory with the gun. I shot [Nat], but I certainly hadn't intended to." Crazy people do irrational things. A few days later, the panel of three women and nine men announced their verdict. "GAS CHAMBER DEATH VOTED JEALOUS SLAYER," the *Times* headline said. Other than gulping once when he heard the sentence, the accused was stoic. Trial observers heard him whistling as he was led away from the courtroom.

The second trial phase automatically kicked off using the same jury to ascertain if Briggs was insane during the murder and thus not responsible. He wanted them to know he was sorry. That he had "never learned to control his emotions." That his comment to police about wishing to re-commit the murder harkened from self-anger to make "everything look as bad for myself as I could." Unlike before, Briggs looked "deathly pale" in court. Rightly. Three alienists testified that he was "entirely sane" throughout his entire debauchery. Briggs' bid to yank the jurors' heartstrings had yanked air.

CYANIDE DREAMS

JUDGE FRICKE SENTENCED HIM to death on August 7th, 1941. Briggs immediately appealed to the California Supreme Court, citing errors with jury instructions, legal interpretations and the verdict itself. The appeal was tossed out in March 1942. In May, the judge signed the death warrant for a state execution in July at the state's oldest prison in Marin in the north San Francisco Bay. San Quentin was ready for him.

When it came to murder sentences in our grandparents' era, Golden State justice felt a little like modern Texas. Capital punishment was incorporated into the penal code in the rough-and-tumble 1870s and county sheriffs were assigned to carry it out in their own jurisdictions. After 1891, the job was transferred from men with badges on their shirts to prison wardens at San Quentin and Folsom. The ultimate punishment, officials understood, required exacting professionalism. Execution by poisonous inhalation, which replaced hanging as the official procedure for government execution, was inaugurated in late 1938. Close to two hundred inmates would be gassed at a facility one writer likened to "an antiseptic form of hell" before lethal injection became Lady Justice's way.

If you were on death row in Briggs' time, you probably would not grow arthritic there. While Hollywood melodramas played up eleventh-hour reprieves from the Governor's office, the reality was a fairly steady use of the gas chamber to mete out punishment, especially for homicides involving kidnapping and cop-killers. Change would soon blow. A reverberating 1972 California Supreme Court ruling that the death penalty constituted cruel and unusual punishment under the state constitution halted executions. The decision, which the U.S. Supreme Court backed the following year, whisked one hundred and seven people off death row. It would take until 1992—fifteen years after California voters approved a sweeping capital punishment law opposed by former state Supreme Justice Rose Bird and other liberal jurists—before another condemned man would exhale his last breath on the public dime. By the time California's death penalty was reinstated, the criminal justice landscape was far more polarized and complex, oiled by lawsuit-happy interest groups, victims' rights organizations, and DNA testing that freed dozens of innocent people.

But none of that was in play for the man who cancelled Nat Ross's life just as it was starting to re-bloom. Briggs' last hope was for a pardon or commutation of his sentence by Governor Culbert Olson, a New Deal Democrat elected in 1939. In a formal statement to Olson's staff, Briggs sought human forgiveness from a world that never much appreciated him. At three, he said, his parents "deserted" him at an abusive orphanage. At thirteen, he had gone to live with a farmer until he died and Briggs lived from place to place, so malnourished he was willing to break into a food store or associate himself with bank robbers. Released from prison, he heard his father was stationed in Washington State and came out to see him. From there he traveled to L.A.

The State Advisory Board agreed to review his application for executive clemency. Governor Olson must have wondered whether Briggs' past infected his head, whether his environment made him a killer, because on July 8th, 1942 he granted Briggs a thirty-day reprieve. At the end of it, Briggs had exhausted his legal avenues. He had to eat his infamous words along with his terror. Much like Gary Gilmore, the double murderer who thirty years later was executed by firing squad in Utah, Briggs had bluntly said he would rather meet his maker on the state clock than rot away in a cinder block box. Wish granted!

The doors of the San Quentin gas chamber were sealed airtight on August 7th when he calmly entered it. The former Cotton Products washing machine foreman glanced around at the witnesses assembled for his state execution and, unrepentant to the end, mock-saluted them with an arm that the prison guards had neglected to strap down. Minutes later, after authorities fixed their oversight, the cyanide pellets were dropped, and Briggs' little goodbye became his last act.

You might be wondering after digesting all this how Nat's blood relations reacted to the drip-drip coverage. Hard as it is to believe, they emotionally covered their eyes and plugged their ears. Nobody can remember them stepping foot in the courtroom to eyeball Briggs, nor were they quoted in any story or a witness at San Quentin.

Nat's big sister (my grandmother, Rose Zahler) had already experienced a snoot-full of personal loss in a hugely publicized trial as a key witness in her father's murder in 1915 El Paso. Besides, when Briggs did his deed, my grandmother and her only son, Gordon, who Nat adored, had their own problems. That's because fourteen year old Gordon was fighting for his life with metal tongs drilled into his skull at County General Hospital in East L.A. after a horrific Pasadena junior high gymnastics accident broke his neck (and nearly decapitated him) in October 1940. Ever since, his mother had been at his bedside trying not to accept the doctor's prognoses that her boy would most certainly die while her husband, veteran Hollywood composer Lee Zahler, tried frantically to pay the medical bills.

Had my grandmother been at the hospital when Briggs unleashed his bullets at Cotton Products, she might have sensed the vibration a short four miles away across the L.A. River. She had now lost her father and brother to murderers, and she dealt with it by dwelling on the darkness as little as possible and trying to serve others.

Years back, I took it upon myself to untangle the killings' misconceptions from their verifiable facts, to crack open the crust of family repression that refused to give the fallen men the sunshine, I felt, their heroism deserved. When I took the birds-eye view of what I had unearthed, I was aghast at the parallel lines. Maurice Rosenberg and his son, Nat Ross, were both murdered at the same age (thirty-six), during the same month (February) by men who hoodwinked them in similar fashions almost exactly a generation apart. My age when I discovered the non-coincidence: thirty-six.

Once I finally shook off my own paranoia that I had researched my way into the family curse that either killed its most promising men or cut them off cruelly from their dreams, an epiphany set me straight. Gordon, the emaciated quadriplegic and former rascal of his hometown Sierra Madre, miraculously made it out of County General and eventually to Hollywood, where despite not feeling a thing from the neck down, he ran a successful post-production company, hobnobbed with famous celebrities, married, and damn near brought television to apartheid-gripped South Africa. Told he would die within weeks of his accident, he lived thirty-five years.

Somehow, the cosmos' plot-points dictated that Gordon should be our family's leading man precisely because of his ridiculous survival, because able-bodied Maurice and his son had dropped long before they hit old age. Nat's murder by bloodthirsty vendetta was, thus, one agonizing clip of his own fruitful journey through the ether. Our creator had to have planned every molecule of it, because the alternative is unbearable. Do you know what the LAPD found in Nat's trouser pocket when they inspected his corpse? It was a contract, a contract to return to moviemaking, as if his life wasn't already cinematic enough.

PAR FOR THE LANDFILL

Golf and other recreational uses are being developed for dumps after they reached their capacity.

—Los Angeles Times, June 20th, 2000

JUST ANOTHER HARD-HAT MONDAY on Strathern Street.

Scrap-yard machines moan into the dreary haze. A big rig jettisons debris into a giant pit filled with concrete skeletons of old buildings. Across the way, close to a methane plant, a young man in Bermuda shorts whacks golf balls onto a driving range built directly over a closed dump.

Golf? In Sun Valley? A place known for its teeming array of landfills, sand-and-gravel excavators, recycling shops and auto junkyards?

Swing away. As area landfills near capacity over the next decade or so, those golf balls rolling around the artificial turf at the old Penrose Landfill may herald the start of something novel in Sun Valley: a recreation industry where there used to be heavy industry.

New attitudes about maximizing scarce open space, combined with the faith that technology and vigilance can all but eliminate public health threats, have made that possibility more than a tease. In California over the last few years, golf courses, soccer fields–even commercial buildings–have sprouted on trash hillocks compressed with coffee grounds, diapers, orange peels, torn socks and other household castoffs.

Los Angeles City Councilman Alex Padilla, who represents Sun Valley, supports the conversion and said he would consider public subsidies for developers. But a sales job may be required first.

"I'd understand the concern about taking your kids to a day at the course on a man-made mountain of trash," Padilla said. "But experienced golfers know this is not uncommon. The safeguards are in place."

While it did not originate the idea, Los Angeles By-Products Co. in January quietly opened its crescent-shaped driving range on fifteen acres of land near Strathern and Tujunga Avenue. Next to it is a bicycle motocross (BMX) track that debuted in April 1999. Both sit atop the dormant Penrose Landfill, which stopped accepting household trash in 1985.

For company President Michael McAllister, the twin projects cap seven years of planning and permit chasing. He said there are 600,000 people living within a five-mile radius of the range, and some are bound to want to work on that handicap.

"We're just glad it's complete," McAllister said. "Through great effort by our engineers, we were able to achieve something people didn't think we could do."

The 300-yard-long range, which is operated by a separate company, and the BMX track cost about $2 million, McAllister said. Depending on their success, a kiddie train, go-cart track, laser-tag arena, bumper cars or a miniature golf course could be added. There is also talk of batting cages or a skateboard park.

The seventy-two acre site, just southwest of San Fernando Road, is zoned for outdoor recreation.

Someday it may not be the only ex-garbage graveyard open for leisure here.

At Sun Valley's Bradley Landfill, one of the largest private landfills in California, officials are mulling over different scenarios for their 100 acres of land. Bradley will reach capacity in three to four years. The company, which is owned by mammoth Waste Management Inc., is considering a small golf course, soccer fields, baseball diamonds, a vehicle-storage yard and other ideas, according to Scott Tignac, the landfill's division manager.

"We're looking at which options are even realistic," he said. "Economics will drive it."

At Vulcan Materials Company, a sand, gravel and rock producer with three facilities around the industrial Tuxford Street/San Fernando Road area in Sun Valley, reuse plans are in the preliminary stage as well. While it is unlikely Vulcan would seed a golf course over its excavation pits, the company may convert some into catch basins to recharge the local ground water basin, said Jim Dean, Vulcan's area market manager.

Civic leaders are somewhat split on the issue of reusing landfills.

Bill Slater, government affairs chairman for the Sun Valley Area Chamber of Commerce, opposes the landfill-to-golf concept, saying the potential for contaminated runoff is too great. He would rather focus on a city redevelopment proposal that could boost the area's anemic retail base.

"We need to do something to make this a better place—not a vacation site for tourists," Slater said.

But state Senator Richard Alarcon (D-Sylmar), who fought to close the Lopez Canyon Landfill when he was on the Los Angeles City Council, said it is an idea worth testing. Alarcon, who grew up in the area, said: "I could ride my bike in any direction and find a landfill. My dad lives a five-iron away" from one today.

According to the city's Environmental Affairs Department, there are seventeen closed or inactive landfills and three active landfills in Sun Valley. Some of them date to the early 1900s. Others were dug when companies mined for construction aggregate—the sand and rock mixed with cement to make concrete.

"On one hand, Sun Valley is an example of the over-concentration of landfills and...how poor, working-class people don't engage in fights against these things," said Alarcon, who chairs the state select committee on environmental justice. "On the other hand, there is a possibility we can do something positive" with a driving range or future parks.

Plenty of existing Sun Valley businesses were built over old dumps, including several auto parts yards, a kennel and a discount clothing store. That golf could now emerge in a dust-caked community where pickup trucks dominate the road isn't lost on some.

"There's no Starbucks in town," kidded chamber member Ron Hall. "And they wouldn't sell anything if they were here."

A CLOSE LANDFILL IS A USED-UP ASSET

IN MANY CASES, MONEY-MAKING ventures built over landfills give owners a way to offset some of the environmental monitoring and maintenance costs.

A closed landfill "is already a used-up asset," said Jim Aardema, vice president of development of En CAP Golf, a Tampa, Florida-based company that specializes in developing golf courses over landfills.

"What's happening is that cities see they can encourage economic development, and waste companies see they can cut some of their expenses while generating political and community goodwill," said Aardema, whose company is consulting with Waste Management about the future of the Bradley dump.

Another emerging factor, he said, is insurance companies. Because of proven mitigation techniques, they are much more willing to underwrite landfill conversions than they were in the 1980s.

McAllister, the Los Angeles By-Products Company president, said he believes his driving range is the only one in Southern California built with a geo-synthetic cover over the refuse. Made from two thick plastic sheets with a special clay sandwiched in between, the cover is designed to keep water out and fumes from escaping into the air.

His company still runs a seventy-five acre landfill across from the driving range. The Strathern Inert Landfill accepts only non-degradable waste, such as old building materials. McAllister said it could very well have recreational facilities atop it when capacity is reached in about 2013.

A major component to any landfill closure is how potential health threats are minimized. Monitoring goes on for thirty years, and any landfill owner eager to tap into the outdoor sports market better be prepared for expensive studies and scrutiny by multiple government agencies, experts say.

Besides the clay blanket over the landfill's outer layer, recently built municipal dumps must be lined with a nonpermeable membrane to prevent potentially hazardous runoff from leaching into ground water and soil. Using detection wells, regulators keep on the lookout for vinyl chloride, the carcinogen benzene and various heavy metals.

But gas is the biggest worry. In the late 1980s, for example, Glendale was forced to close a golf course built atop the Scholl Canyon Landfill because of leaking methane gas generated by degrading household waste. The course was reopened after the city corrected the problem.

At Penrose, enough methane is suctioned to power 10,000 homes, company officials said. The gas is essentially vacuumed out using a latticework of pipes and manifolds running through the trash.

It is "the most critical part of the system to preserve public safety," said Wayne Tsuda, division director for the city's Environmental Department.

"Penrose was the first landfill we were involved with that was turned into a golf course. It required a lot of technical review."

McAllister said the driving range makes the most money, but that the BMX track hosted more than 200 racers and 200 spectators in early June, when a state qualifier was held by the National Bicycle League. The driving range gets about 200 golfers daily.

Originally, the company wanted to build an eighteen-hole championship course covering both Penrose and the nearby Strathern Inert Landfill. The company hired a lobbyist and spent nearly $210,000 to amass the necessary permits and door-to-door support from neighbors.

After the plans were completed, however, McAllister said state regulators shocked him by saying the company needed to add another clay barrier. The company had already put down the geo-synthetic covering, and the new requirement would have cost several million dollars more.

Ultimately, Los Angeles By-Products opted for a low-tech solution. The driving range, for example, is carpeted with lustrous artificial turf, including beige colored material inside the "sand traps."

Full-blown courses built over landfills, while potential cash cows, require sophisticated and expensive drainage systems to staunch underground runoff created by sprinkler water. A plastic-grass driving range, by contrast, gets sunbaked, but never thirsty.

STATE LEARNING TO HANDLE FORMER DUMPS

Linda Moulton-Patterson, chairwoman of the California Integrated Waste Management Board, said the state is still learning how to handle former dump sites.

Back when Los Angeles By-Products applied to build the golf course, she said there were too many unknowns, especially about the gases.

"From my perspective, there are some creative, great uses for this closed land. With what we've learned in the last ten years, we are on a solid ground," Moulton-Patterson said. "And for a community [today], it's the end of the rainbow."

The ground beneath landfills regularly subsides—a fact that generally makes building traditional structures over them off limits.

At Penrose, checking for signs of cracking on the concrete pad where the golfers are and in the clubhouse is a constant chore. The city even refused to allow the steel clubhouse behind the range until Los Angeles By-Products found a modular-unit builder able to allay the city's concerns.

"We did this for the community, but we do hope to make a little money," said McAllister, who doesn't golf. "After awhile, we'll see if we can do other things on the landfill."

GREEN EDIFICE COMPLEX

—Los Angeles Business Journal, September 9th, 1991

WELL BEFORE SOUTHERN CALIFORNIA dismantles the smog ceiling that burns our lungs, fouls our mood and makes even tornado-strewn Kansas sound like prime real estate, Diamond Bar is bound to be the talk of the town.

That is if anybody can find it.

Nearing completion atop a gently sloping mound, in a bedroom community so residential that officials joke mattresses are sold at fundraisers, is the South Coast Air Quality Management District's gleaming new digs. Erected with a mountain of Mother Nature-friendly systems, the $78 million, high-tech affair is sure to make the most ardent environmentalist green with envy.

But in board rooms, cocktail parties and hallways across our hazy landscape, some Southland business leaders are having a whooping good time getting in their own digs–about the AQMD's new home. For those compelled by the air district to slash, phase out or deep-six emissions over the years, it is a bit of payback time, albeit tongue in cheek.

Though AQMD's 1,100 engineers, chemists, planners and staffers will not move into the fifteen acre, 370,000 square foot complex until October, their white-colored, Diamond Bar headquarters has already been christened with plenty of sarcasm-laced humor: The Pollution Palace, the Taj Mahal of the East or the House that (smog czar) James Lents built.

"That building is going to make them the aristocracy of the bureaucracy and they are going to live like kings," fumes outspoken Watson Land Company Chairman William Huston. "And they are going to pay for it right out of our pockets."

Gripes Robert Wendoll, environmental regulations administrator for local paint maker Dunn-Edwards Corporation, "At a time when government at every level in the state is suffering from budget crunches, the district...is purchasing what I can only describe as an extravagant new office—it's a white elephant."

Not so, cry AQMD officials who have been working on the switch since 1988, when stratospheric Los Angeles land prices made Diamond Bar sound inviting.

AQMD's director of administrative services, Jack Guiso, who says a major portion of his life has "been eaten by the move," asserts the relocation is a "heck of a business decision." The $175 million needed to retire the construction bonds and its interest over twenty-five years, he says, will only add $7 million yearly to AQMD's budget, which is subsidized by industry permits, fines and fees.

Besides, AQMD's current El Monte home—235,000 square feet of space spread between two buildings—is "just too small" and the high rent it pays for some offices has helped its landlord weather the recession, Guiso claims. District officials also contend that the move will benefit businesses. The new H.Q. will allow firms to get their permits issued quicker, queries answered faster and pollutants scrutinized more efficiently. "If we didn't do those things, business would accuse us of being in the dark ages," says fifty-three year old Guiso, an engineer by trade. Just do not tell that to Angelenos who will have to chug thirty miles on the Pomona or Orange freeways to a place that will send them scrambling for their Thomas Bros. maps to locate. They will not care that the Diamond Bar site, situated in the innocuously named Gateway Corporate Center, will be ahead of the eastward-moving population shift and convenient for the growing number of district workers who live in the east San Gabriel Valley city.

Why the stink over just another government building? Money and power.

AQMD regulates 30,000 businesses in L.A., Orange, Riverside, and San Bernardino counties, using its regulatory screws on smog sources large and small, from defense contractors to dry cleaners, oil refiners to restaurants. Business people, though publicly alarmed by L.A.'s environmental troubles, privately moan that AQMD has cost them billions of dollars and thousands of jobs. Little wonder that sniping over the new AQMD dwelling is ricocheting through Southland executive suits.

Though many inside AQMD's El Monte building–which they share with the also popular Internal Revenue Service–can't wait for the move, it is not a universal sentiment even there.

"I've objected to it from day one because it isn't near any planned commuter rail routes and we are thus contributing to air pollution," says liberal AQMD Board Member Sabrina Schiller. "It's not consistent with our goals."

Another district board member, Larry Berg, approves of the building's anti-pollution protections but dislikes its location. "I wanted to put it in South Central Los Angeles, but I suppose some of our business critics wouldn't have liked that either," he says.

Both Schiller and Berg say it is pure coincidence that Executive Director Lents happens to reside in Diamond Bar.

Even from a distance, the Diamond Bar complex is impressive, especially considering it was erected in a brisk twenty months and generally on budget. Sure, it will boast modern offices, a child-care center, a small gym, a panoramic-view cafeteria and a spacious 300 seat auditorium. But that's only half of it.

As Guiso will tell you, with some deserved pride, the home will be a practice-what-you-preach endeavor. High-performance glass shaded by specially designed light shelves will reduce AQMD's energy consumption, as will the high efficiency chillers, reflective roofing material and electronic ballasts. The district is also working with Southern California Edison on first-of-its-kind solar panels.

That's not all. The cooling agent in the air conditioning chillers uses precious little ozone-layer-eating chlorofluorocarbons that the district has started to regulate. The 200-kilowatt fuel cells, virtually emission-free, will produce as much as ten percent of the complex's electrical juice. There is even a methanol-fueled backup generator, low-polluting paints and coatings plus landscaping that guzzles recycled water.

Environmentalists say the new office hits the mark for Southern California, where the air is America's worst and the anti-emission strictures are the nation's toughest.

"The AQMD has taken a state-of-the-art building that is an example for others to build on and is consistent with the district's charter," exclaims Tom Soto, president of Coalition for Clean Air.

Chuckles Veronica Kun, a staff scientist with the Natural Resources Defense Council, "If businesses had less violations, the AQMD wouldn't be able to pay for a big fancy building."

Tiring a bit from the business brickbats, the AQMD's Guiso concludes, "This is an A-Number One building. But you won't find any gold-plated faucets. And remember, we're not the problem; smog is."

REQUIEM FOR THE LUNGS

—*New York Times,* August 25th, 2011

IN NATIONAL POLITICS, CALIFORNIA may be seen as Exhibit A for over-regulating the environment. But anyone making that argument must ignore what the state was like before the Environmental Protection Agency—smog-encrusted, water-polluted, and barely able to retain its ecological luster against crushing population gains. Since the agency's creation, its rules and enforcement have made California a livable, thriving, if oft head scratching place still hospitable toward business.

Now, if you are a Republican presidential candidate irate about America's wheezy economy, it is easy to go Queen of Hearts and call for guillotining the E.P.A. Scapegoating regulators as job-killing obstructionists has long been used to pump up the faithful, but it does not reflect well on America's environmental maturity. None of the White House hopefuls mention the expected $2 trillion in health and environmental benefits from the Clean Air Act by 2020. Few of the greenhouse skeptics, in fact, even broach fresh air at all, perhaps because they hail from states where it was never toxic.

So the next time Michele Bachmann promises to dissolve the Nixon-created E.P.A., perhaps she should do it in Burbank, northwest of downtown Los Angeles. Decades earlier, Bachmann might have had trouble even finding the town through the eye-stinging, russet-brown air pollution filled with ozone, heavy metals, lead and other nasty byproducts of the California car culture. After a quarter century battlng the then Big Three Automakers to produce cleaner cars, California lobbied the federal government for the right to set stricter tailpipe exhaust standards than the rest of the country, and that campaign later helped inspire formation of the EPA itself.

Today, the teeming suburb once home to the defense contractor Lockheed Corporation and other industrial behemoths is on the mend. When the defense contractor and others like it packed up, they left dangerous contaminants behind in the soil. Thankfully, the E.P.A. endured years of legal finger-pointing and declared it a Superfund site that led to construction of groundwater filtration systems. Because Burbank and adjoining Los Angeles and Glendale partly depend on local aquifers, hundreds of thousands of people were protected from carcinogenic water that might have otherwise wrecked their lives.

Manufacturers once polluted willy-nilly in California, until it was chastened by the big gun known as the E.P.A. For the last thirty years, the agency has hastened dozens of other cleanups in California, from leaching chemicals at Bay Area military sites to polluted groundwater in the San Gabriel Valley. It has cleaned up rivers, scolded regional agencies when needed, gone after rogue polluters and even helped Southern California establish the planet's first smog cap-and-trade. While anti-regulatory politicians like to mock California for its environmental whackiness, it still boasts the world's eighth-largest economy.

It is actually the agency's cautiousness, and not over-zealotry, where it has taken its lumps here in California. There is still, for instance, no national water health standard for chromium-6, the solvent that Erin Brockovich crusaded against in remote Hinkley, California. The upshot? Susceptible people lack a guardian with regulatory brawn, and state officials are no match for corporate lobbyists.

Imagining a California without an E.P.A. is visualizing a landscape where dangerous smog returns, compromised aquifers are unusable and only the suicidal would live near a factory. Better to have an inconsistent watchdog than none at all, no matter the campaign bluster from politicians with surface understandings of our ecological behavior.

GODFATHER OF SOUTH CENTRAL

He's been called everything from civil rights crusader to shameless poverty pimp. Chip Jacobs goes in search of the real Danny Bakewell.

—*Pasadena Weekly*, November 20th, 2003

THE MAHOGANY DÉCOR OF the Brotherhood Crusade's sunlit boardroom swaddles the place in a cozy ambience, but Los Angeles Mayor Jimmy Han's boys fidget as if they can't wait to get out. Here to nudge support for the mayor's $9 billion makeover plan of Los Angeles International Airport, they tote slick diagrams and fawn for their hosts ideas about how to deal minority contractors into the mix. Can you say whiff?

Danny Joseph Bakewell, the fifty-seven year old activist, entrepreneur and Brotherhood Crusade founder and leader, is still bent out of shape over Hahn's decision not to endorse Bernie Parks for another term as Los Angeles police chief. He toys with the airport consultant, a fellow African-American, like a Bengal tiger with a house cat, spinning him in circles with lacerating questions he can't answer. Why not? This is Bakewell's seat of power, where the community-giving kingdom he built radiated his influence far beyond the bustling grime of Slauson Avenue.

"Look, I'm not that smart," Bakewell says, inflecting a little Southern drawl into a self-deprecation act that no one who knows him really buys. "Tell me, who is going to build the parking lot? Where is the commitment to a black-employed company running it?" When the consultant tries a little street talk to please Bakewell, he pounces. "How come sometimes you talk like a brother, other times like you are from U.S. Motors?"

Everybody busts up. Soon enough, Hahn's deputy mayor and the expert shuffle out of the Brotherhood Crusade's faded brick headquarters as empty-handed as when they arrived. Bakewell has only agreed to consider the mayor's sputtering LAX plan.

Invariably, everybody selling something big around here sees Danny, the Godfather of South Central. The inside joke is that he would run for elected office, but why court demotion?

His daily schedule much like the speeches that enshrined him as a race-loaded bazooka, is packed. By the time he met with the mayor's men, he had been up since 4:30 AM. (his normal hour), hit the Stairmaster at the Pasadena Athletic Club, placed business calls to the East Coast, visited a rundown charter school, then toured one of the job-training centers he's sponsored on a block where many of the "fellas" lack teeth, let alone jobs.

"Get it done!" he cheerleads adult students in an Internet course he visited. "I can't do email and they tell me it's the easiest thing going."

From 55th Street it is back into his chauffeured Lincoln Town Car for a working lunch at P.F. Chang's with Governor Davis' frazzled aides. They ask him about combating the recall and he urges them, and they take note, to organize local rallies tailored for the five o'clock news.

When Danny Bakewell enters a room, it vibrates with a big-man bravado. Say what you will about him, Bakewell inspires neither ambivalence nor cardboard summations.

His spacious, hillside house in a wealthy Pasadena enclave is a one-eighty from the ghetto-area office he commutes to, where concertina wire loops the parking lot. Pugnacious on camera, he is gracious and humble in person, quick to laugh that his wife of thirty-seven years runs the show. Though a devotee of Malcolm X and Martin Luther King, Jr., he claims no organized faith for himself. And if you assumed that New York's Al Sharpton—a man he is often compared to—is his pony in the 2004 presidential campaign, think again. He is on the steering committee of General Wesley Clark.

GIVING SOMETHING BACK

In some African-American quarters, Bakewell is a civil rights superstar. Acting as an umbrella organization, the Brotherhood

Crusade he has led since the early 1970s has doled out roughly $40 million to a hodge-podge of in-the-trenches nonprofits. He has also stuck it to any number of prime institutions, from Paramount Pictures, where he successfully agitated to kill a slavery-tinged television series, to the United Way, which he accused of siphoning more from South Central in donations than it returned.

In other circles, Bakewell's name is radioactive. There is a perception of him as a knee-jerk agitator, faster to draw the race card than his buddy, attorney Johnnie Cochran. Detractors jab that he has plied his connections—or exploited white-man's guilt to corral taxpayer booty for the cause closest to his heart: his own.

Whatever his motivation, the public dollars he has received are substantial, records show. At just three of the shopping centers he owns an interest in, taxpayers contributed $28 million in urban-renewal benefits, making him perhaps one of the richest African-American developers in California with a personal net worth that tops $40 million by some estimates. (He won't confirm the amount.)

The eponymous companies he runs, owns outright or through limited partnerships, control six major inner-city shopping centers in Pasadena, Los Angeles, and Compton, plus two strip malls. Added up, his portfolio exceeds 847,000 square feet, and that does not count a three-story office building in the Crenshaw Avenue area and his share of a $300 million Monterey-area housing project.

Oh yeah, he owns four homes in the Pasadena area, a 373-acre family ranch in Lompoc and a getaway place near Santa Barbara.

His influence seeps elsewhere. Had the American Basketball Association, the high-scoring former league, made a comeback, Bakewell was poised to own the Indiana franchise. He also sits on the board of the *Los Angeles Sentinel*, a black-owned paper that has written some glowing stories about his efforts. (Managing Editor James Bolden said Bakewell has no say in editorial content.)

Meanwhile, the Brotherhood's signature event, a black-tie annual fundraiser that recently honored Magic Johnson, is sponsored by mainstream companies that you would think would be as happy to see Bakewell the activist as they would the IRS. In 2000, the dinner raised a net $245,000. Boeing, Denny's, and Bank of America helped put last year's gala on.

So, the mystery burns: How could the big man be both tireless do-gooder and a self-made multi-millionaire without selling somebody out? Is he the equivalent of ward boss with a heart or a bossy firebrand? Is he loaded because of his activism or peripheral to it? Not that he cares what outsiders, reporters included, speculate.

"There's an old saying that people who love you need no explanation and for those who don't, no explanation can ever do," Bakewell says. "I'm not here to make friends when I'm doing the peoples' business. There is [also] this bill of goods sold to black people that to be relevant, to be it in your community work, you've got to wear combat boots and a field jacket as opposed to a $1,000 suit and a shirt with your name on it. In the '60s, people thought there was some romance in poverty and I'm not advocating it for anyone."

The baggage his name lugs puzzles him just the same. The fist-clenching, don't-cross-us Bakewell people see on television, he says distort his essence. A guy content handing out small business loans or running health expos so women without health insurance can get tested for cancer and other diseases.

But just as there are those who want to champion him for unsung persons generosity and issue-tenacity, a large number do not want to be asked about him. Several respected black leaders and a slew of local officials declined comment for this profile. Mention his name to some politicians and they gasp, "Oh him."

Ted Hayes, a well-known L.A. homeless activist, is one of the few willing to go on record. Hayes says Bakewell broke his promise to assist him with a march because Bakewell was so bitter about Parks, now Los Angeles City Council member, is being re-appointed chief of police.

"I stay away from him now," said Hayes. "His heart is with nobody but Dam Bakewell. I'm surprised he's been able to bamboozle people for thirty years."

For Bakewell's supporters, that's balderdash. Follow his kindness, they say, even he tends to have a my-way-or-the-highway management style.

"The question is what is his record of building institutions," says Maulana Karenga, a black studies professor at Cal State Long Beach and former Brotherhood Crusade board member. "Has he built just placement centers, built shelters for battered woman, helped the homeless? Yes. He's not trying to be a monk. The test one's commitment to the community is he much he gives back and Danny does give back."

THE ELEPHANT BITES BACK

HE CERTAINLY GOT AROUND. Commencing the early 1990s, if there was racial turmoil and a microphone, Bakewell seemed to behind it.

When a Korean-born merchant fatally shot teenager LaTasha Harlins over a dispute about a bottle of orange juice, Bakewell spearheaded a protest at the Compton Courthouse. The demonstrators, angry at Judge Joyce Karlin's sentence of probation and community service for the shop owner, turned unruly as they surged deeper into the building. The District Attorney in early 1992 considered charging Bakewell with inciting a riot. But there was contradictory evidence, even some that he had tried restraining the mob, records show.

Once in the public eye, he was everywhere. He blocked post-riot construction sites. He led actions against United Way-linked utilities. Pasadena's Tournament of Roses was next, followed by rallies against police brutality and sundry outrages, including charges the CIA shepherded crack cocaine into the ghetto.

In 1995, at a ceremony intended to extol a $33 million expansion of the Museum of Science and Industry, he insisted to be on the speaker's list to preach economic justice. It was "preposterous," Bakewell told the crowd, that only four percent of the contractors' workers were black when the black unemployment rate bulged at forty percent.

As usual, his facts were accurate, his presence somewhat annoying, just as they were when Bakewell and his followers stood in front of an oncoming freight train to protest dangerous track conditions through South Central. Conditions improved.

"What differentiates him from other leaders is that he brings a remedy. He doesn't just say what is just wrong," said former Pasadena Assistant to the City Manager Prentice Deadrick, who is now a member of the Pasadena Board of Education. "His ego is satisfied every morning he gets up and puts a pushpin through his tie."

What angers some, however, is that his causes don't always seem as noble as his rhetoric. Bakewell, for instance, pleaded for leniency for Damien Williams, one of the men who pummeled trucker Reginald Denny at the riot's flashpoint. He also stood up for gangsta rap music producer Marion "Suge" Knight when he was hit with a parole violation.

Bakewell said Knight, who had done charity work before his arrest, was more than the sum total of his misdeeds. And if you don't like his stances, if you don't like him pointing out the difference between middle-class L.A., where things work, and the treeless, dirt-poor cement city south of the L.A. Memorial Coliseum, too bad. He doesn't do apologies for defending what he calls "the honor of his people."

It is hard enough, he admits, staying upbeat. Being Danny Bakewell does require that friends and mere acquaintances constantly hover for favors from him.

"If you ever stopped and look at the whole picture and say what of this am I going to change, you might just get so demoralized you'd throw up your hands," he says, slumping down in the car. "You just eat this elephant one bite at a time."

On occasion, that elephant has bitten back.

BRING IT ON

AMONG HIS ACTIONS AGAINST Korean merchants was a backfiring incident in 1996 involving a hat and wig store near Slauson and Vermont avenues. A male customer, the pastor at a prominent church in Pasadena, was told to leave because the shop was for women only.

The Reverend Lee Norris May left all right—right for the Brotherhood Crusade. It sent in other black men with the same result: They were told it was for women only. Bakewell organized a picket to demand time with the proprietor, a petite fifty-three year old woman named In-Suk Lee.

Too cowed to meet, she wrote out an apology in broken English. The reverend spurned it and the woman's life collapsed. The store closed and she had a heart attack. Not long afterward, May embezzled $200,000 of his flock's money and fled. Bakewell, who said he doesn't remember much about the incident, argued the two events were unconnected, though he felt badly about Lee's heart attack and "horrible" about Lee's dishonesty.

"Look, she exercised bad judgment and I moved on. Allowing little things like this to fester can lead to big problems."

If Bakewell's activism was pervasive, so were the people murmuring he was enriching himself off deals leveraged from his convictions. There were questions about why he was awarded a share of a South Central cable franchise with no up-front money down, and why he flowed into the government bond business without any background in high finance.

How the Brotherhood Crusade itself operated also became fair game for those suspicious of Bakewell. In 2000, the last year accounting records were available, the group distributed about $1 million, ninety percent of which went to smaller nonprofits whose boards Bakewell and close associates oversee. One of those groups is the African American Unity Center, a job-training program serving 150 people a day. It receives about half its $2 million budget through the government. After the Northridge earthquake, the AAUC, thanks partly to Bakewell's Democratic Party ties, secured a $4 million federal grant to convert a rotting, old Presbyterian church into a gleaming performing arts center. Because it is an historic building that must meet different preservation and seismic codes, construction has been delayed, according to the center's executive director.

But why it was delayed became less germane than whose initials were behind it.

One day, then-Mayor Richard Riordan hinted that an unnamed black activist was shaking folks down. Jill Stewart, then a columnist at the now-defunct *New Times Los Angeles*, publicized that theme, labeling Bakewell the city's "leading poverty pimp" in a scorching 2001 piece. After brushing off other negative press, he didn't this time. He slapped a libel suit on Stewart and the paper. (She is currently a syndicated columnist for the *Pasadena Weekly*.) Not only did Blackwell lose because a column had tougher libel standards than a news story, he was ordered to pay $25,000 New Times' attorney's fees. Actually, the Brotherhood Crusade paid, because the nonprofit was co-plaintiff. For a guy who often uses litigation as a successful cudgel, it was a bitter defeat, and his detractors danced.

Count popular talk show host Larry Elder as one of those. A few years ago Elder bumped into Bakewell at a Beverly Hills event and recalled that Bakewell could not have been nicer. Altogether, Elder said I and his KABC Radio producer have invited Bakewell twenty to thirty times to come on the show for a feisty debate on race and each time have been rebuffed. Bakewell, who agrees with much of Elder's self-reliance philosophy, asks why would he want to be sand-bagged on air by "the poster child for white conservative types."

Elder asserts Bakewell and cohorts Congresswoman Maxine Waters, Jesse Jackson and the NAACP are panicked that the victim mentality cannot push as many buttons anymore. For him, its teens pregnancies, dismal public schools and the lack of personal responsibility that has shackled blacks, not racism leaching from every pipe.

"There's a term for Danny Bakewell," Elder said, "and that's a race-hustling poverty pimp. I won't apologize."

Blakewell's retort: Bring it on.

"They [still] can't make that dog hunt when they talk about me. Nobody has any traction, no smoking gun. Show it to me."

For the record, he says his companies have never won a contract at a company protested first.

WHATEVER IT TAKES

STATE SENATOR KEVIN MURRAY (D-Culver City), a longtime comrade, said the dot standards are knee deep. For instance, at Riordan and Eli Broad. "When rich white guys get involved with public affairs, they are giving back to the city. When a black guy does it, it's to prop himself up? There are there certain circles where his name is not the one to use? Yes [but] he can generate the troops. *And he runs a legitimate* organization."

Certainly nobody packs them in like Bakewell. When he was seeking $2.6 million in redevelopment subsidies for a Vermont Avenue shopping center, he acknowledged going to the churches and town hall encourage people to attend the hearing. They did. This scene has been repeated and over in his career, with Bakewell understanding the heat the masses can bring.

For years, there was speculation they were interested in him. He had done millions of dollars worth of deals in Compton. Officials there and nearby have been taken away in handcuffs on graft charges as if it were some kind of seasonal rite.

Grinning, Bakewell said he has had two contacts with the FBI. Once was the riots, when he and other black activists logged death threats from white supremacists. The other time was when he was walking back to his car from a rally protesting the killing of Taisha Miller by Riot police. A black man jogged up to him.

"He said, 'Hey brother, I really admire you. I was with the FBI for many years and you're really clean. We'd always be looking at you [for possible charges.]' I kind of laughed. It was so startling that I never got the guy's name or card." An FBI spokeswoman could not corroborate this account.

Here's the kicker on the Riordan angle. Bakewell characterized "Dick as a stand-up guy." The ex-mayor must have felt something too: He sought endorsements from Bakewell for both his '92 and '96 elections, a Riordan spokeswoman confirmed.

For Bakewell's relatives, this upheaval began to wear thin. He's rich enough to walk away. He has his hobbies—bird watching, Italian opera, photography. And he certainly is the patriarch he dreamed of being, the one who keeps family dinners going, even if nobody fights over his fare; after an eat-anything diet that contributed to bypass surgery; he is a strict vegetarian.

"Sometimes we wonder why he continues with his activism," conceded Pamela Bakewell, Danny's sister and Vice President of Operations for the Bakewell Co. "The business is successful. I tell people you can't be a Bakewell and not get sucked in."

Danny Bakewell, Jr., who oversees the Monterey project, said if his dad had his way; every relative would live on his street.

"The perception is that he lives a much grander life than he does. He really is a guy from the South. He likes to hang out with his family and watch the ball game and eat fried tofu, which he tries to convince me is better than real fried chicken. And it is easy to write the poverty pimp thing, or the big negative, but he won the Congressional Black Caucus Man of the Year award. The difference between my dad and most people is that he has the vision and tenacity to turn his wants into a reality."

Make no mistake, either. Obstruct seniors' way and you may be plucking tread out of your teeth. That's why the money spot on his office wall carries a sketch of a menacing 800-pound gorilla. The metaphor reminds him to make everything about his community and his family. If not, why bother?

"Look, I don't live my life seeing how I can get over on people. I live my life trying to make peoples' lives better. And the premises upon which you challenge the system have to be morally correct."

He is right on one count: He is always saying that.

His hard-knuckle focus was needed at the September meeting of the Pasadena NAACP. Ambling in, he funds a dozen community leaders in disarray about their planned invasion of the Pasadena City Council meeting that night. At issue is the $1.5 billion-plus construction boom underway and the paucity of blacks employed.

"White folk," he reminds his restless lieutenants, "don't respond to anything besides advocacy unless you have a lot of money or influence. We must have the moral predicate!" The room quiets as he speaks, all doughnut chomping ceased. Bakewell, it is blatantly obvious, is the cleanup hitter here, and he is choosier about his public moments these days. He also studies "the terms of engagement"—the municipal code, rules about picketing—like nobody's business.

At the council, the room is standing room only because Bakewell and company galvanized the rank and file. Outfitted in a shimmering charcoal suit, he speaks to the council like a chastising parent, and his followers pipe in with "amen" and "that's right" at the crowd-pleasing verses. Some insiders wince. They remember. It was exactly ten years ago that Bakewell led a noisy campaign to open up the then-white male dominated Tournament of Roses Executive Committee to minorities. One tactic was having vehicles parked in the middle of busy Orange Grove Boulevard, so traffic was bottlenecked in front of the Tournament's landmark building. His other move: threatening to hold a counter parade that scared the bejesus out of the locals.

"There is a crisis of confidence," Bakewell growls, and a normally sedate chamber is ionized with tension. "There are people who feel we are locked out of the city and locked out of the system... We don't want to come down for displays like this. But let's be clear: Whatever it takes, we intend to hold you responsible."

When he's done, the city acquiesces to plumb his charges that Affirmative Action policing has slipped. Councilman Chris Holden beams. An older white colleague of his doesn't. He glares at Bakewell with a look of pure what-the-hell-are-you-pulling contempt.

RUN TO DAYLIGHT

HAD IT NOT BEEN for a lovesick heart in the Arizona desert, he might have been famous for terrorizing quarterbacks, not the Establishment.

Bakewell grew up in a small house in a jazz-soaked part of New Orleans with his sister and mom. His parents divorced when he was about nine, yet he saw his dad a lot. Young Danny was a lazy student with ample IQ. He understood why he needed to know that Columbus discovered America, but could not fathom why he needed to recite the name of his ships.

Athletics was his launch vehicle. He was a nimble basketball player who flourished against the older kids. By eighth grade, he was MVP, captain of the team, a seasoned vet. He attended St. Augustine High School, a private Catholic school run by the Josephite Order, and his character took shape.

Along the defensive line in football, he was unstoppable. Teammates nicknamed him the "white whale" because of the special cream-colored helmet he required for his oversized head and because no opponent could harpoon him. The awards came by the armful and he had fifty colleges, including USC, Notre Dame, and Michigan, interested in him despite being one of the punier guys on the team.

"He was a great player—a feared lineman," remembered George McKenna, a boyhood friend who is now assistant superintendent of the Pasadena school district.

People's awe of what he could do on the gridiron fueled his confidence. But rubbing up against that was a coiling resentment. The priests and nuns, he began to think, were only there because they considered blacks "crippled people that needed to be taken care of." He already wondered about his mulatto-like skin and English-sounding last name and assumed whites had sullied the family bloodline during slavery.

His maternal grandfather; Edward Brazile, cast the other impression. A janitor at the *Times-Picayune* newspaper, Brazile didn't act like a mop-and-bucket man in overalls. Before and after work he donned a double-breasted suit, sometimes with a top hat and cane, looking stunningly executive.

"My grandfather always said to take pride in how your dress, you are representing our family and our community and the police won't treat you the same way if you are in a white shirt and tie." His dad, a bricklayer at the time, was much the same way.

After considering a number of colleges, he accepted a football scholarship at the University of Arizona. It was scary time to be alone, what with segregated accommodations and upstart blacks turning up dead in rivers. Only three months later, he quit the Wildcats' freshman squad. He missed his high school sweetheart in New Orleans and intended to marry her.

Back home, now a newlywed, he toiled at a laundry, then as a houseman at a French Quarter hotel. For the hell of it, he applied for a front-desk job and was told he was the wrong color.

His father moved to California and he followed. To pay rent, he worked with a city job training program, then with the UCLA personnel department. But it was the Civil Rights Movement that lit his intellect. He met an older gent named Walter Bremond during a Black Congress meeting, where the talk was about Black Panthers and LBJ's War on Poverty. Bremond and Bakewell, just twenty-two and previously apolitical, gazed around and saw what they could add. There was no group promoting social and educational welfare. So Bremond took out a $15,000 second mortgage and the Brother-hood Crusade came alive.

The days after Martin Luther King was assassinated proved what the kid could do. In a portent, Danny grabbed a bullhorn and pleaded with the students at Emanuel Arts High to boycott their classes. "Register your discontent," he hollered. "We don't go to school on George Washington's birthday..." Most heeded his call.

Even so, the Brotherhood Crusade wobbled. How could they implore others to lift themselves out of poverty when the group was sinking in $190,000 in debt? Bakewell, making $600 a month, sniffed out an opportunity in another charity's bounty. The United Way had a grip around donations from governmental employees, many of whom were minorities. For every dollar the agency took from inner city residents, only a dime was reinvested in services for them, he concluded. Bakewell went to a newly elected Tom Bradley to open up the city payroll deduction campaign to the Brotherhood Crusade. Bradley said no dice. But Bakewell persisted.

"I'd go to the garbage yards in the Valley and other places at 4:00 A.M. to talk to the workers. They couldn't believe I came out. I gave them a rah-rah" about what the Crusade would do.

The rabble rousing succeeded. Then-Councilman Gil Lindsay, who had big hopes for Bakewell, approved making the Brotherhood Crusade a sanctioned charity. That endorsement brought legitimacy and today the Brotherhood Crusade is on a donor list for the L.A. and Santa Monica school districts, the state and federal government, and various utilities, among other places.

The county, with its vast workforce, was the real jackpot. In the late 1970s, Bakewell lobbied Nate Holden, who had just become a state senator after serving as Supervisor Kenny Hahn's chief of staff.

"He whirled around, picked up the phone and said, 'Let me speak with Kenny.' Later on I saw Nate at a reception and he said it's done. We'd [mistakenly] been working at the staff level before. These were all life lessons."

From that bid, the Brotherhood Crusade has generated $11 million from county employees during the last twenty-four years, $387,000 of it last year, county officials say. The Brotherhood Crusade became such a nuisance to the United Way of Greater Los Angeles, with all the protests and bad ink, that the United Way offered to buy the Brotherhood out with $100,000 a year annuity—an offer the group rejected. "We weren't interested," Bakewell said, "in a parent-child relationship."

Today, there's coexistence between the two agencies. They even coordinate donation drives. Asked if it is because of Bakewell intimidation, chapter president Joe Haggerty said no. It is really just common sense in a region where twenty percent of the people live below the poverty line.

Brenda Marsh-Mitchell, who runs Mothers-in-Action, a nonprofit started by the Brotherhood Crusade eleven years ago, remembered the early days when she worked at the Brotherhood Crusade. Its office on Central Avenue would later become a fast food joint.

"Our building leaked during the rain. The KKK would call and say 'Go back to Africa,' and there would be bomb threats and everyone would go home except for Danny. I used to think he was crazy. One day we saw this butt-naked homeless guy who cussed us out when we approached him. Well, Danny saw him another time and brought him back to the office. Danny said to make sure this man had something to eat, someplace to live. 'I want you all to understand' he said 'this is why we have a job—helping the less fortunate.' Danny gave his a job as a handyman and years later, after he got cleaned up, we found him and he got his wish: he got to sing for [Motown producer] Berry Gordy. You have to realize how many people Danny's helped. I'm one of them."

THE SPECULATOR

The mayor's first brush with city hall netted him a windfall.

—*LA Weekly*, April 4th, 1997

THE YEAR WAS 1981, and Richard J. Riordan, along with a small clique of investors and downtown planners saw gravy days ahead for South Park, a dreary industrial area in the shadow of Los Angeles' expanding skyline.

With office construction sizzling a few blocks north and a $750 million redevelopment effort under way, dry officials envisioned South Park as home-sweet-home for the growing legions–an urban village in the land of subdivisions and the long-distance commute. Riordan apparently had a different vision–hefty returns on his real estate dollars.

While bureaucrats rushed to map out their ideas for a tidy latticework of apartments, condos, and amenities there, the low-profile attorney from South Pasadena was displaying the timing of an NBA point guard. Moving methodically over the course of a year, Riordan and his business partners acquired five land parcels near Ninth Street and Grand Avenue, holding them a short time–in one case just three months–before selling them to the city's flush urban renewal entity, the Community Redevelopment Agency (CRA). The bureaucrats got space for a quaint city park. Riordan and company got their own greenery: a windfall of more than $3.6 million, records show.

Just six months later, Riordan bankrolled what still rates as one of the most momentous campaign gifts in Los Angeles political history, a $300,000 loan to a man he had never even met: Tom Bradley. Soon, Riordan would have his first City Hall post, as a Bradley commissioner, whetting an appetite for new conquests that would help carry this enigmatic millionaire from corporate deal making to the mayor's suite.

Besides amplifying on Riordan's still-obscure real estate expertise, the South Park transactions—and subsequent events erase any lingering notion that the mayor was an outsider looking in when he trounced challenger Michael Woo four years ago in the mayoral race. Even one of his own CRA commissioners wonders aloud about the public land sales that preceded his headlong and moneyed entre to Bradley fifteen years ago.

"There is sometimes a confluence between business and politics that results in a significant advantage to political insiders, and it's difficult not to conclude the mayor was a beneficiary of those insider relationships," says Cynthia McClain-Hill; a business land-use attorney and a Riordan appointee to the CRA from 1993 to1995. "You can't say anyone did anything improper, but it doesn't appear to be the result of mere happenstance."

The mainspring to Bradley's dream of a "world class downtown" was the Central Business District redevelopment project, a public works juggernaut that promised to lure in new skyscrapers and rejuvenate Skid Row. Shaking downtown's reputation as a ghost town after the office towers cleared out nightly was key. To achieve it meant establishing a twenty-four hour urban core and fully stocked residential communities capable of winning over the suburbanites. South Park was pinpointed to do just that.

It was not something a bulldozer could fix in a fortnight. South Park was a grab bag of parking lots, ramshackle apartment buildings, garment factories and the like. Bracketed by Eighth Street, the Santa Monica Freeway, Main Street, and the Harbor Freeway, the area was tantalizingly close to L.A.'s bustling financial center to the north and USC to the south, but remained barren nonetheless. "It was absolutely a wasteland," says Chris Stewart, former CEO of the Central City Association, downtown's preeminent business group. "There wasn't really anything going on."

The Community Redevelopment Agency had visions of a sea change, even weighing at one point whether to carve cut a manmade lake. But first things first, and CRA officials hunkered down on housing plans and a park. As far back as 1978, CRA plant tin documents talked of an urban common somewhere along Hope

Street. By January 1980, the agency's work program had honed in on a proposed half-acre park at the corner of Ninth and Hope.

The CRA, though, was several steps behind L.A.'s future mayor. Riordan's first acquisition, near Ninth and Grand, was the Imperial Hotel, an aging three-story structure included on the city's earthquake danger list for unreinforced brick buildings. Using his own money and a partnership's, he paid $1.04 million to a seller called R.L. Krodell, Inc. The deal was done by April 1981.

A nearby parking lot on Hope was next up. Riordan, this time with his own wallet and two partnerships, paid $2.04 million and gained control of the land by August. This time, the seller was the John and Dora Haynes Foundation, which had brushed away offers from two private suitors and even an "expression of interest from the CRA," says Diane Cornwell, director of the foundation, which finances social science research about Los Angeles. Then the Princeton-trained lawyer knocked. "He came in with a very attractive offer," Cornwell says. "It's not stated in our records why he wanted it."

The buying continued through late 1981; when Riordan paid L&R Auto Parks $1.65 million for its lot at Ninth and Grand. L&R executives, who became prodigious Bradley contributors, declined comment.

Riordan's final purchase was recorded on January 6th, 1982. Along with lawyer/colleague Paul Alanis, he bought an empty brick building, also on the quake hazard list, for $1.5 million, closing the transaction only three months before he sold all the parcels to the CRA, documents indicate. Alan Artunian, whose father sold the property, saying it was an amiable deal. Riordan, he says, had bought jewelry from his dad before the land deal; and even attended the man's funeral.

"My father wanted to get rid of" the structure, Artunian says. "He wanted his money, not the building, and Riordan said he'd buy it. My grandfather said, 'A business deal is a business deal. If he can make more money, congratulations!' Riordan knew who to sell to. There were no harsh feelings."

In late April, one calendar year after his first purchase was recorded, Riordan and his partners sold the entire package of South Park assets to the CRA for $9.82 million. That figure yielded them a $3.6 million profit–$500,000 over the appraised value, records show.

That differential raised some eyebrows among business interests who watched the real estate market, says Edward Helfeld, then the agency's administrator. "There was some talk about it, just some sort of downtown gossip." Even so, the transaction did not cause a stir inside the CRA's Spring Street headquarters, because officials had an appraisal and backup paperwork, Helfeld says. Besides, the agency's energies back then were focused on clearing the way for the massive California Plaza skyscrapers on Bunker Hill, the Museum of Contemporary Art and other major developments.

"It certainly is a nice profit." Helfeld said. But "nobody indicated there was any chicanery."

In fact, looking back on Riordan's South Park score, it seems plausible that the New Rochelle native simply took advantage of CRA acquisition practices that left the agency vulnerable to any number of fast-moving investors. Land speculation was rampant in South Park and other blighted downtown areas back then, real estate experts concur.

"There was one guy who would follow the [GRA] agenda and made millions...and there was nothing we could do," recalls Stewart, an ex-CRA commissioner who says he has high regard for Riordan. It would burn me up. We didn't like having to pay a premium for land that six months earlier was selling for half the price. The [Central City] Association even considered buying the land to stop the speculation."

Don Spivak, the agency's deputy administrator and a fourteen-year CRA veteran, believes the short-term acquisitions were one of the factors that bushwhacked redevelopment plans well before the recession and shrinking tax increments stalled projects citywide six years ago, "There was speculation at Ninth, Grand, and Hope, but it wasn't the only place," Spivak says. "The speculation was a factor in land prices going up, which made it difficult to deliver the housing, because it cost the CRA more to buy the land and required us to make larger subsidies to developers than we could make."

Knowing this, why would the CRA publicize its specific land needs, sometimes years in advance? Spivak, Helfeld, and their colleagues say state law requires urban renewal departments to detail their work programs lung before they become brick and mortar—or grass because taxpayer funds are being used. Those blueprints are also necessary for some City Council budget deliberations on the ERA, even if they might tip a valuable hand. "You have to have community participation in a plan. They are public documents," says John Spalding; who recently left the CRA after years as planning director. "There may have been people aware of [them]... But there wasn't much that could be done." Spivak says the agency now uses broader language when it outlines property, demands so speculators will not find such an easy road map. "We try to be more circumspect [today]," he says.

It was an expensive lesson. The park, a grassy two-and-a-half acre enclave in the concrete inner city adjacent to the Fashion Institute of Design, cost taxpayers an eye-popping $27.5 million, a price that include what the CRA paid Riordan and nearby landowners, plus planting and other costs, Spivak says. The figure becomes even more critical because the agency spent between $65 million and $75 million for all of South Park since the business district redevelopment plan was christened in the late 1970s, officials said. For funding and a variety of other reasons, of 12,000 new and renovated housing units in the original plan, just 1,600 now stand.

In the case of Riordan's property, agency Officials had warnings about the land-churning months before they made their buy in South Park. In a report filed in February 1982, CRA appraiser John Monroe said the skyscrapers popping up on Figueroa Street, along with a new hotel and proposed people mover between the Convention Center and Union Station, were contributing to surging land prices. So was speculation, which influenced white-hot land values that in some spots were climbing at four percent a month.

"During our investigation of the market, the overriding factor has been the influence of both developers and speculators on the downtown land market in the past few years," Monroe wrote. "The result has been a relatively high rate of appreciation. The nearby purchases of the redevelopment agency have also contributed to this phenomenon." To derive the fair market value, the agency would pay for the land. Monroe, among other things, studied twenty-six recent sales in South Park. As it turned out, all five of the parcels

Riordan and his partners were selling to the city showed up on that list. Yet Celle Stanford, who negotiated with Riordan in 1982 and now works as a manager for the agency, says news of the ownership turnover had not crossed her desk. Except for two service stations whose land was obtained through eminent domain; all the acquisitions went through voluntary escrow, records show.

"There wasn't hustling and bustling," Stanford says. "These had been longtime property owners in that block." As for Riordan, she says, "He wasn't known to me at this time."

Stanford and other CRA officials say the final price paid to Riordan and his partners was based on the Monroe appraisal and a cattier one—it is just that the first appraisal is now missing, and four important pages are missing from the second.

Stanford also described the negotiations for the property as free of strife, and described Riordan as "very cooperative." There was some dickering over price, however, as evidenced by a January 15th, 1982, letter from a Riordan & McKinzie staff attorney to then-CRA real estate director Virgil McDowell. The letter referenced a January 13th meeting between Riordan and McDowell, and cited recent downtown property transactions in pressing for the highest possible estimate of fair market value.

Today, McDowell recalls the early '80s as a hectic period, especially with Japanese companies buying so much property to the north and the speculation going on around it. "It was pandemonium. Prices were going up like crazy in 1982, and we wanted to tie up that property" for a park, he says. McDowell calls Riordan a "square dealer," saying he even agreed to take a down payment and financing for his land because the agency was still in a money crunch.

Yet even with widespread land speculation, the question of inside information also had resonance. In the late 1980s, the California Building Authority investigated whether L&R, one of the entities Riordan bought from, had somehow received confidential data about CRA plans; Spivak says. Specifically, the state was curious why L&R was buying up land on Main Street that the CRA needed for the $85 million Ronald Reagan State Office Building. The inquiry fizzled, though, after officials concluded L&R was also acquiring other downtown property. They couldn't establish a "systematic pattern" to show that L&R had privileged information, Spivak says.

Similarly, some observers continue to wonder what it was that drew Riordan to sink his money into these dilapidated, forgotten properties.

Several Democratic activists tied to City Hall and Sacramento have long suspected he had inside information about the CRA intentions from someone in the know, prompting him to dash off and buy the suddenly valuable properties needed for the park. Two ex-agency commissioners say the doubts remain today, despite Riordan's vaunted timing.

"Maybe Riordan happened to get lucky and get some information," said one urban renewal commissioner, who spoke on condition of anonymity. "He bought the land for bargain basement prices and maybe sold it at market. That's always in the eye of the beholder."

Real estate lawyer Paul R. Alanis, Riordan's legal colleague who partnered with him to acquire two of the parcels, says the theory that they bought into South Park based on some secret information was ludicrous given Riordan's ethical standards and reflex decision-making style.

"I can assure you that Riordan not only didn't have inside information, he probably had no information," Alanis says. "I was the real estate partner, and I never got any of Dick's time. Dick didn't spend ten minutes on this stuff. It was not his cup of tea. What he loved was the corporate game."

Mike Pfeiffer, executive director of the South Park Stakeholders Group, a nonprofit organization representing landowners there, agrees. "If people say 'secret this, secret that,' they probably don't attend the [CRA] meetings. You don't have to be a brain surgeon to know where redevelopment is going."

Riordan chief of staff Robin Kramer dismisses the notion that the mayor traded on confidential information as "off-base and wrong."

Riordan himself denied repeated requests for interviews about the 1982 deal. Finally, Kramer agreed to relay the questions to him, and he relayed his answers through him. Kramer says her boss told her he simply bought the land and buildings in case he wanted to swap them for other property without paying capital-gains taxes. As for the sale, she says, "A CRA staffer came to him for the [South Park] parcels, and he accepted the gentleman's first offer.

"The mayor purchased many properties downtown beginning in the early 1970s and continuing through the 1980s," she adds.

Riordan partner Alanis makes no mention of a land swap, but says a broker friendly with them pitched the idea as a good investment. "Were we entrepreneurs looking at assembling properties so we could make money in South Park? Yes. But did we anticipate making money off the CRA? No. They have condemnation powers, and it is an uphill battle to prove you paid X one day and should get Y the other." In the end, of course, there was no condemnation, and no haggling over price.

It was also during the early 1980s that Riordan purchased the Original Pantry Café on Figueroa, and adjacent land located on the southeastern flank of the downtown redevelopment project. While he has hung on to the popular eatery, he sold the air rights over it and the block around it to Manufacturer's Life Insurance Company just months after he bought it. Alanis estimates Riordan's profit at $15 million to $20 million.

Downtown real estate "was like the Hong Kong stock market back then," Alanis adds. "Our record wasn't one hundred percent. Dick participated in buying this one large parcel in the Beaudry area, and the-partnership lost several million bucks. But overall he seemed to have the Midas touch."

Six months after his CRA sale, Riordan himself was writing a check, specifically a $300,000 loan to Bradley's gubernatorial campaign. Important for its size alone, the loan takes on an added dimension because Riordan had not given the mayor a dime in the previous three years, city records indicate. On top of that, Riordan and Bradley had never even shaken hands, according to Nelson Rising, Bradley's campaign chairman.

"Dick called me and said he wanted to help," says Rising, now-CEO of Catellus Development Corporation and former partner at Maguire-Thomas, one of the city's most successful developers. Riordan said, "I'm very supportive of Mr. Bradley, [though] I don't know him."

The loan was something of a surprise to others close to Bradley, among them adviser Maureen Kindel. "The loan was the first time

I ever heard of Dick Riordan," says Kindel, who headed Bradley's Board of Public Works and is now a lobbyist. "I do think [Riordan] was genuinely excited about the fact Bradley was going to be governor, and even if he was not, he would be mayor. I think Riordan wanted to be a player."

"It gets your attention, $300,000. I'd be surprised if the Rockefellers gave $300,000," adds one L.A. political consultant. "He wanted to help Bradley substantially and stand out from the pack."

Kramer, again, offers a different version, saying the Bradley camp asked for the money. She says he made the loan, which was repaid, and a subsequent $20,000-plus contribution, because her boss "thought it would be great to have an L.A. mayor with a lot of experience as governor."

Whatever the motivation, the largess was the first gush in a torrent of campaign contributions that Riordan and his law firm made between 1983 and 1993, according to the *Los Angeles Times* and other newspapers. Giving prodigiously as an equal opportunity donor, he and his firm shelled out an estimated $2 million to Republicans and Democrats, from City Hall to the White House.

By the time the Olympics hit L.A., the future mayor was a Bradley commissioner. Were the loan and the slot connected? In a 1993 *Times* article, Riordan himself implied a quid pro quo when he said that after the loan, "He later got a call from a Bradley loyalist asking him what city commission he wanted to serve on."

But Tom Houston, Bradley's deputy mayor from 1984 to 1987, says in an interview that the two events were unrelated. Riordan, according to Houston, was a natural appointee to call upon after a 1984 commission shakeup. "We asked for everyone's resignation and tried to put in new blood," says Houston, now a Sacramento lawyer. "He was one of seven hundred who came in."

Running to unseat Bradley in the 1985 mayoral election, Councilman John Ferraro was not buying that argument. Pointing squarely at the nexus of Rioidan's CRA sale, the loan and the commission post, Ferraro castigated the mayor, saying he would "do anything to be governor. We cannot continue to allow Tom Bradley to get away with selling off Los Angeles parcel by parcel to further his political ambitions," Ferraro was quoted as saying at a March 10th, 1985, press conference.

A livid Bradley denied he had asked Riordan or any campaign contributor for a favor. He labeled the Ferraro brickbat so insulting he "wouldn't dignify" it. Incensed, Riordan himself approached the councilman and told him he thought the attack was "wrong," Kramer says.

Ferraro hammered the mayor again over the issue in a debate four days later. This time, he ambled straight into a trap set by the ex-cop. Riordan's "a good businessman," Bradley said, "just like you were."

Ferraro, it turned out, had built a post office on a piece of vacant Woodland Hills land he bought before joining the council, and leased it to the federal government for more than $100,000 annually. Once this came out, Riordan was a campaign issue no more. Ferraro didn't return calls for this story.

More important for the city he would one day lead, Riordan's first commission job stoked a fire in him that burned as he got more deeply involved with the L.A. Memorial Coliseum, police-bond initiatives and other public endeavors, several of his advisers say. Was he a pol in the making? "The Recreation and Parks job was significant, because he saw how [the system] worked and what he wanted to do to change it," says Richard Lichtenstein, president of Marathon Communications. "It was clearly insufficient to fill his tank," added chief mayoral adviser Bill Wardlaw, "it was the beginning of his involvement."

After nearly twenty years of redevelopment, downtown is a checkerboard of cloud-hugging high-rises, aging apartments, low-slung manufacturing, intermittent retail and grinding poverty. What office construction there is today mainly involves government agencies. And the spectacular private fortunes made by some in the last decade, including those fed by South Park, are but a fading memory.

As mayor, Riordan has been ambivalent about urban renewal, directing the CRA to help earthquake victims but presiding over deep budget cuts and down-sizing. The agency's current spending plan pales against that of the 1980s. "The CRA was really Bradley's baby—he relied on it," says one staffer. "With Riordan, it's a distant relative."

Perhaps it is a case of Riordan under-standing all too well how some people made millions off the CRA during the land rush of the last decade. "A lot of people-made money in the early '80s, and a lot of people lost money in the late '80s," concludes Rising. "People said it was location, location, location. I think it was timing, timing, timing."

Part Three

RETURN OF THE NATIVE

Richard Alatorre's rise from barrio golden boy to bad example and halfway back again.

—*LA CityBeat,* April 7th, 2005

THE TWO HUNDRED FOLKS squished into the VIP lounge of the Henry Fonda Music Box Theater were grinning and yipping as the early poll results blinked on the big screens. It was primary night, March 3rd, and the Antonio Villaraigosa For Mayor bandwagon resembled a Winnebago. A Motown band crooned, the liquor went fast, and if you noticed it, off to the side of the victory buzz, a gaggle of small-town mayors, party operatives, and various believers were embracing a dark-eyed legend many were afraid to be seen with a few years ago. Richard Alatorre was touchable again.

"He was getting hearty hugs, unsolicited, and people wanted their picture with him," recalls Don Justin Jones, a Democratic activist from Pasadena who has known Alatorre since the 1960s. "There's a saying—'You don't shake hands with a dead man or he'll pull you down with him'—and the establishment was treating Richard like the long lost prince of the city. You know he was happy when he was calling people, 'Babe.'"

Had a few things gone differently, it might have been Richard Jose Alatorre taking the oath as Los Angeles' first Latino mayor in modern times, not the slick, cherubic-faced Villaraigosa (should he unseat Jim Hahn May 17th). Had Alatorre not tried to house a little girl who lost her mother nine years ago, some grand building might now bear his name.

Destiny, however, had other ideas. His storybook ascent from barrio kid to Hispanic political royalty collapsed in soap-operatic disgrace in 2001 with a graft conviction and drug allegations. He was banished to the Siberia of house arrest, his legacy tarnished no matter the heartfelt tributes from senators and do-gooders.

Should Villaraigosa need a primer on toughness, the man who has been his unofficial campaign consigliere can go one better. He knows history can be viciously ironic.

In 1992, in a recession-flattened, riot-torn Los Angeles, it was Alatorre, the mainstream Democrat, whom the conservative Richard Riordan most feared as his opponent in the mayoral race. It was Alatorre who masterminded the district reapportionment that enabled Villaraigosa to win Alatorre's old seat that he has used to challenge Hahn. And it was Alatorre, along with County Supervisor Gloria Molina, his longtime nemesis, who hoed the path for a fresh crop of Mexican-American politicians. One of them was Richard Alarcón, the defeated mayoral candidate and Valley Councilman who liked stressing he was no Alatorre (read: corrupt).

Having jogged through hell and back, Alatorre is in his salad days now—happier, healthier, and holier, those close to him say. The impatient snarls that seemed to bubble from a tormented soul—what writer Hunter S. Thompson once called a politician's "inner werewolf"—surface less often. At sixty-three, he is a family guy and elder statesman, both felon and community icon, living sorry for the shame he caused yet convinced that he was hunted.

"I don't condone what I did, but I did it out of desperation," Alatorre explains, slitting his eyes at Camilo's Bistro, one of his Eagle Rock hangouts. "I made a mistake and paid for it. It was a very humiliating experience for my family and friends and the institutions that I was part of. It made me assess the role I'd played in things.

"For five years, I had to wake up wondering what the next story was coming up," he adds. "Because of what happened, I'm the sum of the end of my career, when things were bad. I've got that asterisk on my resume that overshadowed twenty-eight years of work."

That episode now seems like yesterday. Peers don't worry anymore if they are being taped when they call him. A grayer, chubbier Alatorre gets warm smiles at City Hall. Politicians frequently call him for advice, or to help settle feuds. He's also not skating fast over the thin ice of insolvency anymore. Working quietly, tooling around in his steel-gray Jaguar, he consults for the Affordable

Housing Development Corporation, the Los Angeles Port Police, the City of Alhambra, and others. Clients chase him, though he refuses to lobby because of disclosure rules that once got him in hot water as a politician.

"I'm making more money than I ever have," Alatorre confirms. "But I'm not trying to chase the buck. All I want is to support my family and live as privately as humanly possible."

Alatorre, unlike the impeached Bill Clinton or a defrocked televangelist, took his lumps old school: be suffered quietly. Sequestered at home, calling in to his probation officer, he did not court votes or campaign dough. He learned to make beds, empty the garbage, and enjoy the peace of not having to attend endless meetings. There was no image revival campaign, no weepy appearance on Oprah, even if he believed that the media had unfairly portrayed him as a sleazebag.

"I wasn't going to let reporters I had little respect for drive me out of town," he says.

THE NATURAL

Before he died, Jose Alatorre left his son with a nugget: Use your head to make a living, because "you aren't any good with your hands." Young Richard embraced that advice, becoming student body president at Garfield High and part-time collection agent for a Whittier Boulevard jewelry store—a job that taught him when to intimidate people and when to back off.

He was an outgoing teenager, slightly rebellious, sure to attend Mass to check out the girls or pray that his jump shot fell during basketball season.

"I was the typical Catholic hypocrite," Alatorre chuckles. (Today, he is devout.)

At Cal State Los Angeles, Alatorre majored in sociology and then got his master's in public administration from USC, no small feat. While teaching college courses, he happened one day to run into East L.A. Assemblyman Walter Karabian, who knew potential when he saw it. He gave the kid a staff job.

Itching to be the man, Alatorre soon ran and won the assembly seat vacated by David Roberti. His timing sparkled, and he nuzzled in with a fun-loving set of heavy-hitters led by Speaker Willie Brown and his lieutenant, Mike Roos. Brown so liked Alatorre's preternatural cunning that he gave him the committee chairmanship overseeing juiced gambling and liquor interests. Picketing with Chavez, as Alatorre did in 1966 to protest farm workers' conditions, fed the soul. Working at the state capital during the Chicano era on pesticide regulation and rent control fed his conviction that the little guy needed protection.

But it wasn't heaven. Being in Sacramento meant he saw little of his two sons, who were living in Alhambra with his divorced first wife, Stella. He was terrified of flying, and distances required he do it constantly. He had a few harrowing experiences, including one occasion when the plane's nose cone blew off. To soothe his nerves, he drank.

Tired of flying and jonesing to put his stamp on local politics, he ran for L.A. City Council in 1985. He won, oiled by special interest money, joining the flamboyant Nate Holden, the stately John Ferraro, and erudite Zev Yaroslavsky at the Council horseshoe. In a portentous act, he paid a record $142,000 settlement to the City Attorney's office for failing to disclose contributors.

Alatorre savored the pothole politics that Brown had laughingly warned him he would come to despise. He was the king of a fiefdom that ran from Boyle Heights to the Glendale border. In that district's volatile immigrant neighborhoods and yuppified hills, everybody recognized his swarthy, rutted complexion and sandpaper voice.

Mayor Tom Bradley also found his Council point man in Alatorre, even if the two could not be any different personality-wise. Alatorre proved to be masterful at three-dimensional thinking and lining up votes—without an excess of silky oratory.

Yaroslavsky, now a Westside Supervisor, felt a kinship with Alatorre because they both grew up in the same destitute area and understood tough personalities. Their similarities made for some electric combat.

"I judge people in politics by whether their word was good and whether you can depend on them hunkered down in battle, and yeah, I could trust him." Yaroslavsky said. "The thing about him that I always appreciated, even though we don't always agree...he always was the real deal. He cares about people on the margins... I'm not going to defend what he did, [but] when I was up against him, I knew I was in the fight of my life."

By the 1990s, Yaroslavsky's portrait was the general impression of Alatorre: a fighter and even a bully. He would holler at building officials who were not moving fast enough to get repairs done. He would sometimes unload on his own staff, exploding like a volcano while aides were left quivering.

Alhambra Mayor Daniel Arguello was part of Alatorre's assembly staff from 1977 to 1982. He remembers him for his odd mix of tenderness, agile thinking, and combustibility.

"As a boss, he was the most fun I've ever had, and there were other times when I wanted to kick in the door," Arguello remembered. "I'd worked for Tom Bradley, and his control was his presence. When Richard Alatorre was angry, everybody knew it."

This explosiveness, Alatorre now believes, was evidence of buried emotions. He was a dry drunk who missed his dad terribly. He could not uncork his feelings. He regretted what kind of father he had been. Here he was out at ribbon-cuttings, defending the LAPD, shepherding a budget deal, and yet lost inside.

"People had this impression that I was ruthless, or had no blood in my veins," Alatorre said. "I gave nothing up about my emotions, so they said I was mean, cutthroat, backstabbing. You hear that time in, time out, and you become hardened. You become isolated if you've never taken stock of yourself. I didn't realize that I was bleeding internally."

LITTLE HOUSE IN EAGLE ROCK

THE WORLD WOULD FIND out about his hemorrhaging maybe before he did.

In 1997, this reporter wrote a lengthy story in the *LA Weekly* about Alatorre's connections to Samuel Mevorach, an Arcadia-based real estate operator who had bedeviled L.A. housing officials with his dilapidated properties. Among Mevorach's holdings was the Wyvernwood apartments, a sprawling, once-tidy Boyle Heights complex that had degenerated into blistered, crime-infested units coated with dangerous flaking lead paint; a number of children were poisoned from it. Feeling the heat from inspectors, Mevorach needed Alatorre's sway to grease a $91 million, city-subsidized sale of the property.

Alatorre unluckily needed Mevorach just as much as the slumlord needed him.

The previous year, Belinda Ramos, the sister of Alatorre's third and current wife, Angie, had died of colon cancer. Ramos left behind an adorable, seven year old girl whose father was named Henry Lozano. An older man, Lozano was chief of staff to a Democratic congressman and staunchly aligned with Gloria Molina's political machine.

Ramos's dying wish was for Melinda to live with the Alatorres. Melinda loved them, and they loved her back. Two months later, the Alatorres decided to sell their Monterey Hills condo and relocate to an Eagle Rock house with a yard and floor plan roomier for a child.

About this same time, Lozano, who had not had much involvement with Melinda, got upset when the little girl didn't want to spend time with him. Lozano's next move was to initiate a custody fight. It exposed a lot more than parenting techniques.

Soon, the *Los Angeles Times* began writing about how the Alatorres had financed their move into the Spanish-style house. The paper found that Mevorach had given Alatorre tens of thousands of dollars under the table and arranged a sham lease on the condo. Stories about money exchanges at greasy restaurants, bagmen, and mysterious new roofs tied to one of Alatorre's political contributors had a Raymond Chandler feel. When those articles subsided, Alatorre's alleged coke use snatched *Times* headlines.

By 1998, it was unclear whether Alatorre would survive the onslaught. The judge overseeing the ongoing custody fight ordered a surprise drug test, and Alatorre was found to have coke in his system despite his proclamation he was clean. The same judge who had once praised the Alatorres for their care of Melinda ordered her out of their presence. Alatorre's credibility, the judge scolded, had been "totally shredded."

He had ignited the biggest ethics scandal to hit L.A. since the final term of the Bradley administration. Bradley's plunge began when it was revealed that he was a paid adviser to a bank doing business with the city. Alatorre's crisis, by comparison, gave the public an excruciating glimpse into his narcotics use and personal relationships.

Alatorre had once vowed he would not wind up like Bradley had—a broken man sadly walking away from a job after overstaying his welcome—but suddenly Alatorre was lunch meat in a media feeding frenzy. So many television news crews clogged his new front porch that a fence had to be installed. FBI agents pried into his affairs, with the District Attorney's office not far behind. Supposed friends shunned him, unaware of his sinking health or tattered finances. Family members were sucked into the chaos, as well.

For Angie Alatorre, who had stood by her husband during the squall, having Melinda removed was the low point. She had felt guilty that it was her side of the family that had caused her husband's spiral. The drugs, however, were his doing.

"The only time I" got angry "was when we lost Melinda because of Richard's really dumb behavior and the judge sent her to go to my mother's for a week," she recalls. "I told [Richard] that if we didn't get her back, 'I'll never forgive you for this.' I didn't have to say anything else for him to know things had to change."

The next year, Alatorre stunned his backers when he announced he would not seek reelection. He knew that while he would probably win the election, it would be a nasty contest that would cut deeper into his kin. The fact that Melinda was too young to understand the fireworks above her was a blessing they did not want to exploit.

RIDDEN TO THE GROUND

TODAY, PRIVATE-CITIZEN ALATORRE LOOKS healthier than the public one, who often slouched enigmatically at meetings in his fine suits.

Darrell Alatorre, Richard's youngest son, said many people disbelieve him when he says how vibrant his dad has become. With the pressure off, he has time for chatty lunches, USC football games, walks around the Rose Bowl, and doting on Melinda, now a high school junior. Just don't give his dad a home fix-it project because he is all thumbs, Darrell Alatorre laughs.

The late-1990s, conversely, was a wagon-circling time the Alatorre clan would rather forget. The grand jury hauled lots of frightened people before it. Darrell Alatorre lost business clients worried about the stigma. His older brother, Derrick, relocated his family out of the area to relieve the pressure. Alatorre tried reassuring his family he was okay, but he was not sleeping well or looking good. The stress contributed to a ruptured diaphragm requiring surgery in 1997 and 1998. Two years later he got prostate cancer. Today he's hale.

"I didn't worry about his sanity. I worried about his health!" Darrell Alatorre says. "Did I see fear in his eyes? Did he ever break down? Yeah, a couple times. Is that a picture a son wants to see in his father? No! The whole ordeal he went through was bullshit, though there was some truth to his past addiction. I remember asking him during the custody battle why he was doing all this, and he said, 'Mijo, Melinda has nowhere else to go.'"

Meanwhile, as the subpoenas and the stories about him flew, his friends and colleagues were puzzled. Why wasn't he fighting back? His inner circle was baffled that he wasn't holding a press conference to defend himself or announce a libel suit from accusations that many of them believed were untrue or sensationalized. Alatorre was a lot of things, but passive wasn't part of the package.

The *Times*, among other charges, had accused Alatorre's cronies of paying him off through his wife's event-planning business and charities. Where was the context about why they would want the house, his backers asked. Where were the questions about why Richard was abusing? And where was the lowdown on Mevorach, who had copped a deal with the feds, telling them that Alatorre had "extorted" him for cash when Mevorach had been currying Alatorre's favor for years?

Darrell Alatorre says he was ready to take on the *Times* when a writer friend at the paper tipped him off that it'd budgeted $500,000 for stories about the family and had hired private investigators to dig up dirt. A reporter who worked on the stories says there was no such budget item for these stories and no investigators were retained.

"I couldn't believe it," Darrell Alatorre said. "It seemed such an astronomical amount of money. Later, I'd never seen the paper so demonize somebody."

Angie Alatorre says she and her husband's longtime confidante Lou Moret didn't always agree on tactics, but they thought their man should counterpunch. Moret, though, found that Alatorre just wanted out, and didn't believe blood-smelling reporters with preconceptions about ethnic politicians would listen to him.

"He didn't think he took money for anything more improper than anyone else had," says Moret, who ran Alatorre's 1972 and 1974 Assembly campaigns. "He knew he'd been treated differently, and partly that's because he's Mexican and partly because of his reluctance to sell his viewpoint, philosophically. That's how the cookie crumbles... Richard wasn't forced out. He wasn't defeated. He wasn't recalled... But for the *L.A. Times*, he was an easy target."

For his part, Alatorre says it wasn't until he left office and reflected back that he realized his spin into coke, self-doubt, and silence had been building for thirty-odd years.

Early on April 15th, 1964, Alatorre's first son, Derrick, was born at a Boyle Heights hospital. Ten hours later, the ecstasy crumbled when Richard's father suffered a heart attack while painting a crib for his infant grandson and died. For Jose's boy, the loss was ironic, wrenching, and most of all, lasting.

Jose Alatorre, stove repairman and seventh-grade dropout, had always preached hard work and keeping personal problems private. While stoic, he prized ideals. If the national anthem were playing on television, he would make young Richard stand, though he did not always.

In passing away so abruptly, Jose never saw his string-bean son, then twenty-one, mature from a student leader with a sixty-hour-a-week job to one of the nimblest minds in a mostly white state legislature. Nor was he around to dispense wisdom when Richard's weaknesses roared.

"I never knew how much I blamed my dad for dying," Alatorre confides. "It forced me to become something I wasn't ready to be. I had to become head of a household, but I was still a kid. I had no constructive outlet for being hurt later in life. You don't stuff things down in your soul and expect be happy."

Alcoholics Anonymous helped open his eyes, and he accepted that his addictive personality had shown even at age fourteen, when he chug-a-lugged some wine. By his twenties, liquor quieted his rage. He finally quit in 1988 after getting treatment, not allowing himself to lapse when the graft investigations revved up.

It was the drug all over L.A.—cocaine—that he sought. (Drugs, it is worth noting, are the one subject Alatorre refuses to detail except to say stories about him snorting at City Hall or with a buddy looking for city contracts were mostly false.)

"Through AA, I now understand I am a grateful alcoholic," he says. "We're not normal. A normal person can have one drink and not ten to fifteen. I know that if I took one drink, the run would be on... I had so much happening in my life then, when the [stories hit], I didn't know I was powerless."

Nor, some say, did he realize his baggage was slowly entombing him.

"He started locking out friends who would've told him, 'Don't do that! What the fuck is wrong with you?'" Moret adds. "He became a refugee. He wasn't making the right decisions. He got in trouble because he's an addict. Even when he was drinking, it wasn't because he liked it. It wasn't wine or fine Scotch he used. It was 7 and 7. Who drinks that?"

THE AL CAPONE TREATMENT

THICK PRIDE MAY HAVE also contributed to his troubles. By 1996, Alatorre's machinations to funnel government work to Hispanic-run ventures struck many as heavy-handed, as did his connections to the East Los Angeles Community Union, Corboda Corporation, and various MTA contractors seeking a piece of a $1 billion rail line through his district. Newly elected Council members did not fear him as others once had. In what turned out to be his last campaign, a political novice forced him into a runoff.

"He didn't want to give his detractors the pleasure of seeing the mighty stag taken down," says Jones, the Pasadena activist. "He didn't want to let folks in on the pain, and maybe that got him into trouble. Fidel Castro said in his famous speech: 'You can find me guilty, but history will absolve me.' When you look back at this period, people will appreciate that Richard did not cry when his enemies kicked him in the ass, but I guarantee you that his boots were full of blood."

Even after he left office, the bloodletting continued. When Alatorre was lined up with consulting work typical for ex-politicians with the L.A. Department of Water and Power and the Compton Community College District, the *Times* wrote about it, and officials nixed what could have been $70,000-a-year in income. A $114,000-a-year post with a state unemployment insurance board ended, too, when Alatorre settled with the Justice Department.

His legal-defense bills topped $100,000, and to pay them he had to bust open his IRA and pay a $100,000 penalty for early withdrawal. This somewhat undercuts the notion he had been stashing away money as a guy-on-the-take, as detractors suspected; there were no secret bank accounts. Because he had always spent what he made, Alatorre says he "didn't have the luxury of not working" and launched his consulting business.

Dine with him and you glean three things: His cell phone never stops jangling, he wolfs bacon like air, and he can spice cuss words into the most delicate topic. The other f-word—"felon"—he does not use. The idea that he is one scalds him. It just doesn't seem to obsess him.

If he has any satisfaction about his demise, it is that a four year, federal led investigation of his links to people trying to buy his influence did not result in a major corruption charge. Instead, he pled to not disclosing $42,000 in illicit income on his ethics commission and tax filings. Some call this the Al Capone treatment: nailing a high-profile figure on a relatively incidental charge. No other big fish was nabbed, either.

"By prosecuting me, I was making somebody's career," Alatorre says. "We ran the city—me, Zev [Yaroslavsky], and John Ferraro—when Bradley was in trouble. Even the *Times* said that. But certain people did not feel like I was the kind of guy who should be mayor, and what's ironic is that I never wanted that."

Maybe not, but that does not mean he is short on ideas about how to get it. Still very much on his game, Alatorre will unleash a torrent of expletive-laden opinion about this year's race. And if he is really talking to Villaraigosa as much as he says he is, current Mayor Jim Hahn's ears are burning.

"Jimmy is like the T-ball mayor. I go back to when Jimmy first ran for City Controller, and I had the distinct impression he fell into politics. It's not where his gut is," Alatorre says. "Jimmy is a very honest guy. It's just that he's always around the edges on issues. If you asked his ex-aides, they'd say he's lazy. He doesn't live and breathe politics like his sister [Councilwoman Janice Hahn] does. [Former Governor] Gray Davis was evil. He was driven. Jimmy isn't driven. He's just blah."

Alatorre does sees promise in Villaraigosa, saying, "I recognize Antonio's shortcomings, but he has the best chance of getting done what L.A. needs," adding: "We need someone who will work well with the City Council and Sacramento, someone who will get L.A. the goodies."

For instance, he notes that Hahn has not even taken advantage of L.A.'s respected police chief, William Bratton, to get more cops or anti-terrorism money. "Bratton likes the notoriety here, but he's so far up Jimmy Hahn's butt, and Jimmy is so far up his, neither of them can see... If I were mayor, I'd go put my arm around President Bush and say how much I liked his dad if it got us resources."

That is the kind of thinking that got results, and both the residents who recognize him strolling down Garfield Avenue and the powerful remember. Sympathy is another thing.

"Richard Alatorre was clearly the smartest guy on the City Council when I was there; I admire and love him, but I don't feel sorry for him," says former mayor Richard Riordan, now California's Secretary of Education. "Judge him as he is today. [After all], we forgive murderers."

The family's saga has ended better than any of them could have imagined four years ago—happily. Alatorre has work aplenty and time with his family. Melinda, now a spunky teenager, worships "pops," as protective of him as he is of her. Henry Lozano is a non-factor in their lives. The family even reads the *Times*.

There probably won't be the beach-house he had dreamed about as a young man, but c'est la vie.

"I wake up in the morning," he adds, "happy to be alive."

WHEN BUS DRIVERS BEAT THE SHIT OUT OF PEOPLE

Attacks on riders not always punished.
—*Los Angeles Daily News*, June 24th, 1996

BRUISED AND BLEEDING FROM one ear, seventy-nine year old Louis Ross could only mutter "Why?" as the MTA bus he had just staggered off roared away.

The thrashing he took did not add up. Sure, the retired accountant had squabbled with the driver for taking so long to open the bus doors for him at a Rampart area stop, but Ross figured it was just words.

Then driver David Smith rose from behind the wheel, pushed the diminutive Ross into a handrail and roughed him up so badly he had to be helped off the coach and whisked to the emergency room.

A passenger who watched the November 8th battering said she was so shocked by it she refuses to ride MTA buses anymore.

"I never thought a driver who is supposedly working for us would beat up an old man," said witness Linda Streeter. "For [him] to become so violent all of a sudden, he must have had a problem."

Smith, fired and now serving a six-month jail sentence for the crime that City Attorney James Hahn called "unconscionable," refused comment.

Even so, he was not the first driver to lash out against a passenger.

In the past five years, Metropolitan Transportation Authority bus operators have been implicated in roughly 100 passenger beatings, assaults on motorists and other serious on-duty crimes, according to records obtained by the *Daily News*.

Disturbing on their own, the cases spotlight dual problems for America's second-largest bus agency: its inability to shield drivers from the stress and violence spilling in through the bus doors and the fact that the violence has galvanized some bus operators to flout established rules and respond with hostile acts of their own.

"We've got some guys who aren't the best people," said Goldy Norton, spokesman for the union representing MTA drivers. "If they have a confrontation with passengers, they're likely to lose [their tempers]. It's not an excuse, but unfortunately, these things happen."

Those volatile operators, Norton and agency brass note, represent only a fraction of the 4,000 people at the wheel on MTA coaches. The numbers also pale in comparison to the times drivers were victimized by others while on duty.

As they sweated to keep their coaches on time and under control, the agency's bus operators were targeted in nearly 2,000 assaults and other crimes between 1991 and 1995, the *Daily News* recently reported. Drivers have been stabbed and shot, whacked with metal pipes and bottles, sprayed with tear gas and urine, and sexually brutalized.

"When you play a violin too long, it breaks," said MTA board Chairman Larry Zarian. "The public needs to understand the pressure the drivers face."

But once they have been named suspects in on-duty clashes, drivers have received disparate treatment ranging from punitive to preferential, records and interviews show.

At least eighteen operators have been fired and fourteen suspended because of violent or sexual incidents since 1991—proof, officials say, that their employees are held to tough standards.

Nearly twenty cases, however, remain unsolved or cannot be located because of MTA record-keeping lapses. Two operators quit before they could be disciplined, including a driver who police said sexually assaulted a female passenger with Down syndrome in the San Fernando Valley three years ago.

Others suspected of wrongdoing, meantime, were never thoroughly investigated or were given special treatment, according to a number of current and former Transit Police officers who said they were acting on orders from above.

"I [was] on cases where they thumped people and basically nothing happened," said ex-MTA Transit Police Sergeant Scott Pawlicki. "It was like we were handcuffed."

"Sometimes there is pressure by supervisors not to arrest drivers," added Sargeant Mark Jennings. "It's an unwritten thing."

Contending that her department has a good track record of dealing with operators accused of brutality or other misdeeds, MTA Transit Police Chief Sharon Papa said her department typically handles cases fairly, like it would any other.

At the same time, she conceded, some of her sergeants have until recently given directives to officers not to haul drivers to jail.

"It's the politics involving the unions and the fact bus operators are their co-workers," Papa said. "Some still feel that way, but it's not policy."

In the Ross case, an officer was directed by a supervisor not to allow the old man to identify the driver. That, officials said, partly explained why the driver did not go to jail for more than four months after the attack.

Police supervisors today admit they should have made a "different call" but blame it on a sergeant no longer with the force.

Other incidents reviewed by the *Daily News* exhibited what even MTA cops say was bungled follow-up or poor judgment on their part.

Take the driver accused by a female rider of sexually soliciting her in July. He was not formally questioned by Transit Police until he had committed a second, similar offense with an underage patron in October, records and interviews show.

The operator, Dwight Penkey, was ultimately convicted and sentenced to eighteen months in jail for both crimes–but only after MTA detectives had lost a key file for a month and had difficulty tracking down the first victim.

Even when wires are not crossed, transit cops said, it is difficult to locate hot-tempered operators because of the 1,800 MTA buses roaming the Southland every working day. Victims who cannot list badge numbers, give good physical descriptions or return their calls especially hamper things.

Police, for example, still cannot reach a man who claimed a driver kicked him in the chest so hard it sent him tumbling backward onto a Van Nuys sidewalk. The December incident remains unsolved.

In many of the fleshed-out cases, minor disputes were the catalyst.

One experienced driver had felony battery charges lodged against him by the District Attorney's Office after a young house painter was battered near USC over mere pennies.

The passenger, Tello Sabador, came up ten cents short of the $1.35 fare in December and asked if anyone could lend him a dime or break a $20 bill, according to records and eyewitness statements. Fuming over the request, driver Richard Barre handed Sabador a bus transfer, followed him off the bus, threw him to the ground and then hurtled him into a parking meter, according to prosecutors.

"He was trying to break me in two," Sabador said in an interview.

Preparing for Friday's scheduled start of the trial, Barre's lawyer said his client acted only in self-defense and that Sabador had used racial slurs—a charge Sabador denied.

Still, Barre himself told police investigating the incident that a passenger struck him in the head six months ago and, as a result, he "may have lost it a little too much."

Since his overall record is good, he is still driving today, MTA officials say.

Other drivers, meantime, have been sacked for shoving riders, groping female passengers, even threatening a gang member with a hatchet, personnel records indicate. Others have been suspended for less serious scrapes, including an operator who intentionally rammed the car of two undercover state agents because it was parked in a bus layover zone.

Transit Police Officer Carlos Diaz, an eleven-year veteran, has a different story to tell.

Three years ago, he was summoned to a mid-city site where a Latino passenger had claimed an African-American driver slammed her into a concrete wall after the two exchanged racial barbs and bickered over the bus' destination.

Under their union contract, MTA operators are never supposed to fight, particularly when it means getting off the bus.

Witnesses supported the account of the passenger, Glenda Jimenez, who had a swollen arm and other injuries. Diaz figured it was enough to jail the driver on battery charges, but a sergeant instructed him to just have the driver, Calvin Lawton, Jr., agree to a court appearance.

"Lawton should have gone to jail. No one deserves to be beaten like a piece of meat," said Diaz. "I was boiling inside. But drivers are treated differently."

The sergeant was Jennings, who said he was acting on orders from Captain Dennis Conte.

After reviewing the file, Conte said he made the right decision to expedite the case. He said he did not think it was as serious as Diaz indicated.

If anything, Conte noted, many drivers believe transit cops treat them heavy-handedly and expose them to danger by taking so long to reach crime scenes.

Because of that—and with half the MTA's 372-officer force guarding a rail system that transported only five percent of mass transit users last year—some operators have concluded that the best defense is to go on the offensive.

"You have quite a few bus drivers that will take the situation into their own hands," said operator Sidney Carr. "It's not that they're violent. It's that many old-timers won't put up with someone mouthing off. I try to ignore it."

The City Attorney's Office ultimately decided there was not enough evidence to press criminal charges against Lawton. Jimenez has since filed a $25,000 civil lawsuit.

Lawton's attorney, meanwhile, insisted his client never slammed Jimenez into the wall, only grabbing her arm when she tried to strike him.

While acknowledging that bus crime is a major concern, MTA Executive Director Joe Drew said he believes some riders have filed frivolous claims against drivers because of the agency's deep pockets. For him, the way police handle the cases is more of an issue than operators with short fuses.

"I will be absolutely determined, if we are covering up misbehavior whether by the operators or police, to stop it," Drew said.

In recent years, the agency has forked out $215,000 to settle claims from three unspecified cases involving operator brutality. It faces tens of thousands of dollars more in legal defense bills and upcoming lawsuits.

Driver Eddie Reece said he certainly did not get any break from the MTA after a supervisor discovered he had brought a loaded semiautomatic handgun and extra ammunition on board his bus last year. He said the weapon was there accidentally and, like others, hopes to reverse his termination through the agency appeals system.

"The same thing happened to someone else, and they gave him a twenty day suspension," Reece said.

Roughly three years ago, the agency stopped giving prospective drivers psychological tests because testing was not giving them insight into an applicant's mental state, MTA officials say.

According to Sabador's attorney, Phil Kaufman, the agency should be better at dealing with violent drivers and screening prospective ones.

"[Drivers] take a lot of guff, people hassle them and then they overreact," Kaufman said. "It raises questions."

DRINKING THE KOULAX

But don't ever try to copy its original world famous hamburgers or tacky ambience.
—*Los Angeles Business Journal*, March 23rd, 1992

THE SHACK MAY BE a culinary landmark or urban landmine, but Southlanders don't seem to care when its gooey, red-meat fix is at stake.

For decades now at the corner of Beverly and Rampart boulevards, they've stood, they've scarfed, they've belched and they've split.

It is all in the name of a Tommy's double chili cheeseburger, an eating experience that blends car fumes, cholesterol and seedy characters.

On a hazy Friday last month, a lunch-time throng of about seventy-five was gathered for the ritual of quiet salivation and boisterous jabber near the mangy intersection. Undergrads, out-of-towners, businessmen, and day laborers dutifully queue up around the red-and-white shack as Mercedes-Benzes and gas guzzlers risk their bumpers—and insurance rates—entering the snarled parking lot.

Salsa music, meanwhile, blares out of the back of a patron's car and the Taco Bell across the street looks forlorn, despite its day-glo sales beckonings. Nearby, a young man is being arrested, though Tommy's clientele seem more interested in munching than Miranda rights.

Every year, this outpost of L.A.'s great hamburger wars serves enough people to fill the Coliseum and the Sports Arena—ten times over. It is also a living, breathing sociology treatise paper on melting pots.

Snaps one young lawyer, "This place gives us white-collar yuppies a blue-collar feeling."

Migrating west from Oklahoma's Dust Bowl in 1927 in a Model T Ford, Tommy's owner and namesake, Tom Koulax, flopped with two hot-dog stands before eventually finding his niche in L.A.'s junk-food jumble. It all started with a $900 investment at the Rampart eatery in 1946.

Today, it is not the empire that Richard McDonald or Carl Karcher built, but it is a piece of the fast-food mother lode, nonetheless.

The entrepreneur of Greek descent now has 325 workers at sixteen other hamburger joints scattered from El Monte to Long Beach. And his pockets jingle with nearly $20 million in annual sales.

"I'll give you a good sandwich and not just rip you off," blurts Koulax, seventy-three. "We even pick up the sales tax."

If there is any doubt about the triumph that is the chain of Tommy's Original World Famous Hamburgers, peruse the Yellow Pages and then see the dizzying list of wannabe burger deans.

What a difference a letter makes.

There are Tam's Burgers, Tom's Junior Burger, Tom's Super—and Senior—Burgers, Tomy's, Thoma's and Tomein Tommy's. To name a few.

And they have not stopped at just the name. Tommy's meat-based chili, beefsteak tomatoes and specially cured cheese have all been the stuff of emulation. Even Tommy's ambience—the neon sign, script lettering and industrial paper towel racks—have been copied. So have the sofa-cushion-change prices: $1.30 for a regular burger, $2.05 for a double chili cheese.

But in recent times, Koulax has shown rivals he is not sincerely flattered by imitation: It is the quickest path to the court system. Since 1988 alone, Koulax has filed twenty trademark suits and he has yet to lose one. Copy the lettering, name or shack and you will get slapped with a suit, Koulax warns.

Hence the marquee at the Rampart set-up, Koulax's first site: "Tommy's: Many imitate, none compare." And use of the key phrase—Tommy's Original World Famous Hamburgers—is a signal that a local outlet is a true branch of the incomparable original.

The first imitator was a something of an insider—a Koulax business associate who began his own Tommie's in West L.A. and the South Bay.

"He was a nickel-and-dimer," Koulax recalls. "I don't worry about" rivals now "unless they step on my toes, and then I sue them."

At Tommy's iron-gated headquarters on Beverly, there are two inquiries a week about franchising. That's anathema to Koulax, who prefers branching out at his own leisure.

"What the competition is looking for is a simple, cost-efficient, low-investment thing with a name," adds Tommy's General Manager Brent Maire, himself a former Mickey D's management trainee. "But we just won't let people copy us. We get customers who call up and complain about the price or the burger and we have to explain it's not" the real Tommy's, but a competitor.

Tommy's relies on a recipe of low overhead and fresh ingredients, Maire contends with a dash of pride. And the Rampart shack is a twenty-four hour operation.

"Our food costs are thirty-eight percent of our overall expenses and that's high in the food business," Maire says. "Tom is extremely smart. Others can cut, cut, cut, but he knows customers can taste the difference... We don't even weigh our burgers."

At Tom's Number 5 Chiliburger in the 5200 block of Pico Boulevard, Koulax wouldn't seem to have much to fret about. Despite a billing as "The Greatest Chiliburger in the World" and the same accoutrements as Tommy's—right down to the zesty yellow peppers—the pigeons outnumber the customers. If the cooks are working with the same controlled frenzy as Tommy's, the bars over the windows conceal it.

Tom's Number 5 co-owner, Henry Chung, is not sure why the old proprietor used a name that is so popular in the L.A. burger game—or even if his name was Tom.

"We don't think about changing it," he says.

Back at Rampart, newcomers are astounded they can order, pay and get their goodies in fifteen seconds. It is a down-and-dirty affair: burgers, hot dogs and tamales; potato chips only, no fries; Hostess pies and an honor system where customers snatch canned beverages from an old-fashioned cooler after they order.

But it is the 1990s. What about fiber?

"People ask us how much cholesterol or fat is in our burgers and we tell them we don't know," Maire says. "Everyone is concerned about health but what can we say? We sell an old-fashioned chiliburger."

True enough. Fast-food lite this is not, though Koulax experimented with, and later scrapped, nutrition-oriented chicken sandwiches at the La Habra outlet.

(Koulax opened a sitdown Mexican restaurant, Tomecito's across from the Rampart stand in the 1970s, but it tanked. Today, the facility is a lime-green storage area.)

As for the customers, they say Koulax's fare is high living for the palate, if not murder at times on the stomach.

"Someone asked me where I was going to eat," says one downtown businessman. "And I said, 'To grab a good lunch and get sick the rest of the weekend.'"

Adds Steve Westling, a visiting police officer from Albany, Oregon: "The food's great here, especially when you want to prepare for a bowel movement."

Or take attorney Peter Anderson, a middle-aged customer who has his tie draped over his shoulder to avoid an early run to the dry cleaners.

"I started coming here at two A.M. when I was at Loyola law school," he says between bites. "I've been coming here pretty regularly since then...when I get the need for a burger fix."

Indeed, at USC, going a long stretch without a Tommy's run is tantamount to forsaking a football game for lawn bowling.

As it was forty years ago—when Koulax had to use his car trunk as a storage locker for want of space—the weekends are when the cash registers ka-ching the loudest.

Sometimes, though, the Rampart stand, which is celebrating its forty-fifth anniversary this year, is a little too popular.

Gangs, particularly one called Armenian Power, like to frequent Tommy's on Friday and Saturday nights, according to Tommy's security guard Versabey Duque, who sports a billy club at his side. To forestall troublemaking, the parking lots are sometimes roped off and the crowd chemistry is watched closely.

To date, there have been no violent crimes, though the once-proud residential area continues to degenerate into an amalgam of cookie-cutter apartment buildings and graffiti-spattered retail stores.

Does it matter much? Probably not.

Concludes Koulax, "If I had to start over, I couldn't do it now. But I've accomplished what I wanted."

GOT YOUR BACK

Rancho Los Amigos is the last chance for kids, gangsters and other uninsured victims of severe spinal injuries. Now the county wants to shut it down.

—*LA CityBeat,* July 31st, 2003

SOME FOODS PACK FATS, others engorge the soul. Alvaro Morfin's gooey dish of chicken Parmesan does both, bubbling with mouth-watering red sauce and a pinch of hope not always stocked around here.

The former-East L.A. homeboy aced his assignment to prepare the meal, just as he has his entire crash course on adjusting to life as a paraplegic, and the doctors and therapists caring for him regard it as proof his talents can carry him anywhere his deadened legs cannot. Take a whiff of his fare, the staff exclaims. They are drooling over it.

County-run Rancho Los Amigos Medical Center pines for these moments.

Parked in his wheelchair in a classroom-kitchen for the newly disabled, Morfin, eighteen, blanches at all the fuss, nonetheless. He is proud, a might wary. Says he can't foresee a career under a poofy chef's hat. Computer repairs—now that grabs his imagination.

Collaring everyone else is the skinny kid's backstory, how he was supposed to be the exception to the tired story of wayward youth stumbling toward oblivion.

He had lived with a foster family after getting into minor drug trouble. Removed from it, he earned honor-roll grades at Optimist High School Senior and kept his distance from gangland temptations. Back home this summer, though, on a night he lives with everyday, old habits resurged and he was ambushed when he just wanted to party. A bullet fired by someone whose face he never caught ricocheted off his spine.

That's why he is at Rancho.

"Me cook?" Morfin deadpans, his dark, brown eyes swooping the room. "No, I'll get a girlfriend for that. I plan to go home" pretty soon.

Irene Gilgoff, the boy's physician, gladly swallows the un-PC remark as if it were his succulent chicken. Over her career, the diminutive, gray-haired physician has treated 150 juveniles who lost sensation in their bodies because of gang firefights and crummy timing.

"There's a lot of hope for him," Gilgoff said smiling. "He recently went to the movies and noticed girls noticing him. That was big. [Others like him] go out with such rage."

Dotted over 220 acres in the gray, lunch-pail city of Downey, the Spanish stucco buildings here give way to creaky barracks, which yield to shady courtyards. They segue to the only blatantly modern edifice here: the tan-colored Jacquelin Perry neuro-trauma rehab building. You would never know from this sleepy tableau that Rancho grips a world class reputation for research and care of people with devastating spinal cord and brain injuries.

Neither is it obvious the facility itself is on the ventilator, not unless you spot the "Save Rancho" signs wedged in a few windows. In January 2003, the Board of Supervisors voted to close it because of the $60 million-a-year drag it adds to a county health-department deficit, a deficit estimated at $709 million over three years. Unlike previous shortfalls, there are no late-minute federal bailouts expected this round. A sense pervades that Rancho is expendable amid L.A.'s teeming emergency room and dead-bolted community health clinics.

Only an injunction by a federal judge in April prevented Rancho's doors from being chained. One non-profit out of Chicago inquired about administering the hospital so the county could lease indigent services from it, but everything rides on the courts.

Barring any late-hour deals, the spinal-injured will be referred to the county's four general hospitals, none of which specialize in spinal-cord rehab or related complications. Disabled advocates predict doing that will rain down misery among society's most vulnerable and cost taxpayers big in the long run.

"Nobody wants to close Rancho," said health department spokesman John Wallace. "We just have too many uninsured in L.A. County."

ON THE WARD

FOLKS ARE USUALLY SHIPPED here after they have been patched up at other hospitals from whatever laid them out. It is Rancho personnel who must teach them to monitor parts of themselves numb to the touch and, sometimes, dead to everything else. They will be schooled to insert their own catheters and how to guard against kidney infections. They will be lectured to shift legs and butts they cannot feel to prevent pressure sores—the common cold of the wheelchair crowd—and absorb dozens of other tips, caveats and shortcuts about L.A. life from the seat of their pants. Many will be operated on and many, many will return.

The spinal cord—where the brain's instructions to breathe, walk, reach, procreate, disgorge waste and myriad other functions are transmitted via electric impulses—is reliable and brilliant. It is just not terribly forgiving of abuse.

Despite the promise of cures offered by stem-cell research and other neurobiological glimmers, restoring the central nervous system after a wicked jolt is proving to be trickier than some researchers thought six years ago, when actor Christopher Reeves vowed to shake off his paralysis. Even the use of emergency-room steroids to minimize spinal-nerve damage is being revisited.

Think it is a tiny clique affected? There are 450,000 people with spinal cord injuries in America today, thousands of them in Southern California. Just on an outpatient basis, Rancho sees 75,000 patients annually as a sort of Wal-Mart for the disabled.

There are clashing auras about these grounds, grounds that trace to 1888 when a steam locomotive offloaded the sick and Rancho operated a full-blown dairy to sustain itself.

Since then, doctors have trail blazed polio treatments, back fusion surgeries and the halo traction device that is the gold standard around the world. (Rancho, one of eighteen designated regional spinal cord centers in the U.S., is currently part of a national study for paraplegics relearning stepping motions via treadmills.) Hospital alumni have achieved the seemingly impossible themselves, from quadriplegic skydiving to exquisite mouth-brushed Expressionist art that fetches top dollar.

The wards also reflect something less inspiring: the unrelenting drive-by culture of L.A.'s urban warfare and the vast swath of people with little or no health coverage at the low point of their lives. Gunshot wounds are the weapons of common destruction here. They are easily the number one cause of spinal injury with car accidents second—a ratio flip-flopped nationally. Thirty percent of the patients are indigents, the majority of others on Medical or Medicare.

So, unless you have a private insurance card, you are coming to one of the 207 beds here. If a bullet nicks your spinal canal, welcome to your new digs. If your cervical vertebra is compressed on a chain-reaction car wreck, meet your nurses. Should you, on a catastrophic scale, misjudge your ocean dive, jack-knife your motorcycle, get thrown from a horse, trip off a roof, blow your acrobatic landing, or develop a compromised spinal canal through no fault of your own, there is a good bet the rest of your life starts at Rancho.

On your back.

Spend a day here as an outsider and the halls stays with you. Take this day. Outside the weight-lifting room, where wheelchair-shoving biceps are summoned from flab, an adolescent clothed in Oakland Raiders gear propels himself stomach-down on a gurney, staring strangers down. Nearby, but a world away, a kindergarten-age little girl clutching her rag doll rolls by in an electric wheelchair with an exhausted nurse in toe.

Within shouting distance of them a firebrand, Middle Eastern-born surgeon talks about treating foreign nationals and diehard Angelenos. Ask him about ex-patients and he wonders aloud about the man who relocated to Texas to escape gang vendettas.

GO BACK, JACK, AND DO IT AGAIN

MICHAEL SCOTT, FORTY, A soft-spoken disabled specialist with a Zen-like mien and Stanford University pedigree, is hearing the lowdown during morning rounds from an exotic-looking female medical resident.

The first patient is a twenty-seven year old man with multiple gunshot wounds that damaged the middle portion of his spine. He had been shot before, but odds are he will not regain use of his legs this time. Originally treated at Martin Luther King Hospital emergency room, he is glum about his prognosis and still carrying the bullets that nailed him.

The next patient, a thirty-five year old Hispanic man, was shot three times in June. Unlike his ward-mate, he is expected to walk. Still, he has problems—heart problems, hepatitis problems, mood problems, and drug problems. The intricate tattoos adorning his chest gyrate as he writhes in bed. He complains his circulation-aiding socks give him rashes.

Scott predicted the man would be returning to the same "difficult condition" that put him here once he is hale enough to leave. It is a common dilemma for gunshot victims.

"They're more vulnerable in a chair," Scott quips. "They're not going back to Beverly Hills."

It is just about then a toothy African American man in his mid-fifties breaks the somberness. He wheels up the hallway wearing a loud blue-plaid Fedora and matching shorts, inquiring merrily about a nail clipper. He says his toenails "look like tiger claws."

"They're great docs," the man offers, "But the therapists! They're trying to kill me."

With that he rolls off.

A Latino mother of four is the last patient checked. She was ejected from her van during a May highway wreck because she was not wearing a seatbelt. The impact dislocated the most sensitive part of the back—the cervical spine. Upright in a wheelchair, looking content as can be, she reports in Spanish she has nothing negative to report.

"She never complains," says resident Sheila Patel, "If there are any problems, I have to find out through my sneaky ways."

Rancho's adult physical therapy room, a cavernous space with electrical outlets that dangle from the ceiling over a mishmash of gizmos that attack weak muscles and lost coordination, feels like a gym. A patient grunts and a young female therapist cheerleads, "Good job!" Sweet beads and repetition grinds on. What a split-second mishap stole from many may require months laboring here to restore.

The losses seem overwhelming. Off in the corner is a listless burn victim with a bandaged stub where his hand used to be. Ten feet away is a sheepish-looking car accident survivor with a chest brace and deep facial scars. He does not walk as much waddle on the beige-and-white floor, but that is not his only setback. Hyperextension injuries like his jammed nerves controlling the arms, which may never regain full strength and range. A paradox of the limbs results: some patients post-accident are nimble enough to dribble hackeysacks with their feet yet are unable to wash their face.

The spine can baffle. People can fracture their vertebrae without suffering neurological damage and be fine because the cord itself is not damaged. The opposite can be true, too. The worst off tend to have sustained nerve death. As a general rule, the higher up the spine it occurs, the more devastating the loss of function below. Sometimes, only the myelin sheath, the insulation-type coating around the nerve is hurt, and it—unlike the nerve—can regenerate.

Time is the arbiter. Whatever sensation returns after nine months from the point it was lost is typically the best it will get.

"It's a life-changing injury," Scott says. "[Patients have] lost the person they used to be."

Rancho doctors as a result often simultaneously have to play healer, psychologist, social worker and salesman of hope. Aspiring MDs are instructed to look beyond garden-variety complications such as embolisms and spastic limbs that can toss people from their wheelchairs and toward the psyche.

A patient's background often dictates their recovery chances. People with tight knit families and established roles as breadwinners or guardians fare comparatively well. So do the religious. Another thumbnail rule: the younger the victim, the quicker the acceptance of what has befallen them.

Some demand their prognosis immediately. Others say hold off. Type A personalities chomping to reclaim their old mobility can flame out emotionally. Oddly enough, a quadriplegic (someone with no use of their four limbs) on a respirator can be more at peace than a paraplegic (someone with no use of their legs).

"We've had a few dramatic cases where people with no movement in their legs walk out of here," Scott explained. "Even for those with a poor prognosis, hope means different things. I've had some [gang] patients say: 'This is the best thing that could have happened to be. If I weren't paralyzed, I'd be dead.'"

BEYOND GANGLAND

FOR IMAGE-CONSCIOUS ADMINISTRATORS, TALK of Rancho's gang caseload is the one that furrows their brow, one they believe the media has sensationalized. Yes, there are Bloods and Crips here, they acknowledge. Yes, there are baggy pants-wearing homies. But it is not like there are bullets flying in the hallways.

Scott and other physicians do not duck the same subject, perhaps because they cannot. It is county politics they would rather not touch publicly. Just like the strapping firefighter who tore his spine falling off an all-terrain-vehicle, every chart they review bristles with heartbreak, they say.

Rancho doctors have occasionally treated a gang member left a paraplegic after one shooting only to see him return as a quadriplegic after a second incident.

Sometimes it is worse. Roughly ten years ago, a Hispanic teen paralyzed by a gunshot wound and treated at Rancho was handpicked to appear on an ABC network special about adolescent violence. The roundtable show, *Kids In The Crossfire*, was broadcast from a Washington, D.C. high school. Several dozen kids and various luminaries, including then-Attorney General Janet Reno and actor Chuck Norris, attended.

After the program, the former patient vowed he given up his street ways. A rival faction back in L.A. would not abide that promise. Within a year of the show, they ran him down in the street as he sat in his chair and whipped around and shot him to ensure he was dead.

"It was a tragic statement about society," said a Rancho doctor, who asked his name not be used. "It's happened on too numerous an occasion."

Owing to a few harrowing incidents, Rancho has enshrined rules to keep street frictions outside its doors. Some gang patients are assigned aliases. No tribal colors or paraphernalia are permitted on site. Guards are also stationed around the buildings, though a hospital spokeswoman insists it is mainly to dispense directions.

Nonetheless, staffers here know that Saturday is the busiest day for spinal gunshot wounds, summer the busiest of the seasons for them.

"When I came here twenty years ago, there were a few patients with gunshot wounds," Dr. Gilgoff recalled. "Today we get quite a few. Now there can be multiple paraplegics in the same gang. I've had patients with five-six bullet wounds and you realize it's because semi-automatic weapons are in play."

History has taught that pent-up rage is often best diluted with another impulse. Young men from ragged environs, where gang camaraderie can be more solace than family, need a scorch pad to burn anger, and sports has shown it can burn it productively. Hence, the hospital has an extensive wheelchair athletics program, and a bursting trophy case to prove it.

There is basketball, baseball, tennis, and hockey, where getting knocked out of your chair can be a badge of honor, and a magazine—*Sports 'N Spokes*—devoted to it.

The athletics, sponsored by a Rancho support group, have two non-negotiable stipulations. To participate, patients must be in school and clean from drugs.

"They've gotten more out of sports than anything," says Gilgoff. "Of the hundred and fifty gunshot victims I've treated, only about four of them, I thought, should have been incarcerated. The other hundred and forty-six were young men in the wrong situation. With the right assistance" including sports, "they do really well."

Who knows where Alvaro Morfin would be if hadn't been for one epically bad decision?

His storyline is a common one. His mother raised him after she and his dad, a taxi driver, separated. Morfin didn't join a neighborhood gang for sheer mayhem. He joined, he said, because "you don't have nothing else." A couple years ago he was busted on a marijuana charge and sent to live with a foster family. During that time, he said, he earned straight A's, excelling in history, and straightened himself up.

All that willpower buckled this summer back home in East L.A. His friend stole a $1,000 and persuaded Morfin to come party with him. The two sped off on bikes. They pedaled to another pal's house to convince him to join them, and that was when a car carrying a rival gang made a menacing pass. Morfin expected a fistfight, and was not about to shrink from it.

He misjudged intentions. Someone from the car pointed a gun at him and began firing wildly. Morfin tried throwing his gangly frame over a wall to get some cover, but the shooter found his aim. A bullet clipped Morfin in the side, hit his spine and exited from his ribcage. He took a final few steps and dropped.

L.A. County General was the nearest emergency room. He hated it there, nervous about being probed, wondering why it took two hours to get pain medication.

It has been his stay at Rancho where he regained his bearings. He connected with everybody, janitors among them, and learned arm thrusts and cooking. Those new skills developed side-by-side with epiphanies that cost him so much.

"I have to push my [old friends] to the side," he says, struggling to tamp down the lump in his throat. "I can't walk like them (anymore). I came to realize that my family members are my real friends… I had alot of chances before and my luck ran out."

Luck will be immaterial to his graduation from Rancho. On a typical day here, he showers, attends occupational therapy, then physical therapy, rests for an hour, goes to class, eats lunch, hits the weightlifting room, practices wheelchair transfers and finally gets dinner. To unwind, he fancies Playstation (*Grand Theft Auto* is his favorite game) and watching the Angels, which he seems to know more about than skipper Mike Scioscia.

Fixing pressure sores—wounds that result from pelvic-area bones breaking down skin tissue strained from too little circulation—is one of Rancho's fortes. These ulcers can begin the size of a dime and expand to the width of softball. An entire twenty-five bed surgical ward is dedicated to them. Without any sensation down in their legs or butt, patients have to sleuth to detect lesions and always remember to rotate themselves if static for too long. It is tiresome.

ALL NEIGHBORHOODS ALL COLORS

DR. SALAH RUBAYI, AN Iraqi-born surgeon with a rapid-fire tongue, makes it his life's work operating and dealing with these inflamed buggers. Even the most conscientious get them. Once they do, there is forty-seven percent reoccurrence rate. People can develop fatal blood infections if they are left untreated.

For Rubayi, the premise the county's general hospitals could master this specialty should Rancho go under is absurd. It can take twelve weeks to recover from an $80,000 bedsore surgery. In typical cases, the wounds are covered with flaps of muscle exported from the same area as the wound. In extreme cases, when there is no more muscle to scalpel, doctors have to filet a patients' thigh and fold it back over the butt. Wound closed, they live legless.

"Why is Rancho better?" Rubayi said. "We are more rigid with our protocols and dedicated to this injury. We admit patients quickly. We didn't develop this by chasing the big money."

Sam Morris, a blonde-haired, guitar-playing paraplegic who traveled to L.A. from Maine to rehab with a movement specialist, opted for Rancho when a local private hospital twice bungled efforts to heal his pressure wound. Morris is in the minority of patients here with private insurance. A friend told him that Dr. Rubayi was "the best in the business," and had trained other doctors how to do the flap surgery.

"In hindsight, the whole experience at the other hospital was ridiculous," said Morris, twenty-seven. My [first surgeon] "confused confidence with arrogance."

If you think it takes a cataclysmic bonk to disrupt the spine's genius, you have not met eight year old Nelly Benarbashian, a patient in Rancho's pediatric ward. Today a smiling Spongebob Square Pants blanket covers her hospital bed. The little girl can wolf down Taco Bell burritos and do coordination-building puzzles with quiet gusto.

That ordinariness is what people have prayed for.

Nelly's descent to Rancho began last spring at Hazelton Elementary in the San Fernando Valley, where she complained to the school nurse about a sore throat. Hours later, at her bus stop, she collapsed into her mother's arms, and was whisked to an ER in Northridge. She could barely breathe. Her limbs went numb. "Mommy," Nelly wheezed, "I'm dying."

Doctors diagnosed her with transverse myelitis, a puzzling, viral-like condition where the spinal cord swells up and shuts down parts of the body. The Northridge doctors stabilized her, inserting a ventilator and getting her situated in a wheelchair. Afterwards, they transferred her to Rancho because they lacked the know-how to do much more.

"When she first got here, she had a trachea tube and a [feeding tube]," said Nelly's mom, Maral. "Her left foot could only wiggle. I was scared. The therapists got her walking. Without Rancho, I don't know what I would do."

Nelly can walk again. Most who come here will not. To lead them back to a civilization not always as accommodating as those blue handicapped parking spaces, Rancho has set up a model home that looks as if it was thought up by Aldous Huxley. There are gadgets that robotically turn pages, rotate plates and operate spoons. Counters move up and down on a lift, and showers and sinks are free of obstructions. Patients are brought to the house to mull their options, even if they cannot afford all of them.

"I tell patients that I'm teaching them how to be on a barge," said therapist Barbara Phillips. "There were dropped off here [by their accident], so how do they get there?"

WATCHING THE DUMPSTER DIVERS

Park a large, lidless container in front of your house for construction debris or a seasonal de-cluttering and within a few days you may feel like your block's unofficial trash man, if not its junk collector.

—*Los Angeles Times,* July 23rd, 2006

FEW THINGS UNITE A neighborhood like an open dumpster. Park a large, lidless container in front of your house for construction debris or a seasonal de-cluttering and within days you may feel like your block's unofficial trash man, if not its junk collector. Accepting other people's unwanted stuff sure makes you popular.

During the roughly two months a tan, boxcar-sized metal dumpster squatted curbside for the remodel of my Pasadena home, word of the bin's accessibility for public use saturated the area like an ad for free iPods. Suddenly, it was open season for garage clean-outs, liquor-bottle disposal, mystery trash and dog waste, not to mention a place to jettison dearly departed Aunt Tillie's old furniture.

Filthy or not, my dumpster became a sort of waste-disposal Mecca, with neighbors and assorted opportunists visiting it regularly to pay tribute.

As a neat freak, it is not as though I cannot sympathize with the need to rid oneself of excess. Plus an open dumpster has the thrill of pirated cable, a serendipitous chance the universe wants you to seize. Unless, of course, you are the guy who actually paid for the cable line your neighbors rewired for their enjoyment. Or, if you value sleep, and that concussive boom in the wee hours means yet another unauthorized junk tosser has dumped-and-ditched again.

Like owning a home in Southern California, renting a dumpster is not cheap. The monster forty-cubic-yarder I rented cost about $350 for ten days. Once packed to its corrugated rafters, it has to be emptied—also not inexpensive. So when the neighbor's moth-eaten curtains gobble up your highly prized dumpster space, well, it is a call to surveillance.

Not long after my bin was hauled to my house by a flatbed truck, I noticed an ancient-looking, wood-paneled television listing on top of the mound of debris that was supposed to be only the gutted remains of my old patio. The castoff television, which must have taken a hardy heave to clear the container's eight foot wall, piqued my curiosity. So, in the name of suburban sociology, I took my first dumpster dive.

Next to the ancient television was a thick roll of floral carpeting only your grandma would steam clean. Keeping it company was a large jug three-quarters filled with a whitish, watery goo of uncertain composition and undeniable stench. Whoever had planted the container placed it carefully across from other flotsam also not from my remodel: three twelve-pack beer containers, some bag-sealed dog doo, the legs of what appeared to be an old chrome chair, half a couch, a potpourri of twisted fabrics, and grocery bags of junk buried too deep for a look-see without a spacesuit.

I had not known this before, but bin companies catering to home remodelers say that neighbors who stealthily unload their stuff into their customer's rented dumpsters are carrying on a cat-and-mouse tradition as old as the subdivision. To keep your dumpster yours, experts advise covering the top with a tarp. Doing that means accessing your bin through ground-level doors that can be locked at night, when opportunists prowl.

People who ignore this counsel—like me—have found decaying mattresses, construction drywall from somebody else's job, old-fashioned gas stoves, palm fronds, mementos of the recently deceased, and the occasional dead critter in their rentals.

A dumpster is often an easy mark for laborers needing quick disposal of hazardous waste—paint, solvents, asbestos—that's supposed to get special handling under environmental laws.

Elizabeth Randall, the seen-it-all general manager at Chatsworth-based Rent-A-Bin, dubs trash cheats "bin pirates." It is the single biggest customer complaint she hears.

"If you're paying $85 for a bin and somebody fills it up halfway with their stuff," she said, "you've been pirated, ripped off."

Not long ago, Randall said a woman who regularly leased a smallish dumpster phoned Rent-A-Bin in hysterics.

"She said, 'This thiiiing is in my bin. Come take it out!"

When the worker looked inside, he began laughing uproariously. Somebody had deposited a freakishly large paper-mâché clown head and neck in there.

"We put it in the back of the truck [and drove back to our yard], where we promptly set it up on display and had fun with it until it rained and the head melted into a grotesque shape."

Randall's company, as others, will charge more if your bin is found to be over its weight limit at the landfill scale. For one with a six-ton limit, renters can get stuck with a fee of $35 per extra ton.

My across-the-street neighbors own a city-issued mini-dumpster for their large house that serves as my block's private landfill. Everybody unloads in it. Though I have permission to use it for my periodic cleaning blitzes, I feel like a criminal—eyes darting, neck craning—when I do and exhilarated when I'm done. There's just something about de-cluttering at someone else's expense that can twang the guilt and liberate simultaneously.

Dumpster freeloaders, even the renters themselves, can be a resourceful bunch. Steve Pivovaroff, general manager at South El Monte-based General Waste Disposal, said people sometimes line the insides of dumpsters with plywood to extend the height of the walls so they can pile in more debris. The larger the bin, the more inviting it is for abuse.

And abuse there is.

"A lot of times, I'll pull up on a job, and there are neighbors there waiting to dump stuff," Pivovaroff explained. "I'll say that's not yours, and they say no, they are buddies" with the renter when no OK was given. Some "clients will say take the bin away as soon as it's finished because I don't want my neighbors to use it! Some will be asking for a locking lid."

Pivovaroff believes there is probably a subtle form of remodeling NIMBYism playing out. Neighbors annoyed that your new patio or master bedroom construction has slapped them with months' worth of dust, early-morning racket, street-hogging trucks and legions of workers may feel they have some implicit dumpster rights. Or at least an excuse.

Determined to catch a bin pirate in mid-toss, I kept alert when my communal dumpster filled to the point I feared it might tip over. Rustling outside grabbed my attention one Wednesday, so I raced out of my home office to chastise the offender that I am not Pasadena's Fred Sanford.

Some bust: It was merely a worker from across the street using my port-a-potty.

LOCKED OUT FROM LOCKHEED

Burbank-area residents dispute cancer-incident survey.

—*Los Angeles Daily News*, November 3rd, 1996

FOR ALMOST FOUR YEARS, Marjorie Rohrman figured it was the wrenching mystery no doctor could crack: how her husband could contract a quick-striking esophageal cancer normally associated with heavy smokers.

Then August 4th rolled around and she learned that Lockheed Martin Corporation secretly had cut a $60 million settlement with more than 1,300 other Burbank residents who claimed toxic contamination from one of the company's now-defunct aircraft plants damaged their health and property.

Suddenly the Rohrmans, who were not part of that accord, began wondering if those pollutants may have triggered George's death in October 1992 at the age of seventy. A Burbank resident for fifty years, he spent much of his time outdoors on a U.S postal route close to the old plant.

"The first thing the doctors asked was whether he smoked or drank, and he didn't. They were baffled," said Marjorie Rohrman, who now lives in Sylmar.

Company officials repeatedly have said that emissions from their former plant never posed a health risk to the surrounding neighborhood. In their settlement with 1,357 residents, first disclosed by the *Daily News* on August 4th, the company did not admit liability.

In the months since the out-of-court deal became public, many people like the Rohrmans have come forward with stories about illnesses and deaths that they believe could be linked to their proximity to the Lockheed site.

State officials say there is no evidence of unusually high cancer rates around the site to justify a comprehensive study.

Some public health officials, environmentalists and residents are urging the state to conduct such a study to determine whether illnesses in the area can be linked to company-generated pollution.

"The state has an obligation to deal with the issues," said Philip Harber, director of UCLA's School of Occupational and Environmental Medicine. "It needs to be taken seriously, and the state can provide an objective assessment. When there is a public health concern, there is a hazard in doing nothing."

Gail Ruderman Feuer, a senior attorney for the Natural Resources Defense Council, a national environmental group, agreed.

"Companies don't typically pay out $60 million if they don't think they have some responsibility for what happened in the community," she said. "You have significant fears, if not hysteria, in the neighborhoods among people concerned they will get sick. It's appropriate for the government to get involved."

In a prepared statement, company spokeswoman Maureen Curow said Lockheed "would cooperate fully with a meaningful scientific study in Burbank and would be interested in seeing a proposal."

Last week, California health officials said a study is not warranted because a cancer-incident survey of four census tracts ringing the Lockheed's Burbank site, southeast of the Burbank-Glendale-Pasadena Airport, found cancer rates no higher than expected.

"We've had no indication so far that such a study would be a benefit," said Rick Kreutzer, chief of the department's environmental health investigations branch. "The cancer registry has evaluated those concerns and they have indicated there isn't an excess of cancers."

The survey, performed by an epidemiologist at USC's Cancer Surveillance Program, used county databases of reported cancers between 1972 and 1992. It found that there were no measurable excess cancers in the area.

"The cancer incidence rates in the Burbank area in question appear to be average base line rates expected in an older population and there is no evidence of any cancer excess," said Dr. Wendy Cozen, who conducted the survey.

Yolanda McGinnis, a resident of Burbank's Valley Street since the 1950s, is not convinced by those numbers. She and her neighbors long have wondered about the origin of cancers suffered by her husband and half a dozen neighbors, she said.

"Wouldn't you be afraid if your husband died of three types of cancer?" said McGinnis, who said she was treated for colon cancer herself two years ago.

At the heart of the toxic question is the cluster of buildings and sheds—all now razed—that made up Lockheed's 103-acre plant known as B-1.

Used to assemble and develop commercial aircraft and classified Air Force projects, including the U-2 spy plane and F-117A stealth fighter, the plant bustled for six decades until it was shuttered in 1990.

Six years later, that facility became the focus of the settlement and three lawsuits that ensued among people left out of the deal.

In August, retired Justice John Trotter, who mediated the secret accord, confirmed that the company paid the highest settlements—up to $300,000—to eighty people who were sick or who had relatives who died of cancer. Lockheed also set up a medical monitoring program that entitles some settlement recipients to checkups for cancer and other illnesses as well as a medical insurance policy.

Trotter declined comment for this story.

Alan Sigel, a Westwood lawyer who represents roughly 1,800 people who claim Lockheed's contamination also damaged their health and homes, said he would welcome an independent health study.

"We're getting about a hundred calls a day, and of that seventy-five percent evidence some physical illness," Sigel said. "They say, `My husband has a tumor in his lung, and he doesn't smoke and there is no cancer in the family.' We have constant complaints about nose bleeds... If you lived in Burbank for twenty years, are married and have three kids, would you be alarmed? You bet."

Six years ago, the state Department of Health Services wrapped up a $500,000 study of cancer-causing dioxins, heavy metals and lead found near Rosamond, a small, high desert town in southern

Kern County. The city, located a few miles south of nearly two dozen metal recycling businesses and toxic waste sites, had six times the cancer rate normally expected, but state officials concluded there was no clear link between the chemicals and the cancers.

Nevertheless, U.S. Environmental Protection Agency and state toxics officials ordered a major cleanup at the recycling and waste sites.

In the San Joaquin Valley, state experts in 1987 investigated homeowners' fears that pesticides were responsible for twenty cancers in younger people. No link was ever established.

The Health Services Department is expected to release next month an epidemiological report on workers exposed to radioactive and toxic substances at the Santa Susana Field Laboratory in the Simi Hills west of Chatsworth.

Rockwell International Corporation's Rocketdyne Division operates the 2,600-acre facility where rocket engines are tested and where nearly four decades of research with nuclear reactors was carried out. A major cleanup of toxic solvents and low-level radioactive contamination has been under way at the site for more then seven years.

Dan Hirsch, who sits on a citizen panel overseeing the Rocketdyne study, said he believes there is enough evidence to compel DHS to come to Burbank. In the Rocketdyne case, the state refused to study the issue until three influential area state Assembly members, including Panorama City Democrat Richard Katz, held a public hearing and pressured the department, he said.

"They had to be brought in kicking and screaming," Hirsch said. "If it weren't for the intervention by community groups, press coverage and pressure from elected officials, DHS would never have done the...worker epidemiological study. DHS has a reputation as a captured regulatory agency, captured by the industries they are supposed to be regulating."

Independent government commission charged by the legislature with setting and enforcing standards for specific industries in the private sector. The concept was invented by the U.S.

Kreutzer, the Health Department official, disputed that characterization, adding that it is extremely rare for anyone, anywhere to prove an unassailable relationship between cancer and contaminants in a given area.

Experts say there has been only a single cancer cluster traced to chronic exposure to environmental contaminants: a Turkish village where a respiratory cancer epidemic flared because of erionite, an asbestos-like mineral.

"To find an apparent excess of cancer in a small area can sometimes be difficult to establish with certainty," he said. "You don't know if it's a fluctuation in some sort of short period that if examined over a longer window might average out."

Cozen, the USC epidemiologist who did the Burbank cancer survey, said a harbinger of a serious health problem in the city would be if numerous people in the same area contracted the same form of cancer. The survey didn't uncover any such pattern.

"Each cancer is a different disease," Cozen said. "If they had breast cancer or prostate cancer, then it's not related to the environment."

Experts say a full-blown epidemiological study of the area around the Lockheed plant could take five years.

The analysis would require an inventory of what toxics Lockheed used, the amounts pumped into the environment and the ways people were exposed, said Edward Faeder, a chemist and toxicologist who served as Lockheed's environmental protection chief from 1988 to 1990.

Next, trained interviewers might be dispatched into the neighborhoods ringing the former plant to ask residents about their job activities, family medical history, whether they drank, smoked and other lifestyle questions, as well as if they showed symptoms associated with certain maladies, he said.

Once this and other studies were completed, a subgroup of those exposed might be given more in-depth scrutiny, likely with medical examinations, and compared with a similar group that wasn't exposed. The results would then be fed into a computer and interpreted, he said.

Among the hazardous compounds generated by the Lockheed plant was hexavalent chromium, an established human carcinogen that has been linked with lung cancer in workers who breathed high levels of it, according to the Agency for Toxic Substances and Disease Registry.

A 1989 health risk assessment that Lockheed made under a state toxics law concluded that airborne emissions of hexavalent chromium were responsible for eighty percent of the total cancer risk generated by that site.

A byproduct of chrome plating, stainless steel work and painting, the chromium compound can also trigger asthma attacks and allergic skin reactions, the study said. If swallowed, it can result in stomach problems, kidney and liver damage, and even death.

In addition to airborne particles, underground wells that supply an estimated 600,000 people in Burbank, Glendale, La Crescenta, and Los Angeles with water were closed or diluted with clean sources in 1979 after they registered toxic levels significantly above the threshold level.

Under federal Superfund toxics cleanup law, the aerospace firm was identified as the major source of the pollution and is expected to pay the bulk of the estimated $135 million cleanup.

The wells have been sealed, and the polluted water is being flushed through a treatment plant to remove the toxics.

Last year, however, test wells monitored by the U.S. Environmental Protection Agency showed hexavalent chromium levels above the maximum contaminant level, prompting officials to launch an ongoing investigation.

Two other toxic chemicals in the water and Lockheed-owned land are volatile organic compounds called trichloroethylene (TCE) and perchloroethylene (PCE).

Harber, the UCLA doctor, cautioned that even a comprehensive community health study might not solve the central question: whether Lockheed's activities directly caused people to become ill.

"If you showed lung cancer is twice what it is in an unexposed population, how do you know it's caused by smoking or their exposure?" Harber said. "But it's not a situation where one should throw up one's hands and say it's useless. We owe it to people to tell them what we know and don't know."

Co-written with Lee Condon

STEALTH BY THE SUB-DIVISION

Lockheed Corporation's secret brain trust emerges from war smelling like roses.

—*Los Angeles Business Journal*, April 8th, 1991

UNTAINTED BY DEFENSE SCANDALS, distanced from corporate take-over battles, it lives in the hearts of its can-do stalwarts and the minds of America's foes.

When U.S. F-117 aircraft screamed low through a moonless Middle Eastern night, raining laser-guided terror on Iraq's military nerve center in Operation Desert Storm's opening air salvo, Saddam Hussein became a believer.

Lockheed's Skunk Works lives.

Not that Ben Rich, the outspoken engineer who ran the legendary Lockheed Corporation research and development outfit from 1975 to 1990, had any doubts.

"We had a lot of our stuff in the Gulf: F-117s, U-2s, TR-1s. I guess you'd call it tremendous validation," he blurted.

Named after Al Capp's *Li'l Abner* comic strip five decades ago, the Skunk Works is home to 6,000 who toil in cutting-edge confines from Burbank to Palmdale, and is secretly funded by the Pentagon's black budget.

Queries about the facility's security precautions, or its work on the $80 billion Advanced Tactical Fighter program or a twenty-first Century spy plane, are met only with knowing smiles by company officials.

Consider the sleek, V-tail F-117, whose visibility on radar is said to be the equivalent of a small bird. The $42.6 million-per-copy aircraft was flying seven years before its existence was acknowledged in 1988—Manhattan Project-like in its secrecy.

Forty-nine years ago, when a circus tent next to a foul-smelling Burbank plastics factory was its temporary base, Skunk Works became a haven for handpicked scientific hotshots whose only constraints were laws of physics and flight chronicled by Isaac Newton and the Wright brothers.

It was—and continues to be—more a state of mind than a network of plants filled with drafting boards, prototypes and wind tunnels.

"Be quick, be quiet, be on time," remains the organization's mantra.

Back in 1943, no one imagined what the Skunk Works would do—the tens of billions it would make for Lockheed, the technological barriers it would dismantle, the Cold War arms race it would chronicle or the platforms of controlled violence it would assemble. No one except for a hardnosed, aeronautical wizard named Kelly Johnson, who died last December, taking a piece of Skunk Works with him.

Since those heady early days, much has changed with the Advanced Development Projects—Skunk Works' formal name. Like the rest of the now wobbly aerospace world, Skunk Works cannot escape the new found U.S.-Soviet lovefest, declining military budgets or more mundane environmental regulations. High-speed computers long ago replaced the slide rule as the designer's best friend.

Now a stand-alone division, Skunk Works will relocate its manufacturing operations to a new $39 million facility in Palmdale, leaving the once-sleepy town where it grew up in inconspicuous, unmarked buildings near Burbank Airport.

But Johnson's famous fourteen rules still form its backbone. Top-secret military projects are developed best when they are done with small groups of people working on short productions runs, with minimal red tape and tight contractor-government relations. The idea of KISS—Keep It Simple Stupid"—is also attributed to Johnson by Lockheed folk, as was the concept, "Keep all the do-gooders out—including management. They'll help you to death."

Other defense contractors have tried to copy Johnson's creation, but found only limited success. Rich, now a Lockheed consultant, said only one power has effectively taken a page from Skunk Works' management ways: the Japanese.

"It operates with minimum overhead and oversight, permitting it do amazing things in record time," opined Kemper Securities defense analyst Lawrence Harris. "If you want something that has never been done before, the first place to start is the Skunk Works." Last year, the secret organization brought in roughly $800 million to Lockheed's coffers, Harris noted, though it is not the money-maker it used to be.

Johnson was able to spark unconventional thinking by laying down bets with his workers, though he usually won. He said he would give anyone $100 if they could reduce the weight of the SR-71 by ten pounds. Rich first suggested filling the tires with helium. When that failed, he recommended giving the pilots enemas.

It was those type of things that gave Johnson the ability to "lead by charisma," according to Rich.

"He didn't tolerate stupidity or lying, but he was generous with praise," Rich explained. "His success was that he asked a lot of questions and got everyone involved early."

Still, Kelly's first task, assigned during the war to end all wars, was hardly a technological breeze: to develop the first operational U.S. jet fighter for the Army Air Corps. With corporate carte blanche, Kelly literally begged, borrowed and stole engineers from other Lockheed World War II projects.

Working almost around the clock for five months, 136 Skunk Work employees completed the P-80 prototype—dubbed the Lulu Belle—thirty-seven days ahead of schedule. Development cost: $9 million, or a measly $124 million in today's money. Nine thousand were eventually produced.

But the next Skunks Works project, a commercial feeder transport called the Model 75 Saturn, bellyflopped. So did the next plane, the turboprop XFV-1, a strange-looking bird that was part helicopter, part plane. Designed to perform vertical takeoff and landing like the modern-day Harrier jet, it was shot down by the Navy, partly because pilots couldn't look over their shoulders to land.

New Soviet threats opened a window of opportunity for Johnson, though.

When the Air Force spotted a MiG-15 fighter over Korea, Skunk Works won the contract to develop the F-104 Starfighter.

In less than twelve months Skunk Works built two prototypes able to fly at more than Mach 2, twice the speed of sound, forging the F-104s name as a "missile with a man in it."

But Skunk Works' real glory was still ahead. When the Air Force needed a high-altitude spy plane, they came to Johnson. With $20 million in convert money funneled through the Central Intelligence Agency, the Skunks Works took seventy-five people and designed, built and flew the first U-2 in less than eight months. Pentagon officials were even stunned to find Lockheed actually returning $4 million in unused funds.

"Sixteen months after we got the check the U-2 was flying its first mission," Rich gushed. "I can't get a letter out of the Pentagon in that length."

How secret was the U-2?

When Johnson called his test pilot Tony LeVier into a closed-door meeting, he could not tell him about the plane he was asking him to try out. When Johnson told LeVier to find a dry lake bed to put the U-2 through its paces, LeVier had to traipse through three states under an assumed name, passing himself off to everyone as a hunter.

On flying the famous plane: "It was basically a huge metal sailplane that took off like a homesick angel," LeVier recalled.

The U-2s furtive mission, and vulnerability to radar tracking, was exposed on May 1st, 1960, when Francis Gary Powers was shot down 1,000 miles inside U.S.S.R. territory. The incident put U.S.-Soviet detente into the freezer, fueling Nikita Khrushchev's shoe-pounding, anti-West diatribe at the United Nations.

But the U-2 soon redeemed itself, this time in a superpower showdown that tested the world's nerves.

U-2 pilots spotted the Soviets installing long-range nuclear-tipped missiles in Cuba.

The Department of Defense later ordered a tactical version of the U-2—the TR-1—that could find targets behind enemy lines. Decades later, new-generation versions of those frail-looking planes still provide U.S. war planners with information that even the most advanced satellites cannot.

So do three Skunk Work spy planes, designed during the 1960s, able to fly at Mach 3. The most important was the SR-71

Blackbird, a thin delta-winged craft with a fifty-six foot wing span, a sleek fuselage and the ability to fly altitudes exceeding three miles.

A menacing-looking twin engine reconnaissance aircraft stuffed with photographic and electronic sensors, the Blackbird became an integral part of the military's ability to monitor Third World hot spots and other geopolitical developments.

Not everyone is bullish about the future of organizations like the one Johnson pioneered.

"You are going to see black [covert] budget programs under pressure," said Kevin Knobloch, an analyst with the liberal Washington think tank, the Union of Concerned Scientists. "The turning point was the B-2 bomber and the fact that some in Congress thought it was kept under wraps too long."

In the mid-1980s there even was a congressional brouhaha over Skunk Works security procedures, forcing Rich and his staff to go back and classify documents dating back to the U-2.

These days Rich does not fret about whether Skunk Works will flourish in the 1990s. He says he is more concerned about America's eroding industrial base, the loss of Lockheeed faithful to Disney Imagineering or the government's "grindstone" military specifications. He's also seen the organization called the gem of Southern California's aerospace world swell from fourteen departments in 1965 to more than 200 now.

"There will always be niches to fill in for the military and we'll keep asking them what they will need in the next century. Remember, there are only 3,000 days left in this one."

OUTHOUSE LAWYERS

L.A. County pays more for outside legal help than the state; firms donate heavily to curry favor.

—*LA Weekly*, January 13th, 1995

IN THE STREAM OF lawsuits flooding Los Angeles County each year, the $1 million brutality claim seemed just another garden-variety case.

A gang member chased by sheriff's deputies from Lynwood to South Gate charged he had been bitten by a police dog and whacked in the face with an officer's flashlight during his arrest—and he wanted some financial justice. Bracing for a trial, the county hand-picked Eugene Ramirez, a private lawyer with a stellar record defending sheriffs in canine cases.

In the end, however, there was no dramatic court testimony and little publicity. The judge dismissed the suit last fall after the victim's lawyer conceded he had scant chance of winning: his client was back in prison on a parole violation. It was going to be a pretty standard use of force case," says Ramirez.

But that routine round of non-litigation cost the county plenty—Ramirez estimates he billed $32,000 for the job.

Sending that legal work outside Los Angeles' vast bureaucracy was a well-rehearsed exercise in contracting out to the county counsel's office, a *Weekly* investigation has found. While only a handful might realize it, using hired lawyers to defend the county against the cavalcade of suits and claims filed against it is a well-worn practice. In some circumstances it is hard to gauge where the county ends and private law firms on the public payroll begin.

During the past five years, the county counsel's office has shelled out a whopping $190 million to outside attorneys, an average of $38 Million a year, records show. In that same period, the county's own 120-lawyer retinue made do on budgets that averaged just $29.2 million annually. And that doesn't include the $24 million spent on private attorneys last year by the county public defender's office, a practice that has drawn sharp criticism in recent years.

Few public entities inside the Golden State lean on private lawyers the way L.A. County does. Indeed, the entire state government, including the Department of Justice and the California Department of Transportation, forked over just $30 million for outside legal work in 1991, the last time the issue was studied. Those state expenditures prompted Attorney General Dan Lungren to fulminate, "During this time of severe fiscal crisis, the state of California can ill afford $30 million of private legal-services charges at rates of $165 per hour and beyond." Private firms employed by the county that year took in $39 million, according to records.

Over the past year, San Diego County spent between $17,000 to $53,000, or about eight percent, of its $9 million county counsel budget on private legal help. For the same period, Los Angeles County's rate was fifty-five percent. San Francisco officials did not return phone calls.

Even in a town famous for the legal brawn behind high-pressure movie deals, corporate takeovers, and land swaps, some observers believe the county's private army of attorneys constitutes one of the Southland's most powerful firms, albeit its most anonymous. But unlike its paymasters in their drab offices on the sixth floor of the county's Hall of Administration, operations churn away inside luminous skyscrapers with terrazzo lobbies, Ivy League connections, and freshly stocked bars.

When the 1993-94 fiscal year ended, 114 law firms were on the L.A. County Rolodex, all cleared for work. And work they have. When a gigantic Malibu landslide prompted some 250 homeowners to seek hundreds of millions of dollars from government, it was private counsel who settled the county's share for $30 million. When a South Bay property owner challenged Proposition 13 all the way to the Supreme Court, it was outside lawyers carrying the defense load. When a county worker strains his back, or a county truck skids into a car on an icy mountain road, it is a good bet that outside counselors will be plotting court moves.

County officials running this machine argue that using outside attorneys on complex or specialized cases is a taxpayer winner—a way to thwart aggressive plaintiff lawyers without spending heaps on public salaries and benefits once the case plays out. But at a time when tight budgets have forced closure of health clinics and branch libraries, critics are beginning to challenge the outlay of tens of millions in legal fees.

Moreover, when privatization is invoked as a rallying cry against government excess, the county's venture in contracting for legal expertise seems a cautionary experience. In fact, despite the huge sums being spent, there has yet to be a comprehensive study looking at how effective the outside lawyers are, officials concede.

"It's hard understanding exactly why so much is being farmed out," says Barbara Maynard, one of Supervisor Gloria Molina's legislative deputies. "The answer from the county counsel's office is that it's just how much it costs. But nobody is buying into that."

Those doubts were reinforced by the results of an audit Molina requested in 1993. According to the report, prepared by consultants McGladrey & Pullen and Advanced Risk Management Techniques, judgments and settlements against the county climbed from $53.6 million in 1988-89 to $134.3 million three years later, despite the outside help. County lawyers called foul, responding that the audit mixed figures from several separate categories of expenditures and thus reached inaccurate conclusions about total legal payouts and about skyrocketing legal fees.

"We had some concerns over the numbers they used," says Bill Penman, a senior assistant to County Counsel DeWitt Clinton. "We couldn't figure out the source."

According to records Penman provided to the *Weekly*, the county in the last fiscal year paid out $54.8 million for all judgments and settlements, an eight percent hike over the previous year. Records going back further were unavailable.

Yet even if some of the numbers were off, the audit found other disturbing holes in the county counsel's ability to manage and track so many private law firms doing so many different things. "Legal expenses can be substantially reduced through exerting greater control over outside defense-firm activities, handling more cases in-house, and establishing a more aggressive policy for settling claims before they are litigated," it urged managers.

And the criticism didn't stop there.

Seven months ago, the county's own Department of Auditor-Controller jumped into the fray by doing its own study. While it concluded that the county had "adequate procedures" to oversee its private lawyers, it also urged a shopping list of reforms to better track costs and develop "specific criteria" in choosing the firms. Eleven also found that the county fails to periodically evaluate its contract law firms. Pellman says many of the audit's recommendations have since been implemented.

Regardless of those reforms, the question remains: Why is L.A. County so deeply committed to large-scale contracting with private lawyers? Part of the answer may lie in the small fortune pumped into the campaign war chests of Los Angeles politicians by the law firms working for the county. As in the philanthropic slogan, they give and give often: in 1993 alone their generosity surpassed the $350,000 mark.

The strongest argument offered by the bureaucrats in charge of the public purse strings is that firming out complex specialty litigation enables the county counsel's office to better focus on more routine matters—ordinances, departmental contracts, advice to the supervisors and the like.

"There's a lot we can't do here while serving as in-house counsel," says Clinton assistant Penman. "The outside work is so intermittent it wouldn't benefit us having [more] staff attorneys," Penman argues.

But the political largess of the private firms notwithstanding, critics inside and outside the Hall of Administration wonder whether the county's semiprivate judicial squad is the lean, mean operation its advocates purport it to be.

In particular, skeptics point out that the county privatizes such work as automobile liability and medical malpractice, fields where the caseload is fairly regular and could be brought in-house with potentially huge savings. Bob Stern, Co-Director of the Center for Governmental Studies, a Los Angeles based nonprofit research group, believes that is an option that should he looked into posthaste.

"The question is whether there is an ongoing need for specialists, and, if Mete is, why doesn't the county and city develop that?" Stern says. "It may be carrying privatization to an extreme."

Even officials with the Sheriff's Department are critical of the county strategy. They have lobbied for years for their own attorneys so they could develop an in-house specialty lighting charges of brutality, false arrest and other claims. The answer from the county counsel's office has been a steadfast no, a product, some say, of good old turf protection.

"The private lawyers are very good," says Lieutenant Dennis Burns, who runs the Sheriff's Civil Litigation Unit. "[However] we think with in-house lawyers [we] can be more efficient and contain costs. There's no doubt a county counsel lawyer does it cheaper by the hour than a contract firm."

Of the $8 million spent on Sheriff's defense cases last year, about $6 million went to outside lawyers, Burns estimates.

L.A. County lawyers argue their job is more immense than other jurisdictions, a factor of the huge population and sprawling health-care and social-service network administered here. As a barometer of that, all medical malpractice, most automobile liability, and some worker's compensation and general-litigation cases are sent outside. The load is so heavy that the county contracts out with third-party administrators to negotiate smaller claims and oversee private law firms handling malpractice, automobile and general-liability cases. Those administrators made an additional $3 million last fiscal year.

Perhaps surprisingly; it is not L.A.'s blue blood law firms—the old-timers like O'Melveny & Myers or Gibson, Dunn & Crutcher—that gobble up the lion's share of county work. The fattest bills are racked up by firms that only insiders or lawyers might instantly recognize: Parker, Milliken, Clark, O'Hara & Samuelian; Morris, Polich & Purdy; Bonne Bridges, Mueller; Cotkin & Collins.

And for eighteen of those firms, the county contract was worth more than $500,000 annually for at least three of the past five years. (At $22.1 million, Auxiliary Legal Services actually billed the most over the five years studied by the *Weekly*; it is a nonprofit service established to handle child dependency cases.) By contrast, sixty-six of the 114 firms took in less than $200,000 from the county last year.

Who gets chosen, and for how much work, is an opaque process, hard to monitor and hard to challenge. Unlike other public entities, including the Los Angeles City Attorney's Office, the county rarely requires competitive bidding. Instead, interested law firms submit brochures, resumes and such for review, then come in for interviews. It is up to Clinton to decide who makes it in the pool, not the supervisors.

Once there, the firms usually remain indefinitely, since there is no official re-evaluation or mandatory review of their county contract, officials concede; if any one of them missteps, its workload is simply curtailed.

Pellman says he cannot remember a single instance in which a firm was bounced for overbilling or other transgressions—a statement critics find astonishing, given the $190 million figure. On occasion, he adds, a law firm gets referred by a supervisor, though he says that is no guarantee they will be cleared for work.

To hear it from county officials, and from the attorneys doing the work, private law firms give taxpayers a bargain, offering the Hall of Administration a discount of between ten and fifty percent off their normal rates. They fetch $105 per hour for sheriff cases, $88 to $125 for automobile and malpractice work. Bond and general litigation counsel can go much higher, sometimes bringing $290 per hour depending on the seniority of the lawyer involved.

While it is hard to nail down an exact figure for comparison, county staff attorneys bill the departments retaining them between $76 arid $189 an hour, figures that include overhead and staff support. The average salary for a veteran, non-management county barrister, sources say, is $105,000.

What's more, officials and private lawyers assert that the county closely tracks the funds laid out for legal help. Steve Manning, who split off from Morris, Polich & Purdy to form his own firm, frequently represents the Sheriff's Department against excessive-force charges. While he relishes the courtroom confrontations, he says the work is exacting —and "barely profitable."

"It's very difficult money," says Manning, who defended sheriff's deputies accused of racist tactics in Lynwood, a matter that is still pending, "the cases are hard fought, emotionally charged, and the plaintiff attorneys are very strident, true believers we call them...and one can't tell you at how many levels they review the bills."

Few corporate clients are as zealous as the county in ensuring all tabs have been stripped of billing cellulose and gratuitous expenses, agrees Reich Bridges, senior partner at Bonne Bridges, Mueller, O'Keefe & Nichols, which has put in twenty years defending the county's health care system against malpractice suits and which collected $9.7 million in fees last year.

"They do a very thorough job," Bridges says. 'They audit all the time."

So, given the measly rates, eagle-eye scrutiny and bureaucratic obstacles, who would push to be on the county speed-dialing machine? Plenty, that's who, officials and lawyers say.

"Their incentive is that they get work fairly consistently and the pay is guaranteed, even if we look at their bills closely," says Bob Ambrose, an assistant county counsel in charge of general litigation.

And as a door opener, Penman says, showcasing their county work to private clients or smaller governmental entities does not hurt the firms either.

Karl Samuelian, an influential Republican Party stalwart and managing partner at Parker Milliken, says both civic pride and profits come into play. His outfit has received $10.4 million in the last five years, documents show.

"You get into real battles," says Samuelian, whose firm, among other things, defended the county in Malibu's Big Rock mudslide and disputes over jail construction. "In each, it requires a specialist, and the county counsel is not equipped to handle all of it. We've done a good job for the county."

Critics, however, scoff at the notion that big-time law firms hunt down public contracts its exchange for profit-eating discounts. Many public agencies, they suspect, have been bamboozled into paying bills higher than they should have and will eventually emulate corporate America. It is cracking down.

"The county willy-nilly hires outside firms and ends up paying three to four times as much than they would have if they hired in-house lawyers," says Stephen Yagman, a successful and controversial Venice plaintiffs' lawyer who has battled both city and county attorneys in police-brutality cases. "This is a kind of Thatcher-Reagan privatization of legal representation that is unwarranted and shocking...it's a welfare plan for connected lawyers."

Adds another Los Angeles lawyer, like Yagman experienced in dealing with the government but unwilling to speak for the record, "The fiction is that a low billing rate means a low bill, and it doesn't. I believe that at least a good strong minority of lawyers don't have the integrity to make a [billable] hour an hour."

Another attorney, who has worked on numerous government deals, concurs. He believes the private firms working for the county offset their low public rates by stretching out the time it takes to do basic tasks—a claim officials vigorously disagree with. "There's this joke about a lawyer going to St. Peter at the pearly gates and saying, I'm not supposed to be here, I'm only forty-five years old and just a young man.' Well, St. Peter turns back at the guy and says, 'Looking at your billable hours, you're eighty-five.'"

If money is the mother's milk of politics, then the law firms doing business with the city and county of Los Angeles seem to have taken over their own dairy. During a one-year period starting June 30th, 1993, those firms funneled at least $101,335 into the war chests of the five supervisors, campaign records show. In all likelihood, they gave significantly more, but it is impossible to total, because numerous lawyer-contributors did not list their employers on their disclosure forms.

Those same firms donated another $260,000 to L.A. City Council candidates during the 1993 election cycle, according to records on file with the city's Ethics Commission.

At the county, Deane Dana took in $13,400, with checks rolling in from Bonne Bridges and Parker Milliken as well as Jones, Day, Reavis & Pogue, the outfit Supervisor Yvonne Brathwaite Burke used to work for. Burke herself drew in more than $29,000 from the firms, including largess from Bonne, Bridges; powerful westside outfit Manatt, Phelps, Phillips & Kantor; the law offices of former L.A. Police Commissioner Melanie Lomax, and her old employer.

Supervisor Mike Antonovich came in at slightly less, notching $23,800. Among the contributors were Veatch, Carlson, Grogan & Nelson; Cox, Castle & Nicholson; and Latham & Watkins. Parker Milliken chipped in a single $5,000 contribution.

Largely because of his recent supervisorial campaign, Yaroslavsky was buoyed the most by the firms, scoring $43,800. Large chunks came from Christensen, White, Miller, Fink & Jacobs; O'Melveny & Myers; and Latham.

Molina received $3,100.

Officeholders say the contributions are all aboveboard, just citizens expressing their support, even if they are getting contracts from departments they ultimately oversee. Private attorneys chime in that the greenbacks are totally unrelated to the lawsuits, claims, settlements and advice they are laboring on for government.

"It would be foolish for any firm who is working with the county counsel's office to get down and dirty in politics," says Bridges.

Other political watchers are a tad more cynical says one political consultant, who asked to stay off the record, "You match up these law firms and then see the campaign contributions, and the officials are literally getting rich."

KARMA FOR THE CARMAKERS

—*New York Times*, January 26th, 2009

DESPITE THE DRUMBEAT OF grim economic news up and down the state, Californians today no doubt are celebrating President Obama's decision to allow states to enact anti-global warming auto emission standards stricter than federal rules. They're also in a befuddled state of what-took-so-long déjà vu.

For those who don't remember, thick, noxious, russet-hued air pollution from the 1940s on that used to blanket a good part of the Los Angeles area for a goodly part of the year. When it dawned on desperate environmental officials here in the late 1960s that California needed to drop the hammer on the politically powerful, sales-oriented car companies by forcing them to slash ozone-forming compounds with regulations far sterner than the national limits, the industry rolled out the same arguments we have seen on the greenhouse gas front: *It's not fair to do this state by state*; *It'll cost too much*; *It's technologically infeasible*; *Production chaos isn't good for consumers*.

No matter how much southern Californians adored their cars, they began seeing the speciousness of these arguments, and that what the automakers seemed to care most about was the yearly sales ledger, not technological improvements that supposedly would drive certain models out of people's price range. So in 1967, aided by some plucky California politicians, a young Ralph Nader and a well-timed radio documentary titled *A Breath of Death*, about smog's pernicious stranglehold on the L.A. dream, the state built a congressional coalition with other increasingly polluted states and resisted efforts, primarily led by Representative John Dingell, the Michigan Democrat, to put so-called emission standards on the shelf.

And yes, it is the same John Dingell. Not that it was easy. Not that the then Big Four automakers and their lobbyists didn't try everything they could to blunt the attack on their tailpipe waste. Yet when 500,000 pro-waiver letters were dumped on the Capitol steps and dreary pictures of skyline-obliterated Los Angeles went up in the Rotunda, the tide began changing.

Wasn't the health and well-being of millions of Americans in a state with higher industrial output than many countries worth a crackdown on the machine that made the state such a suburban idyll? The answer was a resounding yes. New York, Louisiana, Texas rallied to California's argument, even if then Governor Ronald Reagan figured the state had no shot.

On November 2nd, 1967, when Obama and I were both little kids, the state became the first ever to win the authority to ramp up anti-smog standards, and there was jubilation from Sacramento to Santa Monica. Today, those standards, which many others have copied around the world, have helped make California cars ninety-nine percent cleaner than they used to be.

You would have figured the American automakers would have embraced the message Californians sent. You might have thought they would have done what the Japanese car makers did: start building cleaner cars cleaner from the production lines up. For all that, Ford, General Motors, and Chrysler apparently heard a different tune, and perhaps the distress they are in now is another word for karma.